4th Edition

STUDY GUIDE

▲

FINANCIAL ACCOUNTING

JAMES A. HEINTZ, DBA, CPA
Professor of Accounting
University of Connecticut

COLLEGE DIVISION South-Western Publishing Co.

CINCINNATI DALLAS LIVERMORE

Table of Contents

Chapter 1
Concepts and Principles of Accounting

STUDY GOALS

After studying this chapter, you should be able to:

1. Describe accounting as an information system for business enterprises.

2. Describe financial accounting and managerial accounting.

3. Describe the development of financial accounting concepts and principles.

4. Identify and illustrate the application of the following basic financial accounting concepts and principles:

   Business entity

   Cost principle

   Business transactions

   Unit of measurement

5. Identify the accounting equation and its basic elements.

6. Describe and illustrate how all business transactions can be stated in terms of the resulting changes in the three basic elements of the accounting equation.

7. Describe the nature of an account and its use in recording transactions.

8. Identify and describe the following financial statements:

   Income statement

   Retained earnings statement

   Balance sheet

   Statement of cash flows

GLOSSARY OF KEY TERMS

Account. The type of record used for the purpose of recording individual transactions.

Accounting. The process of identifying, measuring, and communicating economic information to permit informed judgments and decisions by users of the information.

Accounting equation. The expression of the relationship between assets, liabilities, and owner's equity; most commonly stated as Assets = Liabilities + Owner's Equity.

Account form of balance sheet. A balance sheet with assets on the left-hand side and liabilities and owner's equity on the right-hand side.

Account payable. A liability created by a purchase made on credit.

Account receivable. A claim against a customer for sales made on credit.

Asset. Property owned by a business enterprise.

Balance sheet. A financial statement listing the assets, liabilities, and owner's equity of a business entity as of a specific date.

Business entity concept. The concept that assumes that accounting applies to individual economic units and that each unit is separate and distinct from the persons who supply its assets.

Business transaction. The occurrence of an event or of a condition that must be recorded in the accounting records.

Capital stock. Share of ownership of a corporation.

Corporation. A separate legal entity organized in accordance with state or federal statutes and in which ownership is divided into shares of stock.

Cost principle. The principle that assumes that the monetary record for properties and services purchased by a business should be maintained in terms of cost.

Credit. (1) The right side of an account; (2) the amount entered on the right side of an account; (3) to enter an amount on the right side of an account.

Debit. (1) The left side of an account; (2) the amount entered on the left side of an account; (3) to enter an amount on the left side of an account.

Dividend. A distribution of earnings of a corporation to its owners (stockholders).

Double-entry accounting. A system for recording transactions based on recording increases and decreases in accounts so that debits always equal credits.

Equity. The right or claim to the properties of a business enterprise.

Expense. The amount of assets consumed or services used in the process of earning revenue.

Financial accounting. The measuring and recording of transactions for a business enterprise or other economic unit and the periodic preparation of various reports from such records.

Financial Accounting Standards Board (FASB). The current authoritative body for the development of accounting principles.

Generally accepted accounting principles (GAAP). Generally accepted guidelines for the preparation of financial statements.

Governmental Accounting Standards Board (GASB). The current authoritative body for the development of accounting principles for state and municipal governments.

Income statement. A summary of the revenues and expenses of a business entity for a specific period of time.

Journal. The two-column form used to record journal entries.

Ledger. A group of related accounts that comprise a complete unit.

Liability. A debt of a business enterprise.

Managerial accounting. Employs both historical and estimated data which are used in conducting daily operations and in planning future operations.

Net income. The final figure in the income statement when revenues exceed expenses.

Net loss. The final figure in the income statement when expenses exceed revenues.

Owner's equity. The rights of the owners in a business enterprise.

Partnership. A business owned by two or more individuals.

Posting. The process of transferring debits and credits from a journal to the accounts.

Prepaid expense. A purchased commodity or service that has not been consumed at the end of an accounting period.

Report form of balance sheet. The form of balance sheet with the liability and owner's equity sections presented below the asset section.

Retained earnings. Net income retained in a corporation.

Retained earnings statement. A statement for a corporate enterprise, summarizing the changes in retained earnings during a specific period of time.

Revenue. The amount charged to customers for goods sold or services rendered.

Sole proprietorship. A business owned by one individual.

Statement of cash flows. A summary of the cash receipts and cash payments of a business entity for a specific period.

Stockholders. The owners of a corporation.

Stockholders' equity. The equity of the shareholders in a corporation.

T account. A form of account resembling the letter T.

Trial balance. A summary listing of the balances and the titles of the accounts.

CHAPTER OUTLINE

I. Accounting as an Information System.

   A. Accounting is an information system that provides essential information about the financial activities of an entity to various individuals or groups for their use in making informed judgments and decisions.

   B. Accounting information is composed principally of financial data about business transactions, expressed in terms of money.

   C. Accounting provides the conceptual framework for gathering financial data and the language for communicating these data to different individuals and institutions.

   D. Those individuals charged with the responsibility for directing the operations of enterprises, referred to as "management," depend upon and make the most use of accounting information.

   E. The process of using accounting to provide information to users involves (1) identification of user groups and their information needs, (2) the gathering and processing of financial data by the accounting system, and (3) the generation of reports communicating the information to users.

II. Financial and Managerial Accounting.

   A. Financial accounting is concerned with the measuring and recording of transactions for a business enterprise or other economic unit and the periodic preparation of various reports from such records.

   B. Managerial accounting extends beyond financial accounting. Both historical and estimated data are used to provide reports for management's use in conducting daily operations and in planning future operations.

III. Development of Financial Accounting Concepts and Principles.

   A. As the country has developed economically and business organizations have grown in size and complexity, accounting concepts and principles have been developed to serve as guidelines for the preparation of useful financial statements. Accounting principles do not have the same authority as universal principles or natural laws. Rather, they represent guides based on reason, observation, and experimentation.

   B. The Financial Accounting Standards Board (FASB) is presently the dominant body in the development of generally accepted accounting principles.

      1. After issuing discussion memoranda and preliminary proposals and evaluating comments from interest parties, the FASB issues *Statements of Financial Accounting Standards,* which become part of generally accepted accounting principles.

      2. The FASB issues *Interpretations,* which have the same authority as the standards.

      3. The FASB also is attempting to develop a broad conceptual framework for financial accounting, which is being published as *Statements of Financial Accounting Concepts.*

   C. The Governmental Accounting Standards Board (GASB) was formed in 1984 to establish accounting standards to be followed by state and municipal governments.

   D. Other accounting organizations that are influential in establishing accounting principles include the American Institute of Certified Public Accountants (AICPA) and the American Accounting Association (AAA).

   E. Various governmental agencies with an interest in the development of accounting principles include the Securities and Exchange Commission (SEC) and the Internal Revenue Service (IRS).

   F. Other influential organizations in the development of accounting principles include the Financial Executives Institute (FEI), the National Association of Accountants (NAA), the Financial Analysts Federation, and the Securities Industry Associates.

IV. Financial Accounting Concepts and Principles.

   A. Business Entity Concept.

      1. The business entity concept is based on the applicability of accounting to individual economic units in society.

2. These individual economic units include all profit-making businesses, governmental and not-for-profit units, and individual persons and family units.

B. The Cost Principle.

1. Under the cost principle, monetary accounting records are expressed in terms of cost.

2. The exchange price, or cost, agreed upon by buyer and seller, determines the monetary amount to be recorded.

C. Business Transactions.

1. A business transaction is the occurrence of an event or of a condition that must be recorded.

2. A particular business transaction may be relatively simple, involving only two accounts, or more complex, involving three or more accounts.

D. Unit of Measurement.

1. All business transactions are recorded in terms of money. It is only through the record of dollar amounts that the diverse transactions and activities of a business may be measured, reported, and periodically compared.

2. Although the purchasing power of the dollar is unstable, for accounting purposes the monetary unit is assumed to be stable in order to insure objectivity.

V. Assets, Liabilities, and Owner's Equity.

A. The properties owned by a business enterprise are called assets and the rights or claims to the properties are called equities.

B. Equities may be subdivided into two principal types: The rights of creditors (called liabilities) and the rights of owners (called owner's equity).

C. The accounting equation may be expressed in the following ways: assets = equities; assets = liabilities + owner's equity; assets - liabilities = owner's equity.

VI. Transactions and the Accounting Equation.

A. All business transactions can be expressed in terms of the resulting change in the three basic elements (assets, liabilities, and owner's equity) of the accounting equation.

B. To record transactions on a regular basis, separate records are maintained for each major asset, liability, and owner's equity item.

C. A type of record used to record individual transactions is called an account.

D. A group of related accounts is called a ledger.

VII. Nature of an Account.

A. The simplest form of an account is known as a T account, and has three parts: a title, a space for recording increases in the amount of the item, and a space for recording decreases in the amount of the item.

B. The left side of the account is called the debit side and the right side is called the credit side.

C. The process of recording a transaction in the journal is called journalizing. The process of transferring data from the journal to the appropriate accounts is known as posting.

D. Transactions that increase assets are entered on the left side of asset accounts as debits, and decreases are entered on the right side as credits. Increases in liabilities and owner's equity are entered on the right side of those accounts as credits, and decreases are entered on the left side as debits.

E. A purchase on account is a type of transaction that creates a liability, called an account payable, in which the purchaser agrees to pay in the near future.

F. Consumable goods purchased, such as supplies, and advance payments of expenses are considered to be prepaid expenses or assets.

G. The amount charged to customers for goods or services sold to them is called revenue. Increases in revenues are recorded as credits.

H. A sale on account allows the customer to pay later, and the selling firm acquires an account receivable.

I. The amount of assets consumed or services used in the process of earning revenues is called expense. Increases in expenses are recorded as debits.

J. The general rules of debit and credit may be summarized as follows:

	Debit	Credit
Asset accounts	Increase (+)	Decrease (-)
Liability accounts	Decrease (-)	Increase (+)
Owner's equity accounts	Decrease (-)	Increase (+)
Revenue accounts	Decrease (-)	Increase (+)
Expense accounts	Increase (+)	Decrease (-)

K. The normal balances of asset and expense accounts are debits.

L. The normal balances of liability, capital stock, and revenue accounts are credits.

M. When the rules of debit and credit are followed, the total of the accounts with debit balances must equal the total of the accounts with credit balances.

N. A listing of the account balances which verifies the equality of the debits and credits is known as the trial balance.

VIII. Financial Statements.

A. The income statement is the summary of the revenue and expenses of a business entity for a specific period of time.

1. The excess of revenue over expenses incurred in earning the revenue is called net income or net profit.

2. If the expenses of the enterprise exceed the revenue, the excess is a net loss.

3. In the determination of periodic net income, the expenses incurred in generating revenues must be properly matched against the revenues generated.

B. The retained earnings statement is a summary of the changes in the earnings retained in the business entity for a specific period of time.

1. Corporations distinguish between (1) the investments of the owners and (2) the retained earnings or net income retained in the business.

2. On the retained earnings statement, net income increases retained earnings, and net loss and dividends, which are distributions of earnings, decrease retained earnings.

C. The balance sheet lists the assets, liabilities, and owner's equity of a business as of a specific date.

1. The form of balance sheet with the liabilities and owner's equity sections presented below the asset section is called the report form.

2. The form of balance sheet which lists assets on the left and liabilities and owner's equity on the right is called the account form of balance sheet.

D. The statement of cash flows is a summary of the cash receipts and cash payments for a period.

1. It is customary to report cash flows in three sections: (1) operating activities, (2) investing activities, and (3) financing activities.

2. The cash flows from operating activities section includes cash transactions that enter into the determination of net income.

3. The cash flows from investing activities section reports the cash transactions for the acquisition and sale of relatively long-term or permanent-type assets.

4. The cash flows from financing activities section reports the cash transactions related to the sale of capital stock and borrowings and cash dividends paid to shareholders.

E. The sequence in which the financial statements of a business are usually prepared is as follows: income statement, retained earnings statement, balance sheet, and statement of cash flows.

PART 1

Instructions: A list of terms and related statements appear below. From the list of terms, select the term that relates to each statement and print its identifying letter in the space provided.

A. Account   H. Cost principle   O. Net income
B. Account payable   I. Equities   P. Owner's equity
C. Account receivable   J. Expense   Q. Prepaid expenses
D. Accounting equation   K. Income statement   R. Retained earnings statement
E. Assets   L. Journal   S. Revenue
F. Balance sheet   M. Ledger   T. Statement of cash flows
G. Business entity concept   N. Liabilities

_____ 1. The records of properties and services purchased by a business are maintained in accordance with the (?).

_____ 2. The properties owned by a business enterprise.

_____ 3. The rights or claims to the properties owned by a business enterprise.

_____ 4. The rights of creditors represent debts of the business and are called (?).

_____ 5. The rights of the owner or owners.

_____ 6. Assets = Liabilities + Owner's Equity.

_____ 7. The liability created by a purchase on account.

_____ 8. Consumable goods purchased, such as supplies, are considered to be assets, or (?).

_____ 9. The amount charged to customers for goods or services sold to them.

_____ 10. When sales are made on account, allowing the customer to pay later, the business acquires a(n) (?)

_____ 11. The amount of assets consumed or services used in the process of earning revenue.

_____ 12. A list of the assets, liabilities, and owner's equity of a business entity as of a specific date, usually at the close of the last day of a month or year.

_____ 13. A summary of the revenue and the expenses of a business entity for a specific period of time, such as a month or a year.

_____ 14. A summary of the changes in the earnings retained in a business entity for a specific period of time, such as a month or a year.

_____ 15. The excess of the revenue over the expenses incurred in earning the revenue is called (?)

_____ 16. A type of record traditionally used for the purpose of recording individual transactions.

_____ 17. A group of related accounts that comprise a complete unit.

_____ 18. Transaction information is initially entered in a record called a(n) (?)

_____ 19. The concept that assumes that accounting applies to individual economic units and that each unit is separate and distinct from the persons who supply its assets.

_____ 20. A summary of the cash receipts and cash payments of a business entity for a specific period of time.

PART 2

Instructions: Indicate whether each of the following statements is true or false by placing a T or F in the space provided.

_____ 1. Financial accounting employs both historical and estimated data, which management uses in conducting daily operations and in planning future operations.

_____ 2. The Governmental Accounting Standards Board has responsibility for establishing the accounting standards to be followed by state and municipal governments.

_____ 3. Of the various governmental agencies with an interest in the development of accounting principles, the AICPA has been the most influential.

_____ 4. The AICPA has established a code of professional ethics to guide CPAs in the conduct of their practices.

_____ 5. The business entity concept is based on the applicability of accounting to individual economic units in society.

_____ 6. A separate legal entity, organized in accordance with state or federal statutes and in which ownership is divided into shares of stock, is called a corporation.

_____ 7. A partnership is owned by not less than four individuals.

_____ 8. A business transaction is the occurrence of an event or of a condition that must be recorded.

_____ 9. All business transactions are recorded in terms of money.

_____ 10. Shares of ownership interest in a corporation are generally called corporate interests.

_____ 11. Amounts entered on the left side of an account are called debits to the account.

_____ 12. The process of entering a transaction in a journal is called posting.

_____ 13. A listing of account balances which verifies the equality of the total debit balances and the total credit balances is called a trial balance.

_____ 14. The financing activities section of the statement of cash flows includes cash transactions that enter into the determination of net income.

_____ 15. Distributions of earnings to owners (stockholders) are called dividends.

PART 3

Instructions: Complete each of the following statements by circling the letter of the best answer.

1. As part of a project to develop a broad conceptual framework for financial accounting, the FASB is publishing
   a. Statements of Financial Accounting Standards
   b. Interpretations of Statements of Financial Accounting Standards
   c. Statements of Financial Accounting Principles
   d. Statements of Financial Accounting Concepts

2. The dominant body in the development of generally accepted accounting principles today is the
   a. Accounting Principles Commission
   b. Accounting Procedures Committee
   c. Financial Accounting Standards Board
   d. General Accounting Principles Board

3. The records of properties and services purchased by a business are maintained in accordance with the
   a. business entity concept
   b. cost principle
   c. matching principle
   d. proprietorship principle

4. Another way of writing the accounting equation is
   a. Assets + Liabilities = Owner's Equity
   b. Owner's Equity + Assets = Liabilities
   c. Assets = Owner's Equity - Liabilities
   d. Assets - Liabilities = Owner's Equity

5. The form of balance sheet with the liability and owner's equity sections presented below the asset section is called the
   a. report form
   b. balancing form
   c. account form
   d. systematic form

PART 4

Instructions: Some typical transactions of Crowe Company are presented below. For each transaction, indicate the increase (+), the decrease (-), or no change (o) in the assets (A), liabilities (L), and owner's equity (OE) by placing the appropriate sign(s) in the appropriate column(s). More than one sign may have to be placed in the A, L, or OE column for a given transaction.

	A	L	OE
1. Issued capital stock for cash			
2. Purchased supplies on account			
3. Charged customers for services sold on account			
4. Received cash from cash customers			
5. Paid cash for rent on building			
6. Collected an account receivable in full			
7. Paid cash for supplies			
8. Returned supplies purchased on account and not yet paid for			
9. Paid cash to creditors on account			
10. Paid cash dividends to stockholders			

PART 5

Instructions: The assets, liabilities, and owner's equity of Feather Company are expressed in equation form below. Following the equation are 10 transactions completed by Feather. On each of the numbered lines, show by addition or subtraction the effect of each of the transactions on the equation. For each transaction, identify the changes in owner's equity by placing the letter R (revenue), E (expense), D (dividends), or S (sale of shares) at the right of each increase or decrease in owner's equity. On the lines labeled "Bal.," show the new equation resulting from the transaction.

	Assets	= Liabilities +	Owner's Equity
	Cash + Supplies + Land	= Accounts Payable +	Capital Stock

1. Feather sold capital stock for $30,000 cash. (1)

2. Feather purchased $3,000 of supplies on account. (2)

   Bal.

3. Feather purchased land for a future building site for $14,000 cash. (3)

   Bal.

4. Feather paid creditors $1,800 on account. (4)

   Bal.

5. Feather paid $2,000 in dividends. (5)

   Bal.

6. Feather paid $2,800 for building and equipment rent for the month. (6)

   Bal.

7. During the month, another $900 of expenses were incurred on account by the business. (7)

   Bal.

8. During the month, Feather sold another $12,000 of capital stock for cash. (8)

   Bal.

9. Feather received $340 for a cash service call. (9)

   Bal.

10. Feather used $600 worth of supplies. (10)

    Bal.

Name _____

PART 6

Instructions: Using the form provided below, prepare the journal entries to record each of the ten transactions listed in Part 5.

JOURNAL

	DATE		DESCRIPTION	POST. REF.	DEBIT	CREDIT	
1							1
2							2
3							3
4							4
5							5
6							6
7							7
8							8
9							9
10							10
11							11
12							12
13							13
14							14
15							15
16							16
17							17
18							18
19							19
20							20
21							21
22							22
23							23
24							24
25							25
26							26

PART 7

The assets and liabilities of Beyers Company as of December 31, 1991, and the revenues and expenses for the year are as follows:

Cash	$ 19,200
Accounts receivable	9,300
Supplies	2,700
Land	21,600
Accounts payable	2,760
Sales	50,940
Rent expense	10,320
Advertising expense	7,650
Utilities expense	6,000
Supplies expense	2,940
Miscellaneous expense	1,350

Beyers Company had capital stock of $30,000 and retained earnings of $12,120 on January 1, 1991. During the current year, the corporation paid cash dividends of $14,760. Cash received from customers was $47,110 and cash paid for expenses and to creditors was $30,010. The cash balance on January 1, 1991 was $16,860.

Instructions: Using the forms provided, prepare the following:

1. An income statement for the year ended December 31, 1991.

2. A retained earnings statement for the year ended December 31, 1991.

3. A balance sheet as of December 31, 1991.

4. A statement of cash flows for the year ended December 31, 1991.

1.

Beyers Company
Income Statement
For Year Ended December 31, 1991

2.

Beyers Company
Retained Earnings Statement
For Year Ended December 31, 1991

3.

Beyers Company
Balance Sheet
December 31, 1991

4.

Beyers Company
Statement of Cash Flows
For Year Ended December 31, 1991

Chapter 2
Accounting for Service and Merchandising Enterprises

STUDY GOALS

After studying this chapter, you should be able to:

1. Describe the nature of a chart of accounts and illustrate the chart of accounts for a service enterprise.

2. Describe and illustrate the flow of business transaction data through an accounting system for a service enterprise.

3. Describe the nature of merchandising operations and illustrate the chart of accounts for a merchandising enterprise.

4. Describe and illustrate the accounting for merchandising transactions.

5. Describe the procedures for discovering errors in accounts.

GLOSSARY OF KEY TERMS

Cash discount. The deduction allowable if an invoice is paid by a specified date.

Chart of accounts. A listing of all the accounts used by a business enterprise.

Credit memorandum. The form issued by a seller to inform a debtor that a credit has been posted to the debtor's account receivable.

Debit memorandum. The form issued by a buyer to inform a creditor that a debit has been posted to the creditor's account payable.

FOB destination. Terms of agreement between buyer and seller, whereby ownership passes when merchandise is received by the buyer, and the seller absorbs the transportation costs.

FOB shipping point. Terms of agreement between buyer and seller, whereby ownership passes when merchandise is delivered to the shipper, and the buyer absorbs the transportation costs.

Invoice. The bill provided by the seller (who refers to it as a sales invoice) to a buyer (who refers to it as a purchase invoice) for items purchased.

Purchases discounts. An available discount taken by the purchaser for early payment of an invoice; a contra account to Purchases.

Purchases returns and allowances. Reduction in purchases, resulting from merchandise returned to the vendor or from the vendor's reduction in the original purchase price; a contra account to Purchases.

Realization principle. The principle under which sales are generally recorded when title to merchandise passes to the buyer.

Sales discounts. An available discount granted by the seller for early payment of an invoice.

Sales returns and allowances. Reductions in sales, resulting from merchandise returned by customers or from the seller's reduction in the original sales price.

Slide. The erroneous movement of all digits in a number, one or more spaces to the right or the left, such as writing $542 as $5,420.

Transposition. The erroneous arrangement of digits in a number, such as writing $542 as $524.

CHAPTER OUTLINE

I. Nature of the Chart of Accounts.

    A. The number of accounts maintained by a specific enterprise is affected by the nature of its operations, its volume of business, and the extent to which details are needed for taxing authorities, managerial decisions, credit purposes, etc.

    B. A listing of the accounts in the ledger is called a chart of accounts. Generally, the accounts in the chart of accounts should appear in the same order as the accounts are presented on the balance sheet and income statement.

II. Flow of Business Transaction Data.

    A. The flow of business transaction data may be diagrammed as follows:

Business *Transaction* occurs $\Rightarrow$ Business *Document* prepared $\Rightarrow$ Entry recorded in *Journal* $\Rightarrow$ Entry posted to *Ledger*

        1. The initial record of each transaction is a business document.

        2. Transactions are entered in chronological order in the journal.

        3. The amounts of the debits and credits in the journal are posted to the accounts in the ledger.

    B. A formal form of ledger account is the standard account form, which includes balance columns.

    C. The primary advantage of the standard account form is that the account balance is readily available.

    D. The general journal is the formalized device used for recording journal entries in chronological order.

    E. The posting of a debit or credit journal entry to an account ledger is performed in the following manner:

        1. Record the date and the amount of the entry in the account.

        2. Insert the number of the journal page in the Posting Reference column of the account.

        3. Insert the ledger account number in the Posting Reference column of the journal.

III. Nature of Merchandising Operations.

    A. Merchandising enterprises acquire merchandise for resale to customers.

    B. The chart of accounts for a merchandising enterprise is similar to that for a service enterprise. The main difference is that the chart of accounts for a merchandising enterprise includes accounts for transactions related to the acquisition and sale of merchandise.

IV. Accounting for Merchandising Operations.

    A. Purchases of merchandise are usually accumulated in an account called Purchases.

    B. Discounts taken by the buyer for early payment of an invoice are called purchases discounts. They are recorded by crediting the purchases discounts account and are viewed as a deduction from the amount initially recorded as Purchases. In this sense, Purchases Discounts can be thought of as a contra (or offsetting) account to Purchases.

        1. The arrangements agreed upon by the buyer and the seller as to when payments for merchandise are to be made are called the credit terms.

        2. The credit period during which the buyer is allowed to pay usually begins with the date of the sale as shown by the date of the invoice or bill.

        3. If the payment is due within a stated number of days after the date of invoice, for example, 30 days, the terms may be expressed as n/30. If payment is due at the end of the month, the terms may be expressed as n/eom.

        4. The terms 2/10, n/30 mean that, although the credit period is thirty days, the buyer may deduct 2% of the amount of the invoice if payment is made within ten days of the invoice date. This deduction is known as a cash discount.

        5. From the buyer's standpoint, it is important to take advantage of all available discounts, even though it may be necessary to borrow the money to make the payment.

C. If merchandise is returned or a price adjustment is requested by the buyer, the transaction is recorded by a debit to Accounts Payable and a credit to Purchases Returns and Allowances.

1. The details of the merchandise returned or the price adjustment requested are set forth by the buyer in a debit memorandum.

2. A confirmation from the seller of the amount of the merchandise returned or the price adjustment requested is set forth in a credit memorandum.

3. The purchases returns and allowances account can be viewed as a deduction from the amount initially recorded as Purchases. In this sense, Purchases Returns and Allowances can be thought of as a contra (or offsetting) account to Purchases.

4. When a buyer returns merchandise or has been granted an allowance prior to the payment of the invoice, the amount of the debit memorandum is deducted from the invoice amount before the purchases discount is computed.

D. Sales are recorded in the accounting records based upon the realization principle. Under this principle, sales are generally recorded when the title to the merchandise passes to the buyer.

E. Merchandise sales are recorded by the seller by a credit to a sales account.

1. Cash sales are recorded by a debit to Cash and a credit to Sales.

2. Sales to customers who use bank credit cards are recorded as cash sales.

3. Sales of merchandise on account are recorded by a debit to Accounts Receivable and a credit to Sales.

4. Sales made by use of nonbank credit cards are recorded as sales on account. Any service fees charged by the card company are debited to Credit Card Collection Expense.

F. Almost all states and many other taxing units levy a tax on retail sales of merchandise, which becomes a liability at the time the sale is made.

G. The seller refers to the discounts taken by the buyer for early payment of an invoice as sales discounts. These discounts are recorded by debiting the sales discounts account, which is viewed as a reduction in the amount initially recorded as Sales. In this sense, Sales Discounts can be thought of as a contra (or offsetting) account to Sales.

H. Merchandise sold that is returned by the buyer or for which a price adjustment is made is recorded by the seller by debiting a sales returns and allowances account. This account is viewed as a reduction in the amount initially recorded as Sales. In this sense, Sales Returns and Allowances can be thought of as a contra (or offsetting) account to Sales.

I. If the ownership of merchandise passes to the buyer when the seller delivers the merchandise to the shipper, the buyer is to absorb the transportation costs, and the terms are said to be FOB shipping point.

1. Transportation costs paid by the buyer should be debited to Transportation In or Freight In and credited to Cash.

2. The balance of the transportation in or freight in account should be added to net purchases in determining the total cost of merchandise purchased.

3. Sellers may prepay the transportation costs and add them to the invoice, as an accommodation to the buyer. In this case, the buyer should debit Transportation In for the transportation costs and compute any purchases discounts on the amount of the sale rather than on the invoice total. The seller records the prepayment of transportation costs by adding the amount to the total invoice and debiting Accounts Receivable.

J. If ownership of the merchandise passes to the buyer when the merchandise is received by the buyer, the seller is to assume the costs of transportation, and the terms are said to be FOB destination.

1. The amounts paid by the seller for delivery of merchandise are debited to Transportation Out, Delivery Expense, or a similarly titled account.

2. The total of such costs incurred during a period is reported on the seller's income statement as a selling expense.

V. Discovery of Errors.

A. The existence of errors in the accounts may be determined by (1) audit procedures, (2) chance discovery, or (3) preparing a trial balance.

B. The trial balance does not provide complete proof of the accuracy of the ledger. It indicates only that the debits and credits are equal.

C. If the two totals of a trial balance are not equal, it is probably due to one or more of the following types of errors:

1. Error in preparing the trial balance, such as:

   a. One of the columns of the trial balance was incorrectly added.

   b. The amount of an account balance was incorrectly recorded on the trial balance.

   c. A debit balance was recorded on the trial balance as a credit, or vice versa, or a balance was omitted entirely.

2. Error in determining the account balances, such as:

   a. A balance was incorrectly computed.

   b. A balance was entered in the wrong balance column.

3. Error in recording a transaction in the ledger, such as:

   a. An erroneous amount was posted to the account.

   b. A debit entry was posted as a credit, or vice versa.

   c. A debit or a credit posting was omitted.

D. Among the types of errors that will not cause inequality in the trial balance totals are the following:

1. Failure to record a transaction or to post a transaction.

2. Recording the same erroneous amount for both the debit and the credit parts of a transaction.

3. Recording the same transaction more than once.

4. Posting a part of a transaction correctly as a debit or credit but to the wrong account.

E. Two common types of errors are known as transpositions (an erroneous arrangement of digits) and slides (the movement of an entire number erroneously one or more spaces to the right or left).

F. If none of the above errors is found, the general procedure followed is to retrace the various steps in the accounting process.

PART 1

Instructions: A list of terms and related statements appears below. From the list of terms, select the term that relates to each statement and print its identifying letter in the space provided.

A. Cash discount   E. FOB shipping point   H. Sales
B. Credit memorandum   F. Purchases   I. Sales discounts
C. Debit memorandum   G. Purchases discounts   J. Transportation Out
D. FOB destination

_____ 1. As a means of encouraging payment before the end of the credit period, a discount for the early payment of cash is known as a (?)

_____ 2. The general term for discounts taken by the buyer for early payment of an invoice is (?)

_____ 3. When merchandise is returned or a price adjustment is requested, the buyer may inform the seller through the use of a (?)

_____ 4. The document issued by the seller, allowing for returns of merchandise or a price reduction.

_____ 5. The seller refers to the discounts taken by the buyer for early payment of an invoice as (?)

_____ 6. If the ownership of the merchandise passes to the buyer when the seller delivers the merchandise to the shipper, the buyer is to absorb the transportation costs, and the terms are said to be (?)

_____ 7. If ownership passes to the buyer when the merchandise is received by the buyer, the seller is to assume the costs of transportation, and the terms are said to be (?)

_____ 8. Purchases discounts can be thought of as a contra account to (?)

_____ 9. Sales returns and allowances can be thought of as a contra account to (?)

_____ 10. If the terms of sale are FOB destination, the amounts paid by the seller for delivery of the merchandise are debited to (?)

PART 2

Instructions: Indicate whether each of the following statements is true or false by placing a T or F in the space provided.

_____ 1. The initial record of each transaction is evidenced by a business document.

_____ 2. The chart of accounts for a merchandising enterprise will be the same as that for a service enterprise.

_____ 3. A discount offered the purchaser of goods as a means of encouraging payment before the end of the credit period is known as a bank discount.

_____ 4. Credit terms of "2/10, n/30" mean that the buyer may deduct 2% of the amount of the invoice if payment is made within 10 days of the invoice date.

_____ 5. If the seller is to absorb the cost of delivering the goods, the terms are stated FOB (free on board) shipping point.

_____ 6. The purchases returns and allowances account can be viewed as a deduction from the amount initially recorded as Purchases.

_____ 7. Under the realization principle, sales are generally recorded when the title to merchandise passes to the buyer.

_____ 8. The primary advantage of the standard account form is that all debits and credits are listed separately.

_____ 9. The equality of debits and credits in the ledger should be verified at the end of each accounting period, if not more often, through preparing a balance sheet.

_____ 10. A recording error caused by the erroneous rearrangement of digits, such as writing $627 as $672, is called a slide.

PART 3

Instructions: Complete each of the following statements by circling the letter of the best answer.

1. A buyer receives an invoice for $120 dated June 10. If the terms are 2/10, n/30, and the buyer pays the invoice within the discount period, what amount will the seller receive?
   a. $120
   b. $117.60
   c. $96
   d. $2.40

2. The sales discount account is a contra account to:
   a. Accounts Receivable
   b. Sales Discounts
   c. Sales
   d. Purchases

3. When the seller prepays the transportation costs and the terms of sale are FOB shipping point, the seller records the payment of the transportation costs by debiting:
   a. Accounts Receivable
   b. Sales
   c. Transportation In
   d. Accounts Payable

4. If the seller collects sales tax at the time of sale, the seller credits the tax to:
   a. Sales
   b. Accounts Receivable
   c. Sales Tax Payable
   d. Sales Tax Receivable

5. Of the following errors, the one that will cause an inequality in the trial balance totals is:
   a. incorrectly computing an account balance
   b. failure to record a transaction
   c. recording the same transaction more than once
   d. posting a transaction to the wrong account

6. Of the following errors, the one that will *not* cause an inequality in the trial balance totals is:
   a. debit balance recorded on the trial balance as a credit.
   b. account balance entered in the wrong balance column in the trial balance.
   c. credit posting omitted from an account in the ledger.
   d. same erroneous amount recorded for both the debit and credit parts of a transaction.

PART 4

Instructions: Prepare entries for each of the following related transactions of Axel Co. in the journal given below.

1. Purchased $5,000 of merchandise from Wilson Co. on account, terms 2/10, n/30.

2. Paid Wilson Co. on account for purchases, less discount.

3. Purchased $3,500 of merchandise from Farris Co. on account, terms FOB shipping point, 2/10, n/30, with prepaid shipping costs of $80 added to the invoice.

4. Returned merchandise from Farris Co., $750.

5. Paid Farris Co. on account for purchases, less returns and discount.

JOURNAL

	DATE		DESCRIPTION	POST. REF.	DEBIT	CREDIT	
1							1
2							2
3							3
4							4
5							5
6							6
7							7
8							8
9							9
10							10
11							11
12							12
13							13
14							14
15							15
16							16

PART 5

Instructions: Prepare entries for each of the following related transactions of J & B Co. in the journal given below.

1. Sold merchandise on nonbank credit cards and reported accounts to the card company, $3,150.

2. Sold merchandise for cash, $2,850.

3. Received cash from card company for nonbank credit card sales, less $125 service fee.

4. Sold merchandise on account to Rask Co., $4,500 terms, 2/10, n/30, FOB shipping point. Prepaid transportation costs of $150 at the customer's request.

5. Received merchandise returned by Rask Co., $350.

6. Received cash on account from Rask Co. for sale and transportation costs, less returns and discount.

JOURNAL

	DATE		DESCRIPTION	POST. REF.	DEBIT	CREDIT	
1							1
2							2
3							3
4							4
5							5
6							6
7							7
8							8
9							9
10							10
11							11
12							12
13							13
14							14
15							15
16							16
17							17
18							18
19							19
20							20
21							21

PART 6

Selected transactions for the first month of operation of Momper Co. are as follows:

Apr. 3 Sold capital stock for $30,000.
     10 Purchased equipment on account for $10,600.
     14 Purchased merchandise on account for $6,900.
     22 Purchased additional equipment on account for $5,100.
     29 Paid $2,400 to creditors on account.

Instructions: 1. Journalize the transactions in the journal given below.

2. Post to the appropriate ledger accounts on the next page.

3. Prepare a trial balance of the ledger accounts of Momper Co. as of April 30 of the current year, using the form below.

	DATE	DESCRIPTION	POST. REF.	DEBIT	CREDIT	
1						1
2						2
3						3
4						4
5						5
6						6
7						7
8						8
9						9
10						10
11						11
12						12
13						13
14						14
15						15

Momper Company
Trial Balance
April 30, 19--

Name _____

ACCOUNT Cash   ACCOUNT NO. 11

DATE	ITEM	POST. REF.	DEBIT	CREDIT	BALANCE	
					DEBIT	CREDIT

ACCOUNT Equipment   ACCOUNT NO. 18

DATE	ITEM	POST. REF.	DEBIT	CREDIT	BALANCE	
					DEBIT	CREDIT

ACCOUNT Accounts Payable   ACCOUNT NO. 21

DATE	ITEM	POST. REF.	DEBIT	CREDIT	BALANCE	
					DEBIT	CREDIT

ACCOUNT Capital Stock   ACCOUNT NO. 31

DATE	ITEM	POST. REF.	DEBIT	CREDIT	BALANCE	
					DEBIT	CREDIT

ACCOUNT Purchases   ACCOUNT NO. 51

DATE	ITEM	POST. REF.	DEBIT	CREDIT	BALANCE	
					DEBIT	CREDIT

Chapter 3
The Matching Concept and the Adjusting Process

After studying this chapter, you should be able to:

1. Describe and illustrate the application of the accounting period concept.

2. Discuss the matching concept as it relates to the cash basis and the accrual basis of accounting.

3. Describe the nature of the adjusting process and illustrate the preparation of adjusting entries related to: plant assets, prepaid expenses, unearned revenues, accrued assets, and accrued liabilities.

4. Describe and illustrate the effect on the financial statements of the failure to record adjusting entries.

5. Describe and illustrate the application of the materiality concept.

GLOSSARY OF KEY TERMS

Accrual basis. Revenues are recognized in the period earned and expenses are recognized in the period incurred in the process of generating revenues.

Accrued asset (accrued revenue) or accrued liability (accrued expense). An asset (revenue) or a liability (expense) that gradually increases with the passage of time and that is recorded at the end of the accounting period by an adjusting entry.

Accumulated depreciation account. The contra asset account used to accumulate the depreciation recognized to date on plant assets.

Adjusting entry. An entry required at the end of an accounting period to record an internal transaction and to bring the ledger up to date.

Book value. The difference between the balance of a plant asset account and its related accumulated depreciation account.

Cash basis. Revenue is recognized in the period cash is received, and expenses are recognized in the period cash is paid.

Contra account. An account that is offset against another account.

Depreciation. The decrease in usefulness of all plant assets except land.

Fiscal year. The annual accounting period adopted by an enterprise.

Going concern concept. The concept that assumes that a business entity has a reasonable expectation of continuing in business at a profit for an indefinite period of time.

Materiality concept. The concept that recognizes the practicality of ignoring small or insignificant deviations from generally accepted accounting principles.

Natural business year. A year that ends when a business's activities have reached the lowest point in its annual operating cycle.

Plant assets. Tangible assets that are permanent or have a relatively long life and are used in the business.

Prepaid expense. A purchased commodity or service that has not been consumed at the end of an accounting period.

Unearned revenue. Revenue received in advance of its being earned.

CHAPTER OUTLINE

I. Accounting Period.

   A. The going concern concept assumes that a business entity has a reasonable expectation of continuing in business at a profit for an indefinite period of time.

   1. The going concern concept supports the treatment of prepaid expenses as assets, even though they may not be salable.

   2. When there is conclusive evidence that a business entity has a limited life, the accounting procedures should be appropriate to the expected terminal date of the entity. The financial statements should be prepared from a "quitting concern" or liquidation point of view, rather than a "going concern" point of view.

   B. The maximum length of an accounting period is usually one year, which includes a complete cycle of the seasons and of business activities.

   1. The annual accounting period adopted by an enterprise is known as its fiscal year.

   2. An accounting period ending when a business's activities have reached the lowest point in its annual operating cycle is termed the natural business year.

   3. The long-term financial history of a business enterprise may be shown by a succession of balance sheets, prepared every year. The history of operations for the intervening periods is represented in a series of income statements.

II. Matching Concept.

   A. The determination of periodic net income relies on the matching concept, which requires the use of a two-step process.

   1. Revenues are recognized during the period.

   2. Costs of assets consumed (expenses) in generating the revenues must be matched against those revenues to determine the net income.

   B. Revenues and expenses may be reported on the income statement by the cash basis or the accrual basis of accounting.

   C. For most businesses, the cash basis does not measure revenues and expenses accurately enough to be considered an acceptable method.

   D. Generally accepted accounting principles require the use of the accrual basis of accounting.

   1. Under the accrual method, revenues for rendering of service are recognized after the service has been rendered.

   2. Revenues for the sale of merchandise are generally recognized after the ownership of the goods has passed to the buyer.

   3. The costs of assets consumed in generating revenue during a period must be recognized as expenses.

   4. The accrual basis of accounting requires the use of the adjusting process at the end of the accounting period to properly match revenues and expenses for the period.

III. The Nature of the Adjusting Process.

   A. The entries required at the end of the accounting period to bring the accounts up to date and to assure the proper matching of revenues and expenses are called adjusting entries.

   B. Adjustments are required for plant assets, prepaid expenses, unearned revenues, accrued assets, and accrued liabilities.

IV. Plant Assets.

   A. Plant assets are tangible assets that are permanent or have a relatively long life and are used in the business.

   B. The decrease in the usefulness of a plant asset is called depreciation. The adjusting entry to record depreciation is a debit to an expense account and a credit to a contra account, accumulated depreciation.

   C. The difference between the balance of a plant asset account and its related contra asset account (accumulated depreciation) is called the book value of the asset.

V. Prepaid Expenses.

   A. Prepaid expenses are the costs of goods and services that have been purchased but not used at the end of the accounting period. Examples include prepaid insurance, prepaid rent, prepaid advertising, prepaid interest, and various kinds of supplies.

B. At the time the expense is prepaid, it may be recorded initially as an asset.

   1. The amount of the prepaid expense actually used is determined at the end of the accounting period.

   2. An adjusting entry at the end of the accounting period debits an expense account and credits the asset account for the amount of the adjustment.

VI. Unearned Revenues.

A. Items of revenue that are received in advance represent a liability that may be termed unearned revenue. Examples of such revenue include subscriptions received by magazine publishers, rent received in advance, and premiums received on insurance policies.

B. When revenue is received in advance, it may be credited to a liability account.

   1. At the end of the accounting period, the amount of the revenue that has been earned must be determined.

   2. That portion of the revenue that has been earned must be adjusted by debiting the liability account and crediting the revenue account.

VII. Accrued Assets (Accrued Revenues).

A. Because it is common to record some types of revenue only as cash is received during a fiscal period, at the end of the period there may be items of revenue that have not been recorded.

B. The amounts of such unrecorded revenues, called accrued assets or accrued revenues, must be recorded by debiting an asset account and crediting a revenue account.

VIII. Accrued Liabilities (Accrued Expenses).

A. Expenses that accrue from day to day but are recorded only when they are paid are called accrued liabilities or accrued expenses.

B. The adjusting entry for an accrued liability is to debit an expense account and to credit a liability account.

IX. Effect of Omitting Adjusting Entries.

A. Failure to record or an error in recording adjusting entries will result in an incorrect income statement, retained earnings statement, and balance sheet.

B. If the adjusting entry for depreciation expense is omitted, expense will be understated and net income will be overstated on the income statement, the ending balance for retained earnings on the retained earnings statement will be overstated, and the book value of the plant assets and the retained earnings on the balance sheet will be overstated.

C. Unless a correction is made, the same items will be overstated on future balance sheets until the plant assets are disposed of.

D. If the adjusting entry for accrued expense is omitted, expense will be understated and net income will be overstated on the income statement, the ending balance for retained earnings on the retained earnings statement will be overstated, and the liabilities will be understated and the retained earnings will be overstated on the balance sheet.

E. Unless a correction is made, the expense will be overstated and net income will be understated on the following year's income statement.

X. Materiality.

A. The concept of materiality recognizes the practicality of ignoring small or insignificant deviations from generally accepted accounting principles.

B. To determine materiality, the size of an item and its nature must be considered in relationship to the size and the nature of other items.

PART 1

Instructions: A list of terms and related statements appear below. From the list of terms, select the term that relates to each statement and print its identifying letter in the space provided.

A. Accrual basis
B. Accrued assets
C. Accrued expense
D. Accrued liabilities

E. Adjusting entries
F. Book value
G. Depreciation
H. Fiscal year

I. Going concern concept
J. Materiality concept
K. Natural business year
L. Plant assets

_____ 1. An accounting method in which revenues are recognized in the period in which they are earned, and expenses are recognized in the period in which they are incurred.

_____ 2. The entries required at the end of an accounting period to bring the accounts up to date and to ensure the proper matching of revenues and expenses.

_____ 3. The decrease in usefulness in plant assets over time.

_____ 4. An accumulated expense that is unpaid and unrecorded.

_____ 5. The difference between the balance of a plant asset account and its related accumulated depreciation account.

_____ 6. Accrued expenses may also be described on the balance sheet as (?)

_____ 7. Accrued revenues may also be described on the balance sheet as (?)

_____ 8. The annual accounting period adopted by an enterprise.

_____ 9. A period ending when a business's activities have reached the lowest point in its annual operating cycle.

_____ 10. The concept that assumes that a business entity has a reasonable expectation of continuing in business at a profit for an indefinite period of time.

_____ 11. Tangible assets that are permanent and have a relatively long life and are used in the business.

_____ 12. The concept that recognizes the practicality of ignoring small or insignificant deviations from generally accepted accounting principles.

Name _____

PART 2

Instructions: Indicate whether each of the following statements is true or false by placing a T or F in the space provided.

_____   1. Generally accepted accounting principles permit the use of either the cash or accrual basis of accounting.

_____   2. When an adjustment that reduces prepaid expenses is not properly recorded, the asset accounts and expense accounts are overstated.

_____   3. Accumulated depreciation accounts may be called contra accounts.

_____   4. The adjusting entry to record depreciation of plant assets consists of a debit to a depreciation expense account and a credit to an accumulated depreciation account.

_____   5. When services are not paid for until after they have been performed, the accrued expense is recorded in the accounts by an adjusting entry at the end of the accounting period.

_____   6. Every adjusting entry affects both a balance sheet account and an income statement account.

_____   7. The annual accounting period adopted by an enterprise is known as its current year.

_____   8. At the time that an expense is prepaid, it may be debited to an asset account.

_____   9. When a prepaid expense is recorded initially as an asset, an adjusting entry is used to transfer the amount used to an appropriate expense account.

_____ 10. The amount of accrued revenue is recorded by debiting a liability account and crediting a revenue account.

_____ 11. When revenue is received in advance, it may be debited to a prepaid revenue account.

_____ 12. The concept of materiality can be used to justify treating small expenditures for plant assets as an expense of the period rather than as an asset.

PART 3

Instructions: Complete each of the following statements by circling the letter of the best answer.

1. Entries required at the end of an accounting period to bring the accounts up to date and to ensure the proper matching of revenues and expenses are called:
   a. matching entries
   b. adjusting entries
   c. closing entries
   d. correcting entries

2. If a $2,000 adjustment for depreciation is not recorded, which of the following financial statement errors will occur in the current period?
   a. Net income will be understated.
   b. Retained earnings will be understated.
   c. Assets will be overstated.
   d. Expenses will be overstated.

3. If a $250 adjustment for accrued salaries is not recorded in year 1, which of the following financial statement errors will occur in year 1?
   a. Expenses will be overstated.
   b. Net income will be understated.
   c. Assets will be understated.
   d. Retained earnings will be overstated.

4. If a $250 adjustment for accrued salaries is not recorded in year 1 and the error is not corrected, which of the following financial statement errors will occur in year 2?
   a. Net income will be understated.
   b. Assets will be understated.
   c. Expenses will be understated.
   d. Retained earnings will be overstated.

5. The costs of goods and services that have been purchased but not used at the end of the accounting period are called:
   a. deferred charges
   b. prepaid expenses
   c. deferred costs
   d. accrued liabilities

6. The amounts of accrued but unrecorded revenues at the end of the fiscal period are both an asset and a(n):
   a. liability
   b. expense
   c. revenue
   d. deferral

7. When a prepaid expense is recorded initially as an asset, an adjusting entry is used to transfer the amount used to an appropriate:

    a.   liability account

    b.   expense account

    c.   contra account

    d.   accrual account

8. Items of revenue that are received in advance represent a liability that may be termed:

    a.   accrued revenue

    b.   accrued liability

    c.   prepaid revenue

    d.   unearned revenue

9. When unearned revenue is recorded initially as a liability, an adjusting entry is used to transfer the amount earned to an appropriate:

    a.   asset account

    b.   current liability account

    c.   accrual account

    d.   revenue account

10. The amounts of accrued but unpaid expenses at the end of the fiscal period are both an expense and a(n):

    a.   liability

    b.   asset

    c.   deferral

    d.   revenue

PART 4

Jim Wheeler closes his books as of the end of each year (December 31). On May 1 of the current year, Jim insured the busiess assets for three years, at a premium of $5,400.

Instructions:

1. In the T accounts presented below, enter the adjusting entry that should be made by Wheeler as of December 31 to record the amount of insurance expired as of that date. The May 1 premium payment is recorded in the T accounts.

2. Wheeler's balance sheet as of December 31 should show the asset value of the unexpired insurance as $_____

3. Wheeler's income statement for the year ended December 31, should show insurance expense of $_____

Cash	Prepaid Insurance	Insurance Expense
May 1 5,400	May 1 5,400	

PART 5

Stewart Co.'s unearned rent account has a balance of $36,000 at December 31 of the current year. This amount represents the rental of an apartment for a period of three years. The lease began on October 1 of the current year.

Instructions: Record the adjusting entry as of December 31 to recognize the rent income for the appropriate portion of the year.

JOURNAL

	DATE	DESCRIPTION	POST. REF.	DEBIT	CREDIT	
1						1
2						2
3						3

Name _____

PART 6

Goodman Inc.'s salary expense account has a balance of $84,000 at the end of the current year, representing salaries paid in cash through Saturday, December 29. Salaries accrued through December 31 amount to $1,250. Goodman also has interest of $260 earned but not collected as of December 31 on a note receivable.

Instructions:

1. Record the adjusting entry for accrued salaries expense as of December 31.

2. Record the adjusting entry for accrued interest income as of December 31.

JOURNAL

	DATE	DESCRIPTION	POST. REF.	DEBIT	CREDIT	
1						1
2						2
3						3
4						4
5						5
6						6

PART 7

Daniels Co.'s delivery service income account has a balance of $3,200 at the end of the current year, representing cash collections for services performed during the year. The unbilled services at December 31 total $700.

Instructions: Record the adjusting entry as of December 31 and post to the T accounts below.

JOURNAL

	DATE	DESCRIPTION	POST. REF.	DEBIT	CREDIT	
1						1
2						2
3						3
4						4

Delivery Service Receivable

Delivery Service Income

Dec. 31   3,200

PART 8

Klay Co.'s equipment account has a balance of $62,000. Depreciation on this equipment is estimated at $4,100 for the year.

Instructions:

1. Record the adjusting entry for depreciation as of December 31 and post to the T accounts below.

2. If the adjusting entry in (1) were omitted, indicate whether the following items will be overstated or understated by $4,100 by placing a check mark in the appropriate column.

	Overstated	Understated
a. Expenses on the income statement	_____	_____
b. Net income on the income statement	_____	_____
c. Retained earnings on the retained earnings statement ...	_____	_____
d. Assets on the balance sheet	_____	_____
e. Retained earnings on the balance sheet	_____	_____

JOURNAL

	DATE	DESCRIPTION	POST. REF.	DEBIT	CREDIT	
1						1
2						2
3						3
4						4

Equipment	Accumulated Depreciation-Equipment	Depreciation Expense-Equipment
Dec. 31 62,000		

Chapter 4
Periodic Reporting

STUDY GOALS

After studying this chapter, you should be able to:

1. Describe and illustrate the use of the work sheet for summarizing the accounting data needed to prepare the financial statements.

2. Illustrate the preparation of an income statement, retained earnings statement, and balance sheet from the work sheet and describe alternate forms for these statements.

3. Describe and illustrate the preparation of adjusting entries and closing entries.

4. Describe and illustrate the flow of data through the accounting system.

5. Describe and illustrate the use of reversing entries.

GLOSSARY OF KEY TERMS

Account form of balance sheet. A balance sheet with assets on the left-hand side and liabilities and owner's equity on the right-hand side.

Adequate disclosure concept. The concept requiring that financial statements and their accompanying footnotes or other explanatory materials should contain all the data necessary for a reader to understand the enterprise's financial status.

Administrative expense. Expense incurred in the general operation of a business.

Closing entry. An entry necessary to eliminate the balance of a temporary account in preparation for the following accounting period.

Cost of merchandise sold. The cost of the merchandise purchased by a merchandise enterprise and sold.

Gross profit. The excess of net revenue from sales over the cost of merchandise sold.

Income from operations. The excess of gross profit over total operating expenses.

Income summary account. The account used in the closing process for summarizing the revenue and expense accounts.

Multiple-step income statement. An income statement with numerous sections and subsections with several intermediate balances before net income.

Net income. The final figure in the income statement when revenues exceed expenses.

Net loss. The final figure in the income statement when expenses exceed revenues.

Other expense. An expense that cannot be associated definitely with operations.

Other income. Revenue from sources other than the principal activity of a business.

Periodic inventory system. A system of inventory accounting in which only the revenue from sales is recorded each time a sale is made; the cost of merchandise on hand at the end of a period is determined by a detailed listing (physical inventory) of the merchandise on hand.

Perpetual inventory system. A system of inventory accounting that employs records that continually disclose the amount of the inventory on hand.

Physical inventory. The detailed listing of merchandise on hand.

Report form of balance sheet. The form of balance sheet with the liability and owner's equity sections presented below the asset section.

Retained earnings statement. A statement for a corporate enterprise, summarizing the changes in retained earnings during a specific period of time.

Reversing entry. An entry that reverses a specific adjusting entry to facilitate the recording of routine transactions in the subsequent period.

Selling expense. An expense incurred directly and entirely in connection with the sale of merchandise.

Single-step income statement. An income statement with the total of all expenses deducted from the total of all revenues.

Work sheet. A working paper used to assist in the preparation of financial statements.

CHAPTER OUTLINE

I. Work Sheet for Financial Statements.

  A. At the end of an accounting period, a work sheet may be prepared to assist the accountant in accumulating data for preparing the financial statements.

  B. The trial balance data for the work sheet are taken directly from the ledger.

  C. The necessary debit and credit portions of the adjusting entries are entered on the work sheet in the adjustments columns.

  D. The data in the trial balance columns are combined with the adjustments data. Asset, liability, and stockholders' equity amounts are then extended to the balance sheet columns and revenue and expense amounts are extended to the income statement columns. Merchandise inventory is an exception to this practice. Beginning merchandise inventory is extended to the income statement debit column. Ending merchandise inventory is entered in the income statement credit column and extended to the balance sheet debit column.

  E. After all the balances have been extended, each of the four columns is totaled. The net income or the net loss for the period is the difference between the totals of the two income statement columns. Net income is entered on the work sheet in the income statement column and the balance sheet credit column. A net loss is entered in the income statement credit column and the balance sheet debit column.

  F. After the net income or net loss is entered in the appropriate column, the columns are totaled to verify the arithmetic accuracy of the work sheet.

II. Preparation of Financial Statements.

  A. The income statement, retained earnings statement, and balance sheet are prepared from the accounts and data in the work sheet.

  B. In preparing financial statements, the adequate disclosure concept should be followed. This concept requires that financial statements and their accompanying footnotes or other explanatory materials should contain all the data necessary for a reader to understand the enterprise's financial status.

  C. Two widely used forms for the income statement are the multiple-step and single-step.

  D. The multiple-step income statement contains many sections, subsections, and intermediate balances.

    1. The total of all charges to customers for merchandise sold, both for cash and on account, is reported as revenue from sales. Sales returns and allowances and sales discounts are deducted from the gross sales amount to yield net sales.

    2. The cost of merchandise sold section appears next. Determination of cost of merchandise sold depends on whether the perpetual or periodic system of accounting for merchandise is used.

      a. Under the perpetual inventory system, both the sales amount and the cost of merchandise sold amount are recorded when each item of merchandise is sold. In this manner, the accounting records continuously (perpetually) disclose the inventory on hand.

b. Under the periodic inventory system, the revenues from sales are recorded when sales are made, but no attempt is made on the sales date to record the cost of merchandise sold. A detailed listing of merchandise on hand (called a physical inventory) is made at the end of the accounting period. This physical inventory is used to determine the cost of merchandise sold during the period and the cost of inventory on hand at the end of the period.

3. Under the periodic inventory system, the cost of merchandise sold during a period is reported in a separate section of the income statement. Beginning inventory plus net purchases (purchases less returns and allowances and discounts) plus transportation costs equals merchandise available for sale. This amount less the ending inventory yields cost of merchandise sold.

4. The excess of the net revenue from sales over the cost of merchandise sold is called gross profit.

5. Operating expenses are generally grouped into selling expenses and administrative expenses.

6. The excess of gross profit over total operating expenses is called income from operations, or operating income. If operating expenses are greater than gross profit, the excess is loss from operations.

7. Revenue from sources other than the principal activity of a business is classified as other income or non-operating income. In a merchandising enterprise, this category often includes income from interest, rent, dividends, and gains resulting from the sale of plant assets.

8. Expenses that cannot be associated definitely with operations are identified as other expenses, or nonoperating expenses. Interest expense and losses incurred in the disposal of plant assets are examples of items that are reported in this section.

9. The final figure on the income statement is labeled net income (or net loss).

E. The single-step form of income statement derives its name from the fact that the total of all expenses is deducted from all revenues.

F. The retained earnings statement summarizes the changes which have occurred in the retained earnings account during the fiscal period.

1. The retained earnings statement is the connecting link between the income statement and the balance sheet.

2. It is not unusual to add the analysis of retained earnings at the bottom of the income statement to form a combined income and retained earnings statement.

G. The balance sheet is prepared in one of two forms.

1. The arrangement of the assets on the left-hand side of the balance sheet, with liabilities and stockholders' equity on the right-hand side, is called the account form of balance sheet.

2. When the balance sheet is prepared in downward sequence, it is called the report form.

H. The assets section of the balance sheet is commonly divided into current assets and plant assets.

1. Current assets are cash and other assets that are expected to be realized in cash, sold, or used up usually within one year or less through the normal operations of the business.

2. Plant assets include equipment, machinery, and buildings, which depreciate with the passage of time.

I. The liabilities section normally includes two categories, current and long-term liabilities.

1. Current liabilities are liabilities that will be due usually within one year or less and that are to be paid out of current assets.

2. Long-term liabilities (fixed liabilities) are liabilities that will not be due for more than one year.

J. The stockholders' equity section includes capital stock (the investment of the stockholders) and retained earnings (the net income retained in the business).

III. Adjusting and Closing Entries.

    A. The analyses necessary to prepare the adjusting entries are completed during the process of preparing the work sheet.

    B. It is only necessary to refer to the work sheet when recording the adjusting entries in the journal.

    C. The balances of the revenue, expense, and dividends accounts must be removed at the end of the accounting period, so that these accounts will be ready for use in the following period. This is accomplished by means of closing entries.

    D. The four entries required to close the accounts of a corporation are as follows:

        1. The first entry closes all income statement accounts with credit balances by transferring the total to the credit side of Income Summary.

        2. The second entry closes all income statement accounts with debit balances by transferring the total to the debit side of Income Summary.

        3. The third entry closes Income Summary by transferring its balance, the net income or net loss for the year, to Retained Earnings.

        4. The fourth entry closes Dividends by transferring its balance to Retained Earnings.

    E. Closing entries are recorded in the journal immediately following the adjusting entries.

    F. After all closing entries have been recorded and posted, the revenue, expense, and dividend accounts have zero balances. The only accounts with balances are the asset, contra asset, liability, and stockholders' equity accounts. Balances of these accounts in the ledger will correspond exactly with the amounts reported on the balance sheet.

    G. After the adjusting and closing entries have been recorded, it is advisable to take a post-closing trial balance to verify the debit-credit equality of the ledger at the beginning of the following year.

IV. Flow of Data Through Accounting System.

    A. The most significant output of the accounting process is the financial statements.

    B. The phases of the accounting process are as follows:

        1. Transactions are analyzed and recorded in a journal.

        2. Transactions are posted to the ledger.

        3. Trial balance is prepared, data needed to adjust the accounts are assembled, and the work sheet is completed.

        4. Financial statements are prepared.

        5. Adjusting and closing entries are journalized.

        6. Adjusting and closing entries are posted to the ledger.

        7. Post-closing trial balance is prepared.

V. Reversing Entries.

    A. Reversing entries are an optional procedure which exactly reverses adjusting entries made at the end of a preceding fiscal period. The purpose of reversing entries is to make the recording of routine transactions as efficient as possible.

    B. Reversing entries can be used with the adjustments for all accrued liabilities and accrued assets.

PART 1

Instructions: A list of terms and related statements appear below. From the list of terms, select the term that relates to each statement and print its identifying letter in the space provided.

A. Account form   F. Income from operations   J. Perpetual inventory system
B. Administrative expenses   G. Multiple-step   K. Report form
C. Current assets   H. Nonoperating income   L. Selling expenses
D. Current liabilities   I. Periodic inventory system   M. Single-step
E. Gross profit

_____ 1. The form of income statement that has many sections, subsections, and intermediate balances.

_____ 2. The form of income statement in which the total of all expenses is deducted from the total of all revenues.

_____ 3. The excess of the net revenue from sales over the cost of merchandise sold.

_____ 4. Expenses that are incurred directly and entirely in connection with the sale of merchandise are classified as (?)

_____ 5. Expenses incurred in the general operations of the business are classified as (?)

_____ 6. The excess of gross profit over total operating expenses is called (?)

_____ 7. Under this inventory system, the revenues from sales are recorded when sales are made, but no attempt is made on the sales date to record the cost of the merchandise sold.

_____ 8. The form of balance sheet with the assets on the left-hand side and the liabilities and owner's equity on the right-hand side is called the (?)

_____ 9. The form of balance sheet in which the liabilities and stockholders' equity sections are listed below rather than to the right of the asset section is called the (?)

_____ 10. Under this inventory system, both the sales amount and the cost of merchandise sold amount are recorded when each item of merchandise is sold.

_____ 11. Assets that may reasonably be expected to be realized in cash or sold or used up usually within a year or less, through the normal operations of the business.

_____ 12. Liabilities that will be due within a short time (usually one year or less) and that are to be paid out of current assets.

_____ 13. Revenue from sources other than the principal activity of a business.

PART 2

Instructions: Indicate whether each of the following statements is true or false by placing a T or F in the space provided.

_F_   **1.** The adequate disclosure concept requires that financial statements and their accompanying footnotes should reveal the names of all major stockholders.

_F_   **2.** Revenue from sources such as income from interest, rent, dividends, and gains resulting from the sale of plant assets is classified as income from operations.

_T_   **3.** The single-step form of income statement has the advantage of being simple and it emphasizes total revenues and total expenses as the factors that determine net income.

_T_   **4.** Gross profit is not calculated in the single-step form of income statement.

_T_   **5.** The excess of gross profit over total operating expenses is called income from operations.

_T_   **6.** The analysis of retained earnings can be added at the bottom of the income statement to form a combined income and retained earnings statement.

_F_   **7.** The traditional balance sheet arrangement of assets on the left-hand side, with the liabilities and stockholders' equity on the right-hand side, is called the report form.

_F_   **8.** After the adjusting and closing entries have been recorded and posted, the general ledger accounts that appear on the balance sheet have zero balances.

_F_   **9.** When the Income Statement columns of the work sheet are totaled, and the Debit column total is greater than the Credit column total, the excess is the net income.

_F_   **10.** The difference between the debit and credit columns of the Income Statement section of the work sheet is normally larger than the difference between the debit and credit columns of the Balance Sheet section.

_F_   **11.** A type of working paper frequently used by accountants prior to the preparation of financial statements is called a post-closing trial balance.

_T_   **12.** Under the perpetual inventory system, both the sales amount and the cost of merchandise sold amount are recorded when each item of merchandise is sold.

_T_   **13.** The account titled Income Summary is used only at the end of the accounting period during the closing process.

_T_   **14.** In a reversing entry, the accounts and the corresponding amounts in the related adjusting entry are reversed.

_T_   **15.** After the reversing entry for accrued salary expense is posted and the first payroll for January has been posted, the balance of the salary expense account automatically represents the current expense of the new period.

PART 3

Instructions: Complete each of the following statements by circling the letter of the best answer.

1. Beginning merchandise inventory plus net purchases plus transportation equals
   a. cost of merchandise purchased
   b. merchandise available for sale
   c. cost of merchandise sold
   d. gross profit

2. The excess of net revenue from sales over the cost of merchandise sold is called
   a. gross profit
   b. operating profit
   c. net profit from operations
   d. merchandising income

3. Income from operations is computed by subtracting from gross profit the
   a. selling expenses
   b. administrative expenses
   c. total non-merchandising expenses
   d. total operating expenses

4. Items such as income from interest, rent, dividends, and gains resulting from the sale of plant assets are usually classified as
   a. other income
   b. operating income
   c. nonmerchandise income
   d. administrative income

5. Ending merchandise inventory is entered on the work sheet in the
   a. trial balance credit column
   b. income statement credit column
   c. income statement debit column
   d. balance sheet credit column

6. After all adjusting entries are posted, the balances of all asset, liability, revenue, and expense accounts correspond exactly to the amounts in the
   a. work sheet trial balance
   b. general journal
   c. post-closing trial balance
   d. financial statements

7. For which of the following items would a reversing entry not be appropriate?
   a. accrued liabilities
   b. accrued assets
   c. depreciation
   d. accrued revenues

8. In completing the work sheet, all amounts of assets, liabilities, and stockholders' equity are extended to the balance sheet columns except
   a. accounts receivable
   b. long-term notes payable
   c. plant assets
   d. beginning merchandise inventory

PART 4

Levy Co. closes its books each year on December 31. On December 31 of the current year, the salary expense account has a debit balance of $44,500. Levy's last regular payday was Friday, December 28, for the preceding week. Levy Co. owes its employees $230 for working Monday, December 31.

Instructions: Record the following entries in the general journal and post to the general ledger accounts.

1. The adjusting entry for salaries payable as of December 31.

2. The closing entry to close the salary expense account to Income Summary.

3. The reversing entry for salaries payable as of January 1 of the following year.

4. The entry to record the payment of the payroll for the week ended January 4 of the following year. Salaries totaled $1,250 for the week.

JOURNAL

	DATE		DESCRIPTION	POST. REF.	DEBIT	CREDIT	
1							1
2							2
3							3
4							4
5							5
6							6
7							7
8							8
9							9
10							10
11							11
12							12
13							13
14							14
15							15
16							16
17							17
18							18
19							19
20							20

Name _____

ACCOUNT Cash   **ACCOUNT NO.** 111

DATE		ITEM	POST. REF.	DEBIT	CREDIT	BALANCE DEBIT	BALANCE CREDIT
19— Dec.	31	Balance				9 0 0 0	

ACCOUNT Salaries Payable   **ACCOUNT NO.** 213

DATE		ITEM	POST. REF.	DEBIT	CREDIT	BALANCE DEBIT	BALANCE CREDIT

ACCOUNT Income Summary   **ACCOUNT NO.** 313

DATE		ITEM	POST. REF.	DEBIT	CREDIT	BALANCE DEBIT	BALANCE CREDIT

ACCOUNT Salary Expense   **ACCOUNT NO.** 611

DATE		ITEM	POST. REF.	DEBIT	CREDIT	BALANCE DEBIT	BALANCE CREDIT
19— Dec.	31	Balance				4 4 5 0 0	

PART 5

Instructions: On the basis of the following data, prepare the cost of merchandise sold section of the income statement for the fiscal year ended June 30, 1991, for Alman Co.

Merchandise Inventory, June 30, 1991	$155,000
Merchandise Inventory, July 1, 1990	130,000
Purchases	435,000
Purchases Returns and Allowances	3,780
Purchases Discounts	4,590
Transportation In	2,970

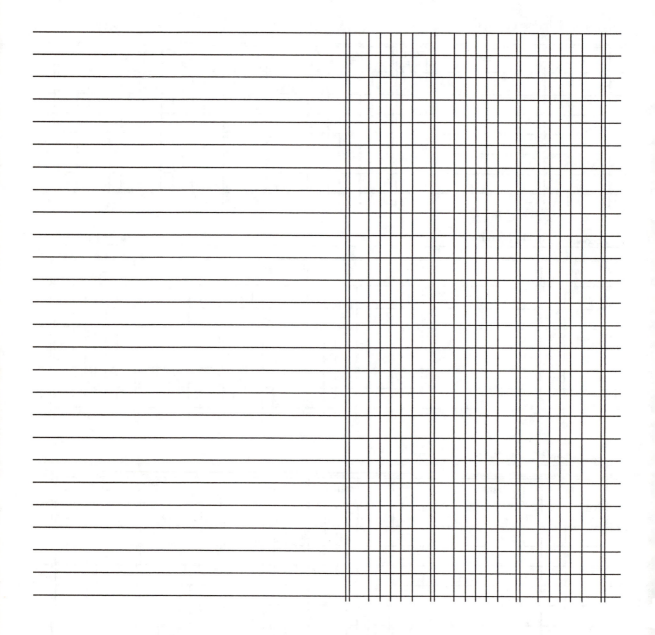

PART 6

Instructions: Record the following adjustments in the Adjustments columns and complete the **work** sheet for Halsey Corporation for the fiscal year ended March 31. The merchandise inventory **on March** 31 is $115,800.

(a) The office supplies on hand March 31 are $1,250.

(b) The insurance expense for the year is $13,980.

(c) Depreciation on delivery equipment for the year is $9,050.

(d) Salaries accrued but not paid, $2,000 (sales salaries, $1,130; office salaries, $870).

Halsey Corporation
Work Sheet
For Month Ended March 31, 19 –

ACCOUNT TITLE	TRIAL BALANCE Debit	TRIAL BALANCE Credit	ADJUSTMENTS Debit	ADJUSTMENTS Credit	INCOME STATEMENT Debit	INCOME STATEMENT Credit	BALANCE SHEET Debit	BALANCE SHEET Credit
Cash	7 3 1 0 0 00							
Accounts Receivable	11 4 0 0 0 00							
Merchandise Inventory	16 0 3 9 0 00							
Office Supplies	1 0 3 5 0 00							
Prepaid Insurance	2 4 7 4 0 00							
Delivery Equipment	6 0 1 5 0 00							
Accum. Dep. - Deliv. Equip.		1 3 9 0 0 00						
Accounts Payable		7 5 3 0 0 00						
Salaries Payable								
Capital Stock		12 8 0 0 0 00						
Retained Earnings		7 5 6 5 0 00						
Income Summary								
Sales		105 6 7 0 0 00						
Sales Returns & Allow.	1 3 0 1 0 00							
Purchases	69 2 9 0 0 00							
Purchases Discounts		6 4 3 0 00						
Sales Salaries Expense	7 7 1 2 0 00							
Advertising Expense	1 3 0 9 0 00							
Delivery Expense	4 2 1 0 0 00							
Dep. Expense - Deliv. Equip.								
Misc. Selling Expense	1 3 9 5 0 00							
Office Salaries Expense	5 4 9 3 0 00							
Office Supplies Expense								
Insurance Expense								
Misc. Administrative Expense	6 8 7 0 00							
Interest Income		7 2 0 00						
	135 6 7 0 0 00	135 6 7 0 0 00						
Net Income								

Name _____

PART 7

Instructions: Use the work sheet in Part 6 for this problem.

1. Record the adjusting entries in the journal below.

2. Record the closing entries in the journal below.

JOURNAL

	DATE		DESCRIPTION	POST. REF.	DEBIT	CREDIT	
1							1
2							2
3							3
4							4
5							5
6							6
7							7
8							8
9							9
10							10
11							11
12							12
13							13
14							14
15							15
16							16
17							17
18							18
19							19
20							20
21							21
22							22
23							23
24							24
25							25
26							26

PART 8

Instructions: Using the Income Statement columns of the work sheet in Part 6, prepare a multiple-step income statement with a cost of merchandise sold section for the year ended March 31, 19—.

Halsey Corporation
Income Statement
For Year Ended March 31, 19—

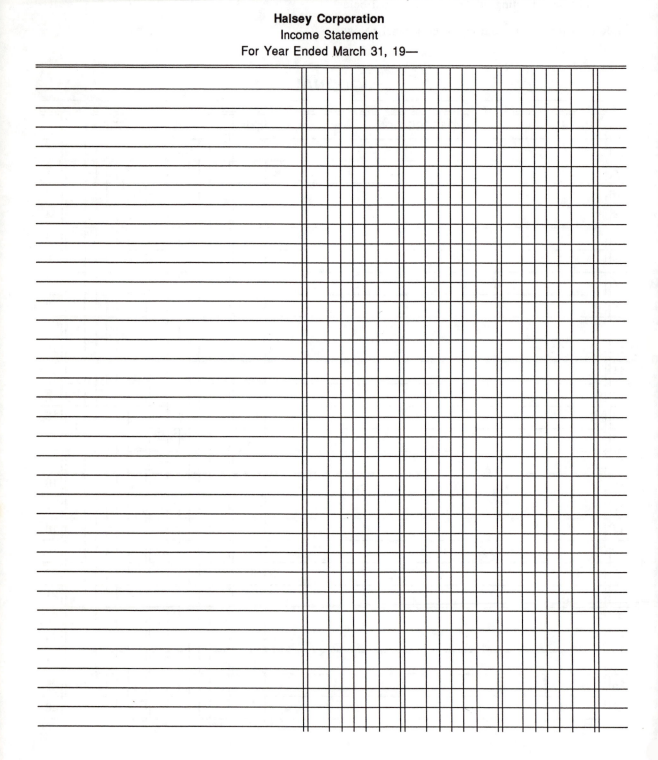

Name _____

PART 9

Instructions: Using the Balance Sheet columns of the work sheet in Part 6, prepare a balance sheet in report form as of March 31, 19—.

Halsey Corporation
Balance Sheet
March 31, 19—

PART 10

Instructions: Using the Income Statement and Balance Sheet columns of the work sheet in Part 6, prepare a retained earnings statement for the year ended March 31, 19—. (Halsey paid no dividends during the current year.)

Halsey Corporation
Retained Earnings Statement
For Year Ended March 31, 19—

Chapter 5
Accounting Systems and Cash

STUDY GOALS

After studying this chapter, you should be able to:

1. Describe the principles of properly designed accounting systems.

2. Describe the three phases of accounting system installation and revision.

3. Describe and illustrate the principles of internal control.

4. Describe and illustrate the use of a bank account for controlling cash, including the preparation of a bank reconciliation.

5. Describe and illustrate internal controls for cash receipts, including: control over mail receipts, use of a cash short and over account, and use of cash change funds

6. Describe and illustrate internal controls for cash payments including use of a voucher system, discounts lost account, and petty cash account.

7. Describe recent trends in the use of electronic funds transfer to process cash transactions.

GLOSSARY OF KEY TERMS

Accounting system. The system that provides the information for use in conducting the affairs of the business and reporting to owners, creditors, and other interested parties.

Bank reconciliation. The method of analysis that details the items that are responsible for the difference between the cash balance reported in the bank statement and the balance of the cash account in the ledger.

Controlling account. The account in the general ledger that summarizes the balances of a subsidiary ledger.

Data base. The entire amount of data needed by an enterprise.

Electronic funds transfer (EFT). A payment system that uses computerized electronic impulses rather than paper (money, checks, etc.) to effect a cash transaction.

General ledger. The principal ledger, when used in conjunction with subsidiary ledgers, that contains all of the balance sheet and income statement accounts.

Internal controls. The detailed policies and procedures used to direct operations and provide reasonable assurance that the entity's objectives are achieved.

Petty cash. Cash set aside in a special fund that is used to pay relatively small amounts.

Subsidiary ledger. A ledger containing individual accounts with a common characteristic.

Voucher. A document that serves as evidence of authority to pay cash.

Voucher system. Records, methods, and procedures employed in verifying and recording liabilities and paying and recording cash payments.

CHAPTER OUTLINE

I. Principles of Accounting Systems.

A. The entire amount of data needed by an enterprise is called its data base. If the data base is relatively small, a manual system might be sufficient. As the data base becomes larger, the manual system can be modified to include such things as subsidiary ledgers, with controlling accounts in the general ledger. As the data base becomes even larger and more complex, a computerized system might be required.

B. Regardless of whether a manual or computerized accounting system is used by an enterprise, there are basic principles of accounting systems that are applicable.

C. Although an accounting system must be tailored to meet the specific needs of each business, reports should not be produced if the cost of the report is more than the benefit received by those who use it (cost effectiveness balance).

D. An accounting system must be flexible enough to meet future needs of the business as the environment in which it operates changes (flexibility to meet future needs).

E. The detailed procedures inherent in an accounting system to control operations are called internal controls (adequate internal controls).

F. An accounting system must provide effective reports in an understandable manner (effective reporting).

G. Only by effectively using and adapting to the human resources of the business can the accounting system meet information needs at the lowest cost (adaptation to organizational structure).

II. Accounting System Installation and Revision.

A. Many large businesses continually review their accounting system and may constantly be involved in changing some part of it.

B. Systems analysis is one phase of accounting system installation and revision. The goal of systems analysis is to determine information needs, the sources of such information, and the deficiencies in procedures and data processing methods presently used.

C. Systems design is a second phase of accounting system installation and revision. Systems designers must have a general knowledge of the qualities of different kinds of data processing equipment, and the ability to evaluate alternatives.

D. The final phase of the creation or revision of an accounting system is to carry out, or implement, the proposals. In the systems implementation phase, all personnel responsible for operating the system must be carefully trained and closely supervised until satisfactory efficiency is achieved.

III. Internal Control Structure.

A. The internal control structure consists of the policies and procedures established to provide reasonable assurance that an enterprise's goals and objectives will be achieved.

B. The internal control structure can be divided into three elements: (1) the control environment, (2) the control procedures, and (3) the accounting system.

C. The policies and procedures of an internal control structure will vary according to the size and type of business.

D. The control environment of an enterprise represents an overall attitude toward and awareness of the importance of controls by both management and other employees.

E. The control procedures are the policies and procedures management has established with the control environment. There are a number of general procedures which apply to all enterprises.

1. The successful operation of an accounting system requires competent personnel who are able to perform the duties to which they are assigned. It is also advisable to rotate clerical personnel periodically from job to job.

2. If employees are to work efficiently, their responsibilities must be clearly defined.

3. To decrease the possibility of inefficiency, errors, and fraud, responsibility for a sequence of related operations should be divided among two or more persons.

4. Responsibility for maintaining the accounting records should be separated from the responsibility for engaging in business transactions and for the custody of a firm's assets.

5. Proofs and security measures such as the use of cash registers and fidelity insurance should be used to safeguard business assets and assure reliable accounting data.

6. To determine whether the other internal control principles are being effectively applied, the system should be periodically reviewed and evaluated by internal auditors.

F. The accounting system generates the information management needs to plan and direct the operations of the enterprise.

IV. Control over Cash.

A. Because of the ease with which money can be transferred, cash is the asset most likely to be diverted and used improperly by employees. Therefore, cash must be effectively safeguarded by special controls.

B. One of the major devices for maintaining control over cash is the bank account.

1. To get the most benefit from a bank account, all cash received must be deposited in the bank and all payments must be made by checks drawn on the bank or from special cash funds.

2. A bank may require a business to maintain in a bank account a minimum cash balance called a compensating balance. Compensating balance requirements should be disclosed in notes to the financial statements.

3. The forms used by business in connection with a bank account are a signature card, deposit ticket, check, and a record of checks drawn.

4. The three parties to a check are the drawer, the one who signs the check; the drawee, the bank on which the check is drawn; and the payee, the one to whose order the check is drawn.

5. Checks issued to a creditor on account usually are accompanied by a remittance advice, which is a notification of the specific invoice that is being paid.

C. Banks usually mail to each depositor a statement of account once a month which shows the beginning balance, checks and other debits (deductions by the bank), deposits and other credits (additions by the bank), and the balance at the end of the period.

D. The balance shown on the depositor's records as cash in bank and the ending balance on the bank statement are not likely to be equal on any specific date because of either or both of the following: (1) delay by either party in recording transactions and (2) errors by either party in recording transactions.

E. To determine the reasons for any difference between the balance according to the bank statement and the bank balance according to the depositor's records, a bank reconciliation is prepared. The bank reconciliation is divided into two sections: one section begins with the balance according to the bank statement and ends with the adjusted balance; the other section begins with the balance according to the depositor's records and also ends with the adjusted balance. The form and the content of the bank reconciliation are outlined as follows:

Bank balance according to bank statement

Add: Additions by depositor not on bank statement
         Bank errors

Deduct: Deductions by depositor not on bank statement
         Bank errors

Adjusted balance

Bank balance according to depositor's records

Add: Additions by bank not recorded by depositor
         Depositor errors

Deduct: Deductions by bank not recorded by depositor
         Depositor errors

Adjusted balance

F. The following procedures are used in finding the reconciling items and determining the adjusted balance of Cash in Bank:

1. Individual deposits listed on the bank statement are compared with unrecorded deposits appearing in the preceding reconciliation and with deposit receipts or other records of deposits. Deposits not recorded by the

bank are added to the balance according to the bank statement.

2. Paid checks are compared with outstanding checks appearing on the preceding reconciliation and with the record of checks written. Checks issued that have not been paid by the bank are outstanding and are deducted from the balance according to the bank statement.

3. Bank credit memorandums, representing additions made by the bank, are traced to the record of cash receipts. Credit memorandums that have not been recorded are added to the balance according to the depositor's records.

4. Bank debit memorandums, representing deductions made by the bank, are traced to the record of cash payments. Debit memorandums that have not been recorded are deducted from the balance according to the depositor's records.

5. Errors discovered during the process of making the foregoing comparisons are listed separately on the reconciliation. For example, if the amount for which a check was written had been recorded erroneously by the depositor, the amount of the error should be added to or deducted from the balance according to the depositor's records. Similarly, errors by the bank should be added to or deducted from the balance according to the bank statement.

G. Bank memorandums not recorded by the depositor and depositor's errors shown by the bank reconciliation require that entries be made in the accounts.

1. The data needed for these adjustments are provided by the section of the bank reconciliation that begins with the balance per depositor's records.

2. After the adjusting entries are posted, the cash in bank account will have a balance which agrees with the adjusted balance shown on the bank reconciliation.

H. The bank reconciliation is an important part of the internal controls because it is a means of comparing recorded cash, as shown by the accounting records, with the amount of cash recorded by the bank.

1. Greater internal control is achieved when the bank reconciliation is prepared by an employee who does not take part in or record cash transactions with the bank.

2. Without a proper separation of duties, cash is more likely to be embezzled.

V. Internal Control of Cash Receipts.

A. At the end of each business day, salesclerks who receive cash over the counter from cash customers should count the cash in their drawer and record the amount on a memorandum form. A cashier's department employee then counts the cash in each drawer and compares the total with the memorandum and the cash register tapes, noting any differences. The cash then is sent to the cashier's office and the tapes and memorandum forms are forwarded to the accounting department for proper recording.

B. The employees who open incoming mail should compare the amount of cash received with the amount shown on the accompanying remittance advice to make sure the two amounts agree. The cash should then be forwarded to the cashier's department and the remittance advices should be delivered to the accounting department for proper recording.

C. When the amount of cash actually received during the day does not agree with the record of cash receipts, the difference should be debited or credited to a cash short and over account.

1. A debit balance in the cash short and over account at the end of the fiscal period is listed as an expense on the income statement. A credit balance is listed as a revenue.

2. If the balance of the cash short and over account becomes larger than may be accounted for by minor errors, management should take corrective measures.

D. Businesses that receive cash directly from customers and that must make change utilize a cash on hand account. At the end of each business day, the total amount of cash received during the day is deposited and the original amount of the cash fund is retained.

VI. Internal Control of Cash Payments.

A. It is common practice for business enterprises to require that every payment of cash be evidenced by a check through use of a voucher system.

B. A voucher system is made up of records, methods, and procedures used in proving and recording liabilities and making and recording cash payments. A voucher system uses (1) vouchers, (2) a file of unpaid vouchers, and (3) a file of paid vouchers.

1. A voucher is a special form on which is recorded relevant data about a liability and the details of its payment. Vouchers are customarily prepared by the accounting department on the basis of an invoice or a memorandum that serves as proof of an expenditure.

2. After approval by the designated official, each voucher is recorded as a credit to accounts payable and a debit to the appropriate asset or expense account or accounts.

3. After the voucher is recorded, it is filed in an unpaid voucher file where it remains until it is paid. The amount due on each voucher represents the credit balance of an account payable. A voucher is filed in the unpaid voucher file according to the earliest date that consideration should be given to its payment.

4. When a voucher is paid, it is removed from the unpaid voucher file and a check is issued for payment. Paid vouchers and the supporting documents should be canceled to prevent accidental or intentional reuse. The payment of a voucher is recorded in the usual manner. After payment, vouchers are usually filed in numerical order in a paid voucher file.

5. The voucher system not only provides effective accounting controls but it also aids management in making the best use of cash resources and in planning cash disbursements.

C. Discounts on the purchase of merchandise are accounted for either as deductions from purchases or as other income.

1. A major disadvantage of recording purchases at the invoice price and recognizing purchases discounts at the time of payment is that this method does not measure the cost of failing to take purchases discounts.

2. By recording purchases at the net amount (assuming that all discounts would be taken) and using a discounts lost account, better control can be maintained over the taking of cash discounts.

3. When the net method of recording purchases is used, all vouchers are prepared and recorded at the net amount. Any discount lost is noted on the related voucher and recorded in the journal when the voucher is paid.

D. A petty cash fund may be used by businesses for which there is frequent need for the payment of relatively small amounts, such as for postage due, etc.

1. In establishing a petty cash fund, the account Petty Cash is debited. If a voucher system is used, Accounts Payable is credited. When the check is drawn to pay the voucher, Accounts Payable is debited and Cash in Bank is credited.

2. The petty cash fund is replenished by a general journal entry debiting the various expense and asset accounts and crediting Accounts Payable. The check in payment of the voucher is recorded in the usual manner.

3. Because disbursements are not recorded in the amounts until the fund is replenished, petty cash funds and other special funds that operate in a like manner should always be replenished at the end of the accounting period.

E. Cash funds may also be established to meet other special needs of a business. These funds are accounted for in a fashion similar to a petty cash fund.

VII. Cash Transactions and Electronic Funds Transfer.

A. Electronic funds transfer is a payment system which uses computerized electronic impulses rather than paper (money, checks, etc.) to effect cash transactions.

B. EFT is beginning to play an important role in retail sales through such systems as the point-of-sale (POS) system.

PART 1

Instructions: A list of terms and related statements appear below. From the list of terms, select the term that relates to each statement and print its identifying letter in the space provided.

A. Bank reconciliation
B. Compensating balance
C. Controlling account
D. Drawer
E. Electronic funds transfer
F. Internal controls
G. Petty cash
H. Remittance advice
I. Unpaid voucher file
J. Voucher

_____ 1. The detailed policies and procedures used to direct operations and provide reasonable assurance that the entity's objectives are achieved.

_____ 2. The subsidiary ledger is represented in the general ledger by a summarizing account called a(n) (?)

_____ 3. The party signing a check.

_____ 4. A required minimum cash balance maintained in a bank account, generally imposed by the bank as part of a loan agreement.

_____ 5. A notification which accompanies checks issued to a creditor that indicates the specific invoice that is being paid.

_____ 6. An accounting record in which the bank balance according to the bank statement is reconciled with the bank balance according to the depositor's records.

_____ 7. A special form on which is recorded relevant data about a liability and the details of its payment.

_____ 8. After approval by the designated official, each voucher is recorded and filed in the (?)

_____ 9. A special cash fund set aside for the payment of relatively small amounts for which payment by check is not efficient.

_____ 10. A payment system using computerized electronic impulses rather than paper to effect a cash transaction.

PART 2

Instructions: Indicate whether each of the following statements is true or false by placing a T or F in the space provided.

_____ 1. The balance in the accounts receivable controlling account in the general ledger will agree with the total of the balances of all of the customers' accounts in the subsidiary ledger.

_____ 2. The goal of systems design is to determine information needs, the sources of such information, and the deficiencies in procedures and data processing methods presently used.

_____ 3. To decrease the possibility of inefficiency, errors, and fraud, responsibility for a sequence of related operations should be assigned to a single person.

_____ 4. Responsibility for maintaining the accounting records should be separated from the responsibility for custody of the firm's assets.

_____ 5. Compensating balance requirements should be disclosed in notes to the financial statements.

_____ 6. The payee is the one to whose order the check is drawn.

_____ 7. In a bank reconciliation, checks issued that have not been paid by the bank are added to the balance according to the bank statement.

_____ 8. Bank memorandums not recorded by the depositor require entries in the depositor's accounts.

_____ 9. For a greater degree of internal control, the bank reconciliation should be prepared by an employee who does not take part in or record cash transactions with the bank.

_____ 10. The employee who opens the incoming mail should compare the amount of cash received with the remittance advice and forward the cash and remittance advice to the accounting department for proper recording.

_____ 11. If there is a debit balance in the cash short and over account at the end of the fiscal period, this represents income to be included in "Miscellaneous general income" in the income statement.

_____ 12. It is common practice for business enterprises to require that every payment of cash be evidenced by a check signed by the owner.

_____ 13. After vouchers are paid, it is customary to file them in numerical sequence in the paid voucher file.

_____ 14. It is a widely accepted view that purchases discounts should be reported as deductions from purchases.

_____ 15. Petty Cash should be debited when the petty cash fund is replenished.

PART 3

Instructions: Complete each of the following statements by circling the letter of the best answer.

1. The job of installing or changing an accounting system is made up of three phases: (1) analysis, (2) design, and (3)
   a. installation
   b. verification
   c. management
   d. implementation

2. To determine whether internal control principles are being effectively applied, the system should be periodically reviewed and evaluated by the
   a. users of the system
   b. internal auditors
   c. employees responsible for operations
   d. EDP service center

3. The bank on which a check is drawn is known as the:
   a. drawer
   b. drawee
   c. payee
   d. creditor

4. In a bank reconciliation, deposits not recorded by the bank are
   a. added to the balance according to the bank statement
   b. deducted from the balance according to the bank statement
   c. added to the balance according to the depositor's records
   d. deducted from the balance according to the depositor's records

5. An important characteristic of the voucher system is the requirement that
   a. vouchers be prepared by the treasurer
   b. vouchers be paid immediately after they are prepared
   c. the face of the voucher show the account distribution
   d. a voucher be prepared for each expenditure

6. In a voucher system, the entry to record the replenishment of the petty cash fund includes a debit to various expense and asset accounts and a credit to
   a. Cash in Bank
   b. Petty Cash
   c. Accounts Payable
   d. various liability accounts

PART 4

On June 30 of the current year, Lambert Inc.'s checkbook showed a balance of $7,795 and the bank statement showed a balance of $8,510. A comparison of the bank statement and Lambert's records as of June 30 revealed the following:

(a) A deposit of $1,820, mailed to the bank by Lambert on June 29, was not included in the bank statement of June 30.

(b) The following checks were outstanding:

Check No. 1255 for $285

Check No. 1280 for $150

Check No. 1295 for $715

(c) Check No. 1289 in payment of a voucher had been written for $140 and had been recorded at that amount by the bank. However, Lambert had recorded it in the check register as $410.

(d) A check for $720 received from a customer was deposited in the bank. The bank recorded it at the correct amount, but Lambert recorded it at $270.

(e) Included with the bank statement was a credit memorandum for $680, representing the proceeds of a $600 note receivable left at the bank for collection. This had not been recorded on Lambert's books.

(f) Included with the bank statement was a debit memorandum for $15 for service charges which had not been recorded on Lambert's books.

Instructions: 1. Complete the following bank reconciliation:

Lambert Inc.

Bank Reconciliation

June 30, 19—

Balance according to bank statement . . . .$

Add:

Deduct:

Adjusted balance . . . .$_____

Balance according to depositor's records . . . .$

Add:

Deduct:

Adjusted balance . . . .$_____

continued

2. In the following journal, prepare the entry or entries that Lambert should make as a result of the bank reconciliation.

JOURNAL

	DATE		DESCRIPTION	POST. REF.	DEBIT	CREDIT	
1							1
2							2
3							3
4							4
5							5
6							6

PART 5

Instructions: Record the following transactions in the journal provided below, assuming that invoices for commodities purchased are recorded at their net price after deducting the allowable discount.

Sept. 8   Voucher No. 1710 is prepared for merchandise purchased from Rose Co., $6,400, terms 2/10, n/60.

10   Voucher No. 1711 is prepared for merchandise purchased from Murphy Co., $10,100, terms 1/10, n/30.

20   Check No. 3210 is issued, payable to Murphy Co., in payment of Voucher No. 1711.

Oct. 9   Check No. 3217 is issued, payable to Rose Co., in payment of Voucher No. 1710.

JOURNAL

	DATE		DESCRIPTION	POST. REF.	DEBIT	CREDIT	
1							1
2							2
3							3
4							4
5							5
6							6
7							7
8							8
9							9
10							10
11							11
12							12

Name _____

PART 6

Instructions: In the journal provided below, prepare the entries to record the following transactions:

1. Voucher No. 312 is prepared to establish a petty cash fund of $500.
2. Check No. 8805 is issued in payment of Voucher No. 312.
3. The amount of cash in the petty cash fund is now $224.40. Voucher No. 443 is prepared to replenish the fund, based on the following summary of petty cash receipts:

   Office supplies, $91.15

   Miscellaneous selling expense, $128.27

   Miscellaneous administrative expense, $59.16
4. Check No. 8844 is issued by the disbursing officer in payment of Voucher No. 443. The check is cashed and the money is placed in the fund.

JOURNAL

	DATE		DESCRIPTION	POST. REF.	DEBIT	CREDIT	
1							1
2							2
3							3
4							4
5							5
6							6
7							7
8							8
9							9
10							10
11							11
12							12
13							13
14							14

Chapter 6
Receivables and Temporary Investments

STUDY GOALS

After studying this chapter, you should be able to:

1. Describe the common classification of receivables.

2. Describe the basic principles of internal control over receivables.

3. Describe the common characteristics of notes receivable.

4. Describe and illustrate the accounting for notes receivable, including the discounting of notes receivable and dishonored notes receivable.

5. Describe the basic concepts in accounting for uncollectible receivables.

6. Describe and illustrate the allowance method of accounting for uncollectible receivables, including the estimation of uncollectibles based on sales and an analysis of receivables.

7. Describe and illustrate the direct write-off method of accounting for uncollectible receivables.

8. Describe and illustrate the installment method of accounting for sales.

9. Describe and illustrate the accounting for temporary investments.

10. Describe and illustrate the presentation of temporary investments and receivables in the balance sheet.

GLOSSARY OF KEY TERMS

Aging the receivables. The process of analyzing the accounts receivable and classifying them according to various age groupings, with the due date being the base point for determining age.

Allowance method. The method of accounting for uncollectible receivables, by which advance provision for the uncollectibles is made.

Carrying amount. The amount at which a temporary or a long-term investment or a long-term liability is reported on the balance sheet; also called basis or book value.

Contingent liability. A potential obligation that will materialize only if certain events occur in the future.

Direct write-off method. A method of accounting for uncollectible receivables, whereby an expense is recognized only when specific accounts are judged to be uncollectible.

Discount. The interest deducted from the maturity value of a note.

Dishonored note receivable. A note which the maker fails to pay on the due date.

Installment method. A method of accounting for installment sales which allocates gross profit on installment sales according to the amount of installment receivables collected in each year.

Marketable security. An investment in a security that can be readily sold when cash is needed.

Maturity value. The amount due at the maturity or due date of a note.

Note receivable. A written promise to pay, representing an amount owed by a business.

Point of sale method. A method of accounting for installment sales under which revenue is realized at the time title passes to the buyer.

Proceeds. The net amount available from discounting a note.

Promissory note. A written promise to pay a sum in money on demand or at a definite time.

Temporary investment. An investment in securities that can be readily sold when cash is needed.

CHAPTER OUTLINE

I. Classification of Receivables.
   A. The term receivables includes all money claims against people, organizations, or other debtors.
      1. A promissory note is a written promise to pay a sum of money on demand or at a definite time. The enterprise owning a note refers to it as a note receivable and records it as an asset at its face value.
      2. Accounts and notes receivable originating from sales transactions are called trade receivables.
      3. Other receivables include interest receivable, loans to officers or employees, and loans to affiliated companies.
   B. All receivables that are expected to be realized in cash within a year are presented as current assets on the balance sheet. Those not currently collectible, such as long-term loans, are shown as investments.

II. Control Over Receivables.
   A. The broad principles of internal control should be used to establish procedures to safeguard receivables.
   B. Business operations should be separated from the accounting for receivables. In addition, responsibility for related functions should be separated.
   C. All credit sales should be approved by a responsible official of the credit department. There also should be procedures for proper approval of all sales returns and allowances and sales discounts. Finally, effective collection procedures should be established to minimize losses from uncollectible accounts.

III. Characteristics of Notes Receivable.
   A. The one to whose order the note is payable is called the payee, and the one making the promise is called the maker.
   B. The date a note is to be paid is called the due date or maturity date.
      1. The period of time between the issuance date and the maturity date of a short-term note may be stated either in days or months.
      2. When the term of a note is stated in days, the due date is a specified number of days after its issuance.
      3. When the term of a note is stated as a certain number of months after the issuance date, the due date is determined by counting the number of months from the issuance date. For example, a three-month note dated July 31 would be due on October 31.
   C. A note that provides for payment of interest is called an interest-bearing note. If a note makes no provision for interest, it is said to be non-interest-bearing.
      1. Interest rates are usually stated in terms of a period of one year, regardless of the actual period of time involved.
      2. The basic formula for computing interest is as follows: Principal x Rate x Time = Interest
      3. For purposes of computing interest, the commercial practice of using 1/12 of a year for a month and a 360-day year will be utilized.
   D. The amount due at the maturity or due date of a note is called the maturity value.

IV. Accounting for Notes Receivable.

   A. When a note is received from a customer to apply on account, notes receivable is debited and accounts receivable is credited for the face amount of the note.

   B. At the end of the fiscal year, an adjusting entry is necessary to record the accrued interest on any outstanding interest-bearing notes receivable.

   C. To facilitate recording the receipt of the maturity amount of the note and interest on the due date, a reversing entry is made as of the first day of the accounting period for any accrued interest recorded from the prior period.

   D. At the time a note matures and payment is received, Cash is debited, Notes Receivable is credited for the face amount of the note, and Interest Income is credited for the amount of interest due.

   E. Instead of retaining a note until maturity, notes receivable may be transferred to a bank by endorsement, a process known as discounting notes receivable.

     1. The interest (discount) charged by the bank is computed on the maturity value of the note for the time the bank must hold the note, namely the time that will pass between the date of the transfer and the due date of the note.

     2. The amount of the proceeds paid to the endorser is the excess of the maturity value over the discount.

     3. The entry to record the discounting of notes receivable is to debit Cash for the proceeds, credit Notes Receivable for the face value of the note, and either debit Interest Expense or credit Interest Income for the amount to balance the entry.

     4. The endorser of a note that has been discounted has a contingent liability to the holder of the note for the face amount of the note plus accrued interest and any protest fee. Any significant contingent liabilities should be disclosed on the balance sheet or in an accompanying note.

   F. If the maker of the note fails to pay the debt on the due date, the note is said to be dishonored. The entry for a dishonored note is to debit Accounts Receivable for the maturity amount of the note, and credit Interest Income for the amount of interest due on the note at maturity. When a discounted note receivable is dishonored, the holder usually notifies the endorser and asks for payment. If request for payment and notification of dishonor are timely, the endorser is legally obligated to pay the amount due on the note, including any accrued interest and protest fee.

V. Uncollectible Receivables.

   A. When merchandise or services are sold on credit, a part of the claims against customers usually proves to be uncollectible.

   B. The operating expense incurred because of the failure to collect receivables is called uncollectible accounts expense, doubtful accounts expense, or bad debts.

   C. The two methods of accounting for receivables believed to be uncollectible are the allowance method and the direct write-off method.

VI. Allowance Method of Accounting for Uncollectibles.

   A. Under the allowance method of accounting for uncollectibles, advance provision for uncollectibility is made by an adjusting entry at the end of the fiscal period.

     1. The adjusting entry to record the allowance for uncollectibles is to debit Uncollectible Accounts Expense and credit Allowance for Doubtful Accounts. The account Allowance for Doubtful Accounts is a contra asset account offsetting accounts receivable.

     2. The balance of the accounts receivable account less the contra account, Allowance for Doubtful Accounts, determines the expected realizable value of the receivables as of the end of the fiscal period.

     3. Uncollectible accounts expense is recorded on the income statement as a general expense and is closed to Income Summary.

   B. When an account is believed to be uncollectible, it is written off against the allowance account by debiting Allowance for Doubtful Accounts and crediting the customer's account receivable.

   C. An account receivable that has been written off against the allowance account may later be collected.

1. The account should be reinstated by an entry that is the exact reverse of the write-off entry—a debit to the customer's account receivable and a credit to Allowance for Doubtful Accounts.

2. The cash received in payment would be recorded in the usual manner as a debit to Cash and a credit to Accounts Receivable.

D. The estimate of uncollectibles at the end of the fiscal period is based on past experience and forecasts of future business activity. Two methods of estimating uncollectibles are as follows:

1. The amount of uncollectibles may be estimated based upon the percentage of sales.

   a. Based upon past experience or industry averages, the percentage of sales which will prove to be uncollectible is estimated.

   b. The estimated percentage of uncollectible sales is then multiplied by the sales for the period, and Uncollectible Accounts Expense is debited and Allowance for Doubtful Accounts is credited for this amount.

   c. Ideally, the estimated percentage should be based upon credit sales, but total sales may be used if the portion of credit sales to total sales is relatively stable.

2. Uncollectibles may be estimated by analyzing the individual account receivable accounts in terms of length of time past due.

   a. An aging of accounts receivable is prepared which lists accounts by due date.

   b. Percentages are applied to each category of past due accounts to estimate the balance of the allowance for doubtful accounts as of the end of the accounting period.

   c. The amount of the adjusting entry at the end of the fiscal period for uncollectible accounts expense is determined by that amount necessary to bring the allowance account to its estimated balance as of the end of the period.

E. Estimates of uncollectible accounts expense based on analysis of the receivables are less common than estimates based on sales.

VII. Direct Write-Off Method of Accounting for Uncollectibles.

A. Under the direct write-off method of accounting for uncollectibles, no entry is made for uncollectibility until an account is determined to be worthless. At that time, an entry is made debiting Uncollectible Accounts Expense and crediting the individual customer's account receivable.

B. If the account that has been written off is later collected, the account should be reinstated by reversing the earlier entry to write off the account.

C. The receipt of cash and payment of a reinstated account is recorded in the usual manner.

VIII. Receivables from Installment Sales.

A. In the typical installment sale, the purchaser makes a down payment and agrees to pay the remainder in specified amounts at stated intervals over a period of time. Such sales should be treated the same as any other sale on account.

B. In some exceptional cases, collection of the receivables is not reasonably assured. In these cases, the installment method of accounting may be used.

C. The installment method allocates gross profit according to the amount of receivables collected in each year, based on the percent of gross profit to sales.

IX. Temporary Investments.

A. Most businesses invest idle or excess cash in temporary investments or marketable securities. These securities can be quickly sold when cash is needed.

B. Temporary investments and securities include stocks and bonds. Stocks are equity securities issued by corporations and bonds are debt securities issued by corporations and various government agencies.

C. A temporary investment in a portfolio of debt securities is carried at cost.

D. A temporary investment in a portfolio of equity securities is carried at the lower of its total cost or market value determined at the date of the balance sheet.

1. The carrying amount is based upon the total cost and total market value of the portfolio, rather than the lower of cost or market price of each individual equity security.

2. If the total market value of the equity securities is less than cost, an unrealized loss is recorded and reported on the income statement as a separate item.

3. If the market value of the portfolio later rises, the unrealized loss is reversed and included in the income, but only to the extent that it does not exceed the original cost. In such cases, the increase is reported separately in the Other Income section of the income statement.

X. Temporary Investments and Receivables in the Balance Sheet.

A. Temporary investments and all receivables that are expected to be realized in cash within a year are presented in the current assets section of the balance sheet.

B. It is customary to list the assets in the order of their liquidity, that is, in the order in which they can be converted to cash in normal operations.

PART 1

Instructions: A list of terms and related statements appear below. From the list of terms, select the term that relates to each statement and print its identifying letter in the space provided.

A.	Aging the receivables	E.	Discount	I.	Promissory note
B.	Allowance method	F.	Dishonored	J.	Temporary investments
C.	Contingent liabilities	G.	Expected realizable value		
D.	Direct write-off method	H.	Proceeds		

__I__ **1.** A written promise to pay a sum of money on demand or at a definite time.

__E__ **2.** The interest charged by a bank for discounting a note receivable.

__H__ **3.** The amount received from selling a note receivable prior to its maturity.

__C__ **4.** Potential obligations that will become actual liabilities only if certain events occur in the future.

__F__ **5.** If the maker of a note fails to pay the debt on the due date, the note is said to be (?)

__B__ **6.** A method of accounting for receivables which provides in advance for uncollectible receivables through the use of an allowance for doubtful accounts.

__D__ **7.** A method of accounting for uncollectible receivables in which no expense is recognized until individual accounts are determined to be worthless.

__G__ **8.** The balance of the accounts receivable following the deduction of the allowance for doubtful accounts.

__A__ **9.** The process of analyzing the receivable accounts in terms of the length of time past due.

__J__ **10.** Securities that may be quickly sold when cash is needed.

PART 2

Instructions: Indicate whether each of the following statements is true or false by placing a T or F in the space provided.

__T__ **1.** Accounts and notes receivable originating from sales transactions are sometimes called trade receivables.

__T__ **2.** For good internal control, an employee who handles the accounting for notes and accounts receivable should not be involved with credit approvals or collections of receivables.

__F__ **3.** When a note is received from a customer on account, it is recorded by debiting Notes Receivable and crediting Cash.

__F__ **4.** When the holder transfers a note to a bank by endorsement, the discount (interest) charged is computed on the face value of the note for the period the bank must hold the note.

__T__ **5.** When the proceeds from discounting a note receivable are less than the face value, the difference is recorded as interest expense.

__T__ **6.** The endorser of a note that has been discounted has a contingent liability that is in effect until the due date.

__F__ **7.** The method of accounting which provides in advance for receivables deemed uncollectible is called the reserve or net realizable value method.

__F__ **8.** The process of analyzing the receivable accounts in order to estimate the uncollectibles is sometimes called aging the receivables.

__F__ **9.** The installment method allocates gross profit according to the amount of receivables collected in each year, based on the percent of net income to sales.

__T__ **10.** The carrying amount of a temporary investment in equity securities is the lower of its total cost or market value.

PART 3

Instructions: Complete each of the following statements by circling the letter of the best answer.

1. On a promissory note, the one making the promise to pay is called the
   a. payee
   b. creditor
   c. maker
   d. noter

2. The amount that is due on a note at the maturity or due date is called the
   a. terminal value
   b. face value
   c. book value
   d. maturity value

3. When a note is discounted, the excess of the maturity value over the discount is called the
   a. gain
   b. proceeds
   c. interest
   d. present value

4. When the allowance method is used in accounting for uncollectible accounts, any uncollectible account is written off against the
   a. allowance account
   b. sales account
   c. accounts receivable account
   d. uncollectible accounts expense account

5. Assume that the allowance account has a credit balance at year end of $270 before adjustment. If the estimate of uncollectible accounts based on aging the receivables is $3,010, the amount of the adjusting entry for uncollectible accounts would be
   a. $270
   b. $2,740
   c. $3,010
   d. $3,280

6. In its first year of operations, Rose Company had sales of $189,000, cost of sales of $132,300, and collections of $98,000. All sales are made on the installment plan and gross profits are calculated by the installment method. The gross profit for the year was
   a. $29,400
   b. $34,300
   c. $56,700
   d. $68,600

7. In its first year of operations, Perez Company had sales of $189,000, cost of sales of $132,300, and collections of $98,000. All sales are made on the installment plan but gross profits are calculated using the point of sale method. The gross profit for the year was
   a. $29,400
   b. $34,300
   c. $56,700
   d. $68,600

PART 4

Instructions: Using the basic formula for interest and assuming a 360-day year, compute the interest on the following notes.

1. $6,000 at 12% for 30 days . . . . $_____
2. $2,500 at 6% for 60 days . . . . $_____
3. $1,000 at 12% for 90 days . . . . $_____

Instructions: Using the 60-day, 6% method, complete the following interest calculations. (Problems 4 and 5 and the same as 1 and 2, so that the two methods of computing interest may be compared.)

4. The interest on $6,000 at 12% for 30 days is . . . $_____
5. The interest on $2,500 at 6% for 60 days is . . . $_____
6. The interest on $8,000 for 90 days at 9% is . . . $_____
7. The interest on $4,500 for 120 days at 12% is . . $_____

PART 5

Instructions: Based on the information given, fill in the blanks below.

1. A 12%, 90-day note receivable for $5,000 was discounted at 14%, 25 days after date.

Face value . . . .   _____
Interest on face value . . . .   _____
Maturity value . . . .   _____
Discount on maturity value . . . .   _____
Proceeds . . . .   _____

2. An 8%, 120-day note receivable for $9,000 was discounted at 10%, 20 days after date.

Face value . . . .   _____
Interest value . . . .   _____
Maturity value . . . .   _____
Discount on maturity value . . . .   _____
Proceeds . . . .   _____

Name _____

PART 6

Instructions: Prepare the journal entries to record the following transactions. (Omit explanations.)

(a) Nugent Co. received a 60-day, 12% note for $6,500 from a customer, Bev Davidson, in settlement of Davidson's account.

JOURNAL

	DATE		DESCRIPTION	POST. REF.	DEBIT	CREDIT	
1							1
2							2

(b) Thirty days after the date of the note in (a), Nugent discounted Davidson's note at the bank at 10%.

3							3
4							4
5							5

(c) Davidson failed to pay the note in (a) and (b) at maturity. Nugent paid the bank.

6							6
7							7
8							8

(d) Ten days after the maturity of the note in (a), (b), and (c), Davidson paid Nugent in full, including interest at 11% for this 10-day period.

9							9
10							10
11							11
12							12
13							13

(e) Nugent received a 90-day, 10% note for $1,000 from a customer, Mary Douglass, in settlement of Douglass' account.

14						14
15						15
16						16

(f) The note in (e) was dishonored at maturity.

17						17
18						18
19						19
20						20

PART 7

Instructions: Prepare the appropriate journal entries for each of the following situations.

(a) Net sales for the year are $550,000, uncollectible accounts expense is estimated at 3% of net sales, and the allowance account has a $425 credit balance before adjustment. Prepare the adjusting entry at year end for the uncollectibles.

JOURNAL

	DATE	DESCRIPTION	POST. REF.	DEBIT	CREDIT	
1						1
2						2

(b) Based on an analysis of accounts in the customers ledger, estimated uncollectible accounts total $5,270, and the allowance account has a $325 credit balance before adjustment. Prepare the adjusting entry at year end for the uncollectibles.

3						3
4						4
5						5

(c) A $4,300 account receivable from Milton, Inc. is written off as uncollectible. The allowance method is used.

6						6
7						7
8						8

(d) A $1,625 account receivable from Gordon Co., which was written off three months earlier, is collected in full. The allowance method is used.

9						9
10						10
11						11
12						12
13						13

PART 8

Dynamo, Inc. uses the direct write-off method of accounting for uncollectibles. On July 31, 1990, Dynamo deemed that an amount of $210 due from Don Moore was uncollectible and wrote it off. On September 8, 1990, Moore paid the $210.

Instructions:

1. Prepare the entry to write off the account on July 31.

JOURNAL

	DATE		DESCRIPTION	POST. REF.	DEBIT	CREDIT	
1							1
2							2

2. Prepare the entry to reinstate the account on September 8, and to record the cash received.

3							3
4							4
5							5
6							6
7							7
8							8
9							9

PART 9

ABC, Inc. had a temporary investment in a portfolio of equity securities as of December 31, 1990, as follows:

	Cost	Market
Security A	$12,000	$10,000
Security B	$16,000	$16,800
Security C	$21,000	$23,000
Security D	$18,000	$17,400

Instructions: Compute the proper carrying amount of these securities on ABC's December 31, 1990 balance sheet . . . . $_____

Chapter 7
Inventories

STUDY GOALS

After studying this chapter, you should be able to:

1. Describe and illustrate the effect of inventory on the financial statements of the current period and the following period.

2. Identify and describe the two principal inventory systems.

3. Identify and illustrate the procedures for determining the actual quantities in inventory.

4. Describe and illustrate the determination of the cost of inventory.

5. Describe and illustrate the most common inventory costing methods under a periodic system, including the comparison of the effect of the methods on operating results.

6. Describe and illustrate the accounting for inventory under the perpetual system.

7. Describe and illustrate the valuation of inventory at other than cost, including valuation at the lower of cost or market.

8. Identify and illustrate the proper presentation of inventory in the financial statements.

9. Describe and illustrate methods of estimating the cost of inventory.

10. Describe and illustrate inventories of manufacturing enterprises.

11. Describe and illustrate accounting for long-term construction contracts.

GLOSSARY OF KEY TERMS

Average cost method. The method of inventory costing that is based on the assumption that costs should be charged against revenue in accordance with the weighted average unit costs of the commodities sold.

Direct labor. Wages of factory workers who convert materials into a finished product.

Direct materials. The cost of materials that enter directly into the finished product.

Factory overhead. All of the costs of operating the factory except for direct materials and direct labor.

Finished goods. Goods in the state in which they are to be sold.

First-in, first-out (fifo) method. A method of inventory costing based on the assumption that the costs of merchandise sold should be charged against revenue in the order in which the costs were incurred.

Gross profit method. A means of estimating inventory on hand without the need for a physical count.

Last-in, first-out (lifo) method. A method of inventory costing based on the assumption that the most recent merchandise costs incurred should be charged against revenue.

Lower of cost or market. A method of costing inventory or valuing temporary investments that carries those assets at the lower of their cost or current market prices.

Materials. Goods in the state in which they were acquired for use in manufacturing operations.

Merchandise inventory. Merchandise on hand and available for sale.

Net realizable value. The amount at which merchandise that can be sold only at prices below cost should be valued, determined as the estimated selling price less any direct cost of disposition.

Percentage-of-completion method. The method of recognizing revenue from long-term contracts over the entire life of the contract.

Periodic inventory system. A system of inventory accounting in which only the revenue from sales is recorded each time a sale is made; the cost of merchandise on hand at the end of a period is determined by a detailed listing (physical inventory) of the merchandise on hand.

Perpetual inventory system. A system of inventory accounting that employs records that continually disclose the amount of the inventory on hand.

Physical inventory. The detailed listing of merchandise on hand.

Retail inventory method. A method of inventory costing based on the relationship of the cost and retail price of merchandise.

Work in process. Goods in the process of manufacture.

CHAPTER OUTLINE

I. Importance of Inventories.
   A. Inventory has an important effect on the current period's financial statements.
      1. Inventory determination plays an important role in matching expired costs with revenues of the period.
      2. The cost of merchandise at the end of the period will appear on the balance sheet as a current asset.
      3. The inventories at the beginning and the end of the period will affect the cost of merchandise sold, which is deducted from net sales to yield gross profit.
      4. An overstatement in the determination of inventory at the end of the accounting period will cause an overstatement of gross profit and net income on the income statement and an overstatement of assets and owner's equity on the balance sheet.
      5. An understatement of inventory at the end of the accounting period will cause an understatement of gross profit and net income on the income statement, and an understatement of assets and owner's equity on the balance sheet.
   B. Since the inventory at the end of one period becomes the beginning inventory for the following period, misstatements of inventory will affect the following period's financial statements.
      1. If the inventory is incorrectly stated at the end of the period, the net income of that period will be misstated and so will the net income for the following period.
      2. The amount of the two misstatements of net income will be equal and in opposite directions. Therefore, the effect on net income of an incorrectly stated inventory, if not corrected, is limited to the period of the error and the following period. At the end of the period subsequent to the period of an uncorrected error, the balance sheet will be properly stated. This is because the two misstatements of net income will cancel each other.
   C. Misstatements of beginning inventory have the opposite effect on the income statement and balance sheet as the same misstatements of ending inventory would have on the income statement and balance sheet.

II. Inventory Systems.
   A. The two principal systems of inventory accounting are the periodic and perpetual inventory systems.
      1. When the periodic inventory system is used, only the revenue from sales is recorded each time a sale is made. No entry is made at the time of the sale to record the cost of the merchandise that has been sold. A physical inventory must be taken in order to deter-

mine the cost of the inventory at the end of the accounting period and the associated cost of merchandise sold for the period.

2. The perpetual inventory system uses accounting records that continuously disclose the amount of inventory. Purchases of inventory items are recorded at the time of purchase as debits to the proper inventory accounts, and sales of inventory are recorded as credits at the time of sale. The balances of the accounts are called book inventories of the items on hand.

B. Although much of the discussion in this chapter applies to both systems, the use of the periodic inventory system will normally be assumed.

III. Determining Actual Quantities in the Inventory.

A. The actual quantities of inventory at the end of an accounting period are determined by the process of "taking" an inventory.

B. All the merchandise owned by the business on the inventory date, and only such merchandise, should be included in the inventory.

C. It may be necessary to examine purchase and sales invoices of the last few days of the accounting period and the first few days of the following period to determine who has legal title to merchandise in transit on the inventory date.

1. When goods are purchased or sold FOB shipping point, title usually passes to the buyer when the goods are shipped. Therefore, these items should be included in inventory by the purchaser on the shipping date.

2. When goods are purchased or sold FOB destination, title usually does not pass to the buyer until the goods are delivered. Therefore, goods shipped under these terms should be included in inventory by the purchaser only when the goods have been received.

D. Special care should be taken for accounting for merchandise that has been shipped on a consignment basis to a retailer (the consignee). Even though the manufacturer does not have physical possession, consigned merchandise should be in-

cluded in the manufacturer's (the consignor's) inventory.

IV. Determining the Cost of Inventory.

A. The cost of merchandise inventory is made up of the purchase price and all expenditures incurred in acquiring such merchandise, including such costs as transportation, customs duties, and insurance.

B. If purchases discounts are treated as a deduction from purchases on the income statement, they should also be deducted from the purchase price of the items in the inventory.

V. Inventory Costing Methods Under a Periodic System.

A. One of the most significant problems in determining inventory cost comes about when identical units of a certain commodity have been acquired at different unit cost prices during the period. In such cases, it is necessary to determine the unit prices of the items still on hand.

B. Under specific identification procedures, it may be possible to identify units with specific expenditures if both the variety of merchandise carried in stock and the volume of sales are relatively small. Ordinarily, however, specific identification procedures are not used.

C. If specific identification procedures are not used, an arbitrary assumption as to the flow of costs of merchandise through the enterprise must be made. The three most common assumptions of determining the cost of merchandise sold are as follows:

1. Cost flow is in the order in which the expenditures were made—first-in, first-out.

2. Cost flow is in the reverse order in which the expenditures were made—last-in, first-out.

3. Cost flow is an average of the expenditures.

D. The first-in, first-out (fifo) method of costing inventory is based on the assumption that costs should be charged against revenue in the order in which they are incurred.

1. The inventory remaining at the end of the period is assumed to be made up of the most recent costs.

2. The fifo method is generally in harmony with the physical movement of merchandise in an enterprise. To this extent, the fifo method approximates the results that would be obtained by the specific identification of costs.

E. The last-in, first-out (lifo) method is based on the assumption that the most recent costs incurred should be charged against revenue.

   1. The inventory remaining at the end of the period is assumed to be composed of the earliest costs.

   2. Even though it does not represent the physical flow of the goods, the lifo method is widely used in business today.

F. The average cost method, sometimes called the weighted average method, is based on the assumption that costs should be charged against revenue according to the weighted average unit costs of the goods sold.

   1. The same weighted average unit costs are used in determining the cost of the merchandise remaining in the inventory and the cost of merchandise sold.

   2. For businesses in which various purchases of identical units of a commodity are mixed together, the average method has some relationship to the physical flow of goods.

G. A comparison of the inventory costing methods reveals that each method is based on a different assumption as to the flow of costs.

   1. If the cost of units and prices at which they are sold remain stable, all three methods yield the same results.

   2. Prices do change, however, and as a consequence the three methods will yield different amounts for ending inventory and the cost of merchandise sold for the period.

   3. In periods of rising prices, the fifo method yields the lowest cost of merchandise sold, the highest net income, and the highest amount for ending inventory.

   4. In periods of rising prices, the lifo method yields the highest cost of merchandise sold, the lowest net income, and the lowest ending inventory.

   5. In periods of changing prices, the average cost method yields results that are in between those of fifo and lifo.

H. During periods of rising prices, most companies prefer to use the last-in, first-out method to reduce the amount of income taxes.

I. It is not unusual for businesses to apply different inventory costing methods to different types of inventory. The method used by a company for inventory costing purposes should be properly disclosed in the financial statements. In addition, any changes in methods should also be disclosed.

VI. Accounting For and Reporting Inventory Under a Perpetual System.

A. Under the perpetual inventory system, all merchandise increases and decreases are recorded in a manner similar to the recording of increases and decreases in cash. The merchandise inventory account at any point in time reflects the merchandise on hand at that date.

B. The basic accounting entries for a perpetual inventory system are as follows:

   1. Purchases of merchandise are recorded by debiting Merchandise Inventory and crediting Accounts Payable or Cash.

   2. Sales of merchandise are recorded by debiting Cost of Merchandise Sold and crediting Merchandise Inventory.

   3. Unlike the periodic inventory system, no adjusting journal entries are necessary for beginning and ending inventory under the perpetual inventory system.

   4. The balance in the merchandise inventory account at the end of the accounting period would be the amount reported on the balance sheet on that date.

   5. The balance of the cost of merchandise sold account would be the amount reported on the income statement for the period.

C. Under a perpetual inventory system, details of the inventory transactions are maintained in a subsidiary inventory ledger. Whether this ledger is computerized or maintained manually, it is customary to use one of three costing methods (first-in, first-out; last-in, first-out; or average).

D. Under the first-in, first-out method of cost flow in a perpetual system, the number of units sold and number of units on hand after each transaction are accounted for on the fifo basis. The items received first are assumed to be the first sold.

E. Under the last-in, first-out method of cost flow in a perpetual system, the number of units on hand after each transaction are accounted for on the last-in, first-out basis. The items received last are assumed to be the first sold.

F. When the average cost method is used in a perpetual inventory system, an average unit cost for each type of commodity is computed each time a purchase is made. Sometimes this averaging technique is called a moving average.

G. The use of a perpetual inventory system for merchandise provides the most effective means of control over inventory. Although it is possible to maintain a perpetual inventory in the memorandum records only or to limit the inventory to quantities, a complete set of records integrated with the general ledger is preferable. Through the use of computers, integrated perpetual inventory systems are being used by more and more companies.

H. The control feature is the most important advantage of a perpetual inventory system. The subsidiary ledger shows the amount of each type of inventory on hand at any given point in time. A comparison of the recorded (book) inventory with the physical quantities on hand can be used to determine the existence and seriousness of any inventory shortages.

I. The subsidiary inventory ledger also can aid in maintaining inventory quantities at an optimal level by facilitating the timely reordering of merchandise and the avoidance of excess inventory.

J. If there is a large number of inventory items and/or transactions, businesses will often computerize the perpetual system for faster and more accurate processing of data.

K. By computerizing a system, additional data may be entered into the inventory records so that inventory may be ordered and maintained at optimum levels.

VII. Valuation of Inventory at Other than Cost.

A. Although cost is the primary basis for the valuation of inventories, under certain circumstances inventory may be valued at other than cost.

B. If the market price of an inventory item is lower than its cost, the lower of cost or market method may be used.

1. Market means the cost to replace the merchandise on the inventory date, based on quantities purchased from the usual source of supply.

2. The use of the lower of cost or market method provides two advantages: the gross profit is reduced for the period in which the decline occurred, and an approximately normal gross profit is realized during the period in which the item is sold.

3. It is possible to apply the lower of cost or market basis to each item in the inventory, major classes or categories, or the inventory as a whole.

4. The method elected for inventory valuation (cost, or lower of cost or market) must be followed consistently from year to year.

C. Obsolete, spoiled, or damaged merchandise and other merchandise that can only be sold at prices below cost should be valued at net realizable value. Net realizable value is the estimated selling price less any direct cost of disposition, such as sales commissions.

VIII. Presentation of Merchandise Inventory on the Balance Sheet.

A. Merchandise inventory is usually presented on the balance sheet immediately following receivables.

B. Both the method of determining the cost of the inventory (fifo, lifo, or average) and the method of valuing the inventory (cost, or lower of cost or market) should be shown. The details may be disclosed by a parenthetical notation or a footnote.

IX. Estimating Inventory Cost.

A. In practice, an inventory amount may be needed to prepare an income statement when it is impractical or impossible to take a physical inventory or to maintain perpetual inventory records. In such cases, inventory estimation methods may be used.

B. The retail method of estimating inventory costs is based on the relationship of the cost of merchandise available for sale to the retail price of the same merchandise.

1. The retail prices of all merchandise acquired are accumulated in supplementary records.

2. The inventory at retail is determined by deducting sales for the period from the retail price of the goods that were available for sale during the period.

3. The inventory at retail is then converted to cost on the basis of the ratio of cost to selling (retail) price for the merchandise available for sale.

4. An inherent assumption in the retail method of inventory estimation is that the composition or "mix" of the commodities in the ending inventory, in terms of percent of cost to selling price, is comparable to the entire stock of merchandise available for sale.

5. One of the major advantages of the retail method is that it provides inventory figures for interim statements.

6. The retail method can be used in conjunction with the periodic system when a physical inventory is taken at the end of the year.

C. The gross profit method of estimating inventory costs uses an estimate of the gross profit realized during the period to estimate the inventory at the end of the period.

1. Merchandise available for sale is accumulated in the accounting records.

2. An estimate of gross profit percentage is multiplied by the sales for the period to determine the estimated cost of merchandise sold.

3. Estimated inventory is then determined by subtracting from the merchandise available for sale the estimated cost of merchandise sold for the period.

4. The estimate of the gross profit rate is ordinarily based on the actual rate for the preceding year, adjusted for any changes made in the cost and sales prices during the current period.

5. The gross profit method may be used in estimating the cost of merchandise destroyed by fire or other disaster, or in preparing interim statements.

X. Inventories of Manufacturing Enterprises.

A. Manufacturing businesses maintain three inventory accounts instead of a single merchandise inventory account. Separate accounts are used for (1) goods in the state in which they are sold (finished goods), (2) goods in the process of manufacture (work in process), and (3) goods in the state in which they were acquired (materials).

B. There are three separate categories of manufacturing costs.

1. Direct materials represent the delivered cost of the materials that enter directly into the finished product.

2. Direct labor represents the wages of the factory workers who change the materials into a finished product.

3. Factory overhead includes all remaining cost of operating the factory.

XI. Long-term Construction Contracts.

A. Enterprises engaged in large construction projects may devote several years to the completion of a single contract or project. In such cases, the cost may be accumulated in Construction in Progress until the project is completed. At that time the full revenue and related net income are recognized, using what is known as the completed-contract method.

B. Whenever the total cost of a long-term contract and the extent of completion of a project can be reasonably estimated, it is preferable to recognize the revenue over the entire life of the contract.

1. The percentage-of-completion method does this by recognizing revenue in any particular period based on the estimated percentage of the contract that has been completed during the period.

2. Costs actually incurred during the year are deducted from the revenue recognized to determine the income.

PART 1

Instructions: A list of terms and related statements appear below. From the list of terms, select the term that relates to each statement and print its identifying letter in the space provided.

A. Average cost	E. Last-in, first-out (lifo)	I. Periodic inventory system
B. Direct materials	F. Lower of cost or market	J. Perpetual inventory system
C. First-in, first-out (fifo)	G. Merchandise inventory	K. Retail inventory method
D. Gross profit method	H. Net realizable value	L. Work in process

_____ 1. The inventory of merchandise purchased for resale is commonly called (?)

_____ 2. An inventory system in which only the revenue from sales is recorded each time a sale is made.

_____ 3. An inventory system in which both the revenue and cost of sales are recorded each time a sale is made.

_____ 4. An inventory costing method that treats the first merchandise acquired as the first merchandise sold.

_____ 5. An inventory costing method in which the ending inventory is assumed to be composed of the earliest costs.

_____ 6. An inventory costing method in which the weighted average unit costs are used in determining both ending inventory and cost of goods sold.

_____ 7. A method of inventory pricing in which goods are valued at original cost or replacement cost, whichever is lower.

_____ 8. The estimated selling price of inventory less any direct cost of disposition.

_____ 9. An inventory method based on the relationship of the cost of merchandise available for sale to the retail price of the same merchandise.

_____ 10. An inventory method which uses an estimate of the gross profit realized during the period to estimate the inventory at the end of the period.

_____ 11. A manufacturing business maintains three inventory accounts: finished goods, materials, and (?)

_____ 12. In a manufacturing business, the delivered cost of the materials that enter directly into the finished product is called (?)

PART 2

Instructions: Indicate whether each of the following statements is true or false by placing a T or F in the space provided.

_____ 1. If merchandise inventory at the end of the period is understated, gross profit will be overstated.

_____ 2. The two principal systems of inventory accounting are periodic and physical.

_____ 3. When terms of a sale are FOB destination, title usually does not pass to the buyer until the commodities are delivered.

_____ 4. During a period of rising prices, the inventory costing method which will result in the highest amount of net income is fifo.

_____ 5. If the cost of units purchased and the prices at which they were sold remain stable, all three inventory methods will yield the same results.

_____ 6. When the rate of inflation is high, the larger gross profits that result are frequently called inventory profits.

_____ 7. As used in the phrase lower of cost or market, "market" means selling price.

_____ 8. When the retail inventory method is used, inventory at retail is converted to cost on the basis of the ratio of cost to replacement cost of the merchandise available for sale.

_____ 9. Merchandise inventory is usually presented on the balance sheet immediately following receivables.

_____ 10. The percentage-of-completion method permits revenue to be recognized based on an estimate of the percentage of a contract that has been completed during a period.

PART 3

Instructions: Complete each of the following statements by circling the letter of the best answer.

1. If merchandise inventory at the end of the period is overstated,
   a. gross profit will be understated
   b. owner's equity will be overstated
   c. net income will be understated
   d. cost of merchandise sold will be overstated

2. If merchandise inventory at the end of period 1 is understated, and at the end of period 2 is correct,
   a. gross profit in period 2 will be overstated
   b. assets at the end of period 2 will be overstated
   c. owner's equity at the end of period 2 will be understated
   d. cost of merchandise sold in period 2 will be overstated

3. During a period of rising prices, the inventory costing method which will result in the lowest amount of net income is
   a. fifo
   b. lifo
   c. average cost
   d. perpetual

4. If the replacement price of an item of inventory is lower than its cost, the use of the lower of cost or market method
   a. is not permitted unless a perpetual inventory system is maintained
   b. is recommended in order to maximize the reported net income
   c. tends to overstate the gross profit
   d. reduces gross profit for the period in which the decline occurred

5. When lifo is strictly applied to a perpetual inventory system, the unit cost prices assigned to the ending inventory will not necessarily be those associated with the earliest unit costs of the period if
   a. a physical inventory is taken at the end of the period
   b. physical inventory records are maintained throughout the period in terms of quantities only
   c. at any time during a period the number of units of a commodity sold exceeds the number previously purchased during the same period
   d. moving average inventory cost is maintained

PART 4

Jayhawk Co. is a small wholesaler of basketball shoes. The accounting records show the following purchases and sales of the Ski-Hi Model during the first year of business.

SKI-HI MODEL

	Purchases						Sales	
Date		Units	Price	Total Cost		Date		Units
Jan.	10	15	$48	$ 720		Feb.	10	10
May	15	100	54	5,400		Apr.	1	95
July	3	60	55	3,300		Aug.	10	65
Nov.	1	35	57	1,995		Nov.	15	20
Total		210		$11,415				190

A physical count of Ski-Hi Model at the end of the year reveals that 20 are still on hand.

Instructions:

1. Determine the cost of Ski-Hi inventory as of December 31 by means of the average cost method with a periodic system:

   INVENTORY (Average Cost)

   Average unit cost = $ _____ = $ _____
   _____units in the inventory @$_____ = $ _____

2. Determine the cost of Ski-Hi inventory as of December 31 by means of the first-in, first-out (fifo) method with a periodic inventory system.

   INVENTORY (Fifo Periodic)

Date Purchased	Units	Price	Total Cost

3. Determine the cost of Ski-Hi inventory as of December 31 by means of the last-in, first-out (lifo) method with a periodic inventory system:

   INVENTORY (Lifo Periodic)

Date Purchased	Units	Price	Total Cost

4. Determine the cost of Ski-Hi inventory as of December 31 by means of the last-in, first-out (lifo) method with a perpetual inventory system.

INVENTORY (Lifo Perpetual)

Date Purchased	Units	Price	Total Cost

PART 5

Bearcat Co. began operating on January 1, 1990. During 1990, Bearcat sold 25,000 units at an **average** price of $78 each, and made the following purchases:

Date of Purchase	Units	Unit Price	Total Cost
January 1	5,400	$50	$270,000
March 1	4,100	54	221,400
June 1	4,800	56	268,800
September 1	8,400	61	512,400
November 1	5,400	69	372,600
December 1	1,900	73	138,700
	30,000		$1,783,900

Instructions: Determine the ending inventory, the cost of merchandise sold, and the gross profit for Bearcat, using each of the following methods of inventory costing: **(1)** fifo, **(2)** lifo, and **(3)** average cost. (Round unit cost to two decimal places.)

	(1) Fifo	(2) Lifo	(3) Average Cost
Sales	$_____	$_____	$_____
Purchases	$ 1,783,900	$ 1,783,900	$ 1,783,900
Less ending inventory	_____	_____	_____
Cost of merchandise sold	$_____	$_____	$_____
Gross profit	$_____	$_____	$_____

PART 6

Instructions: Complete the following summary, which illustrates the application of the lower of cost or market rule to individual inventory items of Unzicker Inc.

Description	Quantity	Unit Cost Price	Unit Market Price	Total Cost	Total Lower of C or M
Commodity A	750	$5.00	$4.80	$_____	$_____
Commodity B	450	7.00	7.50	_____	
Commodity C	210	6.00	5.50	_____	_____
Commodity D	300	4.80	4.30	_____	
Total				$_____	$_____

PART 7

Knoll Inc. operates a department store and takes a physical inventory at the end of each calendar year. However, Knoll likes to have a balance sheet and an income statement available at the end of each month in order to study financial position and operating trends. Knoll estimates inventory at the end of each month for accounting statement preparation purposes. The following information is available as of May 31 of the current year:

	Cost	Retail
Merchandise inventory, May 1	$121,300	$170,000
Purchases in May	271,400	481,400
Purchases returns and allowances—May	6,000	6,900
Sales in May		493,200
Sales returns and allowances—May		10,300

Instructions:

1. Determine the estimated cost of the inventory on May 31, using the retail method.

	Cost	Retail
Merchandise inventory, May 1 .... $	_____	$ _____
Purchases in May (net)	_____	_____
Merchandise available for sale .... $	_____	

Ratio of cost to retail:

$$\frac{\$\underline{\qquad}}{\$\underline{\qquad}} = \underline{\qquad}\%$$

Sales in May (net)		_____
Merchandise inventory, May 31, at retail		$ _____
Merchandise inventory, May 31, at estimated cost		
($_____ x ____%)		$ _____

2. Determine the estimated cost of inventory on May 31, using the gross profit method. On the basis of past experience, Knoll estimates a rate of gross profit of 40% of net sales.

Merchandise inventory, May 1		$ _____
Purchases in May (net)		_____
Merchandise available for sale		$ _____
Sales in May (net)	$ _____	
Less estimated gross profit ($_____ x ____%)	_____	
Estimated cost of merchandise sold		_____
Estimated merchandise inventory, May 31		$ _____

PART 8

During the current year, Salem Construction Company contracted to build a new basketball arena for the local university. The total contract price was $6,800,000 and the estimated construction costs were $5,250,000. At the end of the current year, the project was estimated to be 30% completed and the costs incurred totaled $1,430,000.

Instructions: Using the percentage-of-completion method of recognizing revenue, determine the following amounts:

(1) Revenue from the contract . . . . $_____

(2) Cost associated with the contract . . . . $_____

(3) Income from the contract recognized for the current year . . . . $_____

Chapter 8
Plant Assets and Intangible Assets

STUDY GOALS

After studying this chapter, you should be able to:

1. Describe and illustrate the accounting for the acquisition of plant assets.

2. Describe the nature of depreciation.

3. Describe and illustrate the accounting for depreciation.

4. Describe and illustrate the composite-rate depreciation method.

5. Describe and illustrate the accounting for capital and revenue expenditures.

6. Describe and illustrate the accounting for plant asset disposals.

7. Describe and illustrate the accounting for the leasing of plant assets.

8. Describe and illustrate the accounting for depletion.

9. Describe and illustrate the accounting for intangible assets.

10. Describe and illustrate the reporting of depreciation expense, plant assets, and intangible assets in the financial statements.

11. Describe and illustrate the use of replacement cost of plant assets.

GLOSSARY OF KEY TERMS

Accelerated depreciation method. A depreciation method that provides for a high depreciation charge in the first year of use of an asset and gradually declining periodic charges thereafter.

Amortization. The periodic expense to recognize the decline in usefulness of an intangible asset.

Betterments. Expenditures that increase operating efficiency or capacity for the remaining useful life of a plant asset.

Boot. The balance owed the supplier when an old asset is traded for a new asset.

Capital expenditure. A cost that adds to the utility of an asset for more than one accounting period.

Capital lease. A lease which includes one or more of four provisions that result in treating the leased asset as a purchased asset in the accounts.

Composite-rate depreciation method. A method of depreciation based on the use of a single rate that applies to entire groups of assets.

Declining-balance method. A method of depreciation that provides declining periodic depreciation charges to expense over the estimated life of an asset.

Depletion. The cost of metal ores and other minerals removed from the earth.

Depreciation. The periodic expense to recognize the decrease in usefulness of all plant assets except land.

Extraordinary repairs. Expenditures that increase the useful life of an asset beyond the original estimate.

Goodwill. An intangible asset that attaches to a business as a result of such favorable factors as location, product superiority, reputation, and managerial skill.

Intangible asset. A long-lived asset that is useful in the operations of an enterprise, is not held for sale, and is without physical qualities.

Operating lease. A lease which does not meet the criteria for a capital lease, and thus which is accounted for as an operating expense, so that neither future lease obligations nor future rights to use the leased asset are recognized in the accounts.

Plant asset. A tangible long-lived asset used in the operations of the business and not held for sale in the ordinary course of business.

Residual value. The estimated value of a depreciable asset as of the time it is to be retired from service.

Revenue expenditure. An expenditure that benefits only the current period.

Straight-line method. A method of depreciation that provides for equal periodic charges to expense over the estimated life of an asset.

Sum-of-the-years-digits method. A method of depreciation that provides for declining periodic depreciation charges to expense over the estimated life of an asset.

Units-of-production method. A method of depreciation that provides for depreciation expense based on the expected productive capacity of an asset.

CHAPTER OUTLINE

I. Acquisition of Plant Assets.

  A. Plant assets are assets which are tangible in nature, used in the operations of the business, and are not held for sale in the ordinary course of business. Other descriptive titles frequently used are fixed assets and property, plant, and equipment.

  B. The initial cost of acquiring a plant asset includes all expenditures necessary to get it in place and ready for use. Such expenditures include sales taxes, transportation charges, insurance, etc.

  C. The cost of constructing a building includes the fees paid to architects and engineers for plans and supervision, insurance, etc. Interest incurred during the construction should also be included in the cost of the building.

  D. The cost of land includes not only the negotiated price but also broker's commissions, title fees, surveying fees, etc. If delinquent real estate taxes are assumed by the buyer, they are also chargeable to the land.

  E. Expenditures for improvements that are neither as permanent as land nor directly associated with the building may be set apart in a land improvements account and depreciated accordingly. Such items include trees and shrubs, fences, and paved parking areas.

II. Nature of Depreciation.

  A. As time passes, all plant assets with the exception of land lose their capacity to yield services. Accordingly, the cost of such assets should be transferred to the related expense accounts through depreciation.

  B. Factors contributing to a decline in usefulness of an asset may be divided into two categories: physical depreciation, which includes wear from use and deterioration from the action of the elements, and functional depreciation, which includes inadequacy and obsolescence.

  C. The meaning of the term "depreciation" as used in accounting may be misunderstood because depreciation is not necessarily associated with declines in the market value of an asset. In addition, depreciation does not provide cash for the replacement of assets.

III. Accounting for Depreciation.

  A. In determining periodic depreciation expense, three factors need to be considered: the plant asset's (a) initial cost, (b) residual value, and (c) useful life. Estimates of both the residual value and useful life of plant assets can vary greatly.

  B. The straight-line method of determining depreciation provides for equal periodic charges to expense over the estimated life of the asset.

   1. The depreciable cost of the asset is determined by subtracting the estimated residual value from the initial cost of the asset.

   2. The useful life of the asset is then divided into the depreciable cost.

   3. The resulting amount is an annual depreciation charge which remains constant over the life of the asset.

   4. Straight-line depreciation is often expressed by a percentage rate. The straight-line depreciation rate is equal to 100 divided by the useful life of the asset.

   5. The straight-line method is widely used because of its simplicity.

C. The units-of-production method yields a depreciation charge that varies with the amount of asset usage.

   1. The depreciable cost of the asset is determined by subtracting the estimated residual value from the initial cost of the asset.

   2. The estimated life of the asset, expressed in terms of productive capacity, is then divided into the depreciable cost to arrive at the unit or hourly depreciation charge.

   3. The actual amount of production usage is then multiplied by this rate to determine the depreciation charge.

D. The declining-balance method yields a declining periodic depreciation charge over the estimated life of the asset.

   1. The double-declining balance method uses a rate of depreciation which is double the straight-line depreciation rate.

   2. The declining-balance depreciation rate is then applied to the original cost of the asset for the first year, and thereafter to the book value (cost minus accumulated depreciation).

   3. The residual value of the asset is not considered in determining the depreciation rate or the depreciation charge each period, except that the asset should not be depreciated below the estimated residual value.

E. The sum-of-the-years-digits method yields depreciation results which are similar to those of the declining-balance method.

   1. The depreciable cost of the asset is determined by subtracting the estimated residual value from the initial cost of the asset.

   2. The depreciation rate per year is determined by a fraction; the numerator is the number of years of remaining life at the beginning of the year and the denominator is the sum of the years of useful life.

   3. The depreciation charge for the period is determined by multiplying the sum-of-the-years-digits rate by the depreciable cost of the asset.

F. If the first use of the asset does not coincide with the beginning of the fiscal year, each full year's depreciation should be allocated between the two years benefited.

G. The depreciation method chosen affects the amounts reported on the financial statements.

   1. The straight-line method provides uniform periodic charges to depreciation expense over the life of the asset.

   2. The units-of-production method provides for periodic charges to depreciation expense that may vary considerably depending upon the amount of use of the asset.

   3. Both the declining-balance and sum-of-the-years-digits methods provide for a higher depreciation charge in the first year of use of the asset and a gradually declining periodic charge thereafter. For this reason, these methods are called accelerated depreciation methods.

H. Each of the four depreciation methods described above can be used to determine the amount of depreciation for federal income tax purposes for plant assets acquired prior to 1981.

I. For plant assets acquired after 1980 and before 1987, either the straight-line method or the Accelerated Cost Recovery System (ACRS) may be used to determine depreciation deductions for federal income tax purposes.

J. Under the Tax Reform Act of 1986, Modified ACRS (MACRS) provides for 8 classes of useful life for plant assets acquired after 1986. The depreciation deduction for the two most common classes—the 5-year class (automobiles and light-duty trucks) and the 7-year class (most machinery and equipment)—approximates the use of the 200-percent declining-balance method.

K. ACRS and MACRS are not usually acceptable for computing depreciation under generally accepted accounting principles.

L. Changes in the estimated useful lives and residual values of assets are accounted for by using the revised estimates to determine the amount of remaining undepreciated asset cost to be charged as an expense in future periods.

M. The correction of minor errors in the estimates used in the determination of depreciation does not affect the amounts of depreciation expense recorded in earlier years.

N. Depreciation may be recorded by an entry at the end of each month, or the adjustment may be delayed until the end of the year.

   1. Depreciation is recorded by using a contra asset account, Accumulated Depreciation, or Allowance for Depreciation, so that the original cost of the asset can be reported along with the accumulated depreciation to date.

   2. An exception to the general procedure of recording depreciation monthly or annually is made when a plant asset is sold, traded in, or scrapped, in which case depreciation must be brought up to date as of the date the asset is disposed of.

O. When depreciation is to be computed individually on a large number of assets making up a functional group, it is advisable to maintain a subsidiary ledger.

   1. The sum of the asset balances and the sum of the accumulated depreciation balances in all of the accounts should be compared periodically with the balances of their respective controlling accounts in the general ledger.

   2. Subsidiary ledgers for plant assets are useful to the accounting department in:

      a. Determining the periodic depreciation expense.

      b. Recording the disposal of individual items.

      c. Preparing tax returns.

      d. Preparing insurance claims in the event of insured losses.

   3. Regardless of whether subsidiary equipment ledgers are maintained, plant assets should be inspected periodically in order to determine the state of repair and whether or not they are still in use.

P. Subsidiary ledgers usually are not maintained for classes of plant assets that are made up of individual items of low unit cost. In such cases, the usual depreciation methods are not practical. One common method of determining cost expiration is to take a periodic inventory of the items on hand, estimate their fair value based on original cost, and transfer the remaining amount from the asset account to an appropriately titled expense account.

IV. Composite-Rate Depreciation Method.

A. The composite-rate depreciation method determines depreciation for entire groups of assets by use of a single rate. The basis for grouping may be similarity in life estimates or other common traits.

B. When depreciation is computed on the basis of a composite group of assets of differing life spans, a rate based on averages must be developed using the following procedures:

   1. The annual depreciation for each asset is computed.

   2. The total annual depreciation is determined for the group of assets.

   3. The total annual depreciation divided by the total cost of the assets determines the composite rate.

C. Although new assets of differing life spans and residual values will be added to the group of assets and old assets will be retired, the "mix" of assets is assumed to remain relatively unchanged.

D. When a composite rate is used, it may be applied against total asset cost on a monthly basis, or some reasonable assumption may be made regarding the timing of increases and decreases in the group. A common practice is to assume that all additions and retirements have occurred uniformly throughout the year.

E. When assets within the composite group are retired, no gain or loss should be recognized. Instead, the asset account is credited for the cost of the asset and the accumulated depreciation account is debited for the excess of cost over the amount realized from the disposal.

V. Capital and Revenue Expenditures.

A. Expenditures for additions to plant assets or expenditures that add to the utility of plant assets for more than one accounting period are called capital expenditures.

1. Expenditures for an addition to a plant asset should be debited to the plant asset account.

2. Expenditures that increase operating efficiency or capacity for the remaining useful life of a plant asset are called betterments and should be debited to the plant asset account.

3. Expenditures that increase the useful life of the asset beyond the original estimate are called extraordinary repairs and should be debited to the appropriate accumulated depreciation account.

B. Expenditures that benefit only the current period and that are made in order to maintain normal operating efficiency of plant assets are called revenue expenditures.

1. Expenditures for ordinary maintenance and repairs of a recurring nature are revenue expenditures and should be debited to expense accounts.

2. Small expenditures are usually treated as repair expense, even though they may have characteristics of capital expenditures.

VI. Disposal of Plant Assets.

A. A plant asset should not be removed from the accounts only because it has been depreciated for the full period of its estimated life. If the asset is still useful to the enterprise, the cost and accumulated depreciation should remain in the ledger.

In this way, accountability for the asset is maintained.

B. When plant assets are no longer useful to the business and have no market value, they are discarded.

1. If the asset has been fully depreciated, then no loss is realized.

2. The entry to record the disposal of a fully depreciated asset with no market value is to debit Accumulated Depreciation and credit the asset account.

3. If the asset is not fully depreciated, depreciation should be brought up to date before the accumulated depreciation account is debited. The difference between the cost of the plant asset and its accumulated depreciation (book value) is recognized as a loss.

4. Losses and gains on disposals of plant assets are nonoperating items and may be reported in the Other Expense or Other Income section of the income statement.

C. The entry to record the sale of a plant asset is similar to the entry to record the disposal of a plant asset as set forth above.

1. The first entry should be to update the depreciation expense for the period.

2. The cash received from the sale of the plant asset should be recorded.

3. The accumulated depreciation account should be debited for its balance, and the plant asset account should be credited for its cost. Any difference in the debits and credits to balance the entry will be reported as a gain (credit) or loss (debit) on the sale of the plant asset.

D. Plant assets may be traded in for new equipment having a similar use.

1. The trade-in allowance is deducted from the price of the new equipment. The balance owed is paid according to credit terms and is called boot.

2. If the trade-in allowance is less than the book value of the old plant asset, the loss on the trade-in is recognized immediately.

3. If the trade-in value of the plant asset is greater than its book value, the gain is not recognized for financial report-

ing purposes. Instead, the amount of the gain is deducted from the cost of the new equipment. In effect, this gain is recognized over the life of the new asset as a reduction in the periodic depreciation charges which would otherwise be recognized.

4. The Internal Revenue Code requires that neither gains nor losses be recognized on trade-ins of assets of similar use. Any gain or loss on the exchange is treated as a reduction in or addition to the cost of the new asset acquired.

VII. Acquisition of Plant Assets Through Leasing.

A. Instead of owning a plant asset, a business may acquire the use of a plant asset through a lease.

1. A lease is a contractual agreement that conveys the right to use an asset for a stated period of time.

2. The two parties to a lease are the lessor (the party who legally owns the asset and who conveys the rights to use the asset to the lessee) and the lessee (the party that leases the asset for its use).

B. Capital leases are defined as leases that include one or more of the following provisions:

1. The lease transfers ownership of the leased asset to the lessee at the end of the lease term.

2. The lease contains an option for a bargain purchase of the leased asset by the lessee.

3. The lease term extends over most of the economic life of the leased asset.

4. The lease requires rental payments which approximate the fair market value of the leased asset.

C. Leases which do not meet the preceding criteria for capital leases are classified as operating leases.

D. A capital lease is accounted for as if the lessee has, in fact, purchased the asset. The lessee will debit an asset account for the fair market value of a leased asset and credit a long-term lease liability account.

E. In accounting for operating leases, rent expense is recognized as the leased asset is used.

F. Financial reporting disclosures require the presentation of future lease commitments in footnotes to the financial statements.

VIII. Depletion.

A. The periodic allocation of the cost of metal ores and other minerals removed from the earth is called depletion.

B. The amount of periodic cost allocation (depletion expense) reported each period is based on the relationship of the cost to the estimated size of the mineral deposit and on the quantity extracted during the particular period.

C. The adjusting entry for depletion is a debit to Depletion Expense and a credit to Accumulated Depletion. The accumulated depletion account is a contra account to the asset to which the cost of the mineral deposit was initially recorded.

IX. Intangible Assets. —AMORTIZE – NO CONTRA

A. Long-lived assets that are useful in the operations of an enterprise, not held for sale, and without physical qualities are classified as intangible assets.

1. The basic principles of accounting for intangible assets are like those described earlier for plant assets.

2. The major accounting issues involving intangible assets are the determination of the initial costs and the recognition of periodic cost expiration, called amortization, due to the passage of time or a decline in usefulness of the intangible asset.

3. Intangible assets include patents, copyrights, and goodwill.

B. Patents provide exclusive rights to produce and sell goods with one or more unique features.

1. Patents are granted by the federal government and continue in effect for 17 years.

2. An enterprise may obtain patents on new products developed in its own research laboratories or it may purchase patent rights from others.

3. The initial cost of a purchased patent should be debited to an asset account and then written off, or amortized, over the years of its expected usefulness.

4. The straight-line method of amortization should be used unless it can be shown that another method is more appropriate.

5. A separate contra asset account is normally not credited for the write-off of patent amortization and the credit is recorded directly to the patent account.

6. Current accounting principles require that research and development costs expended in the development of patents should be written off as incurred.

7. Legal fees related to patent purchase or development should be recognized and amortized over the useful life of the patent.

C. The exclusive right to publish and sell a literary, artistic, or musical composition is obtained by a copyright.

1. Copyrights are issued by the federal government and extend for 50 years beyond the author's death.

2. The costs assigned to a copyright include all costs of creating the work plus the cost of obtaining the copyright.

3. A copyright that is purchased from another should be recorded at the price paid for it.

4. Copyrights should be amortized over their useful lives.

D. Goodwill is an intangible asset that attaches to a business as a result of such favorable factors as location, product superiority, reputation, and managerial skill.

1. Goodwill should be recognized in the accounts only if it can be objectively determined by an event or transaction, such as the purchase or sale of a business.

2. Goodwill should be amortized over the years of its useful life, which should not exceed 40 years.

X. Reporting Depreciation Expense, Plant Assets, and Intangible Assets in the Financial Statements.

A. The amount of depreciation expense or amortization should be set forth separately in the income statement or disclosed in some other manner.

B. A general description of the method or methods used in computing depreciation or amortization should also accompany the financial statements.

C. The balance of each major class of depreciable assets should be disclosed in the balance sheet or in notes thereto, together with the related accumulated depreciation, either by major class or in total.

D. Intangible assets are usually presented in the balance sheet in a separate section immediately following plant assets.

XI. Replacement Cost of Plant Assets.

A. In spite of inflationary trends, historical-cost financial statements are considered better than statements based on movements in the price level.

B. Many accountants recommend that businesses provide supplemental information that indicates the replacement cost of plant assets and depreciation based on such cost. Current costs for depreciation would be matched against current revenues and would give a net income figure that would be useful in evaluating operating results.

C. Because the measurement of current costs is both difficult and more subjective than historical cost, the use of replacement costs for plant assets generally has been restricted to experimental situations involving supplemental data.

PART 1

Instructions: A list of terms and related statements appear below. From the list of terms, select the term that relates to each statement and print its identifying letter in the space provided.

✓A. Amortization	F. Composite-rate method	K. Lease
✓B. Betterments	G. Declining-balance method	L. Residual value
✓C. Boot	✓H. Depletion	M. Revenue expenditures
D. Capital	I. Depreciation	N. Straight-line method
✓E. Capital expenditures	J. Extraordinary repairs	O. Units-of-production method

___I___   **1.** The allocation of the cost of an asset to expense over its expected useful life.

___L___   **2.** The estimated value of a plant asset at the time that it is to be retired from service.

___N___   **3.** A method of depreciation which provides for equal periodic charges to expense over the estimated life of the asset.

___G___   **4.** A method of depreciation which yields a declining periodic depreciation charge over the estimated life of the asset.

___E___   **5.** Expenditures that add to the utility of the asset for more than one accounting period.

M ___B___   **6.** Expenditures that benefit only the current period, and that are made in order to maintain normal operating efficiency.

___C___   **7.** The balance owed after the trade-in allowance is deducted from the price of new equipment acquired in a trade for equipment having similar uses.

D ___K___   **8.** A lease which is accounted for as if the lessee has purchased the asset is called a (?) lease.

___H___   **9.** The periodic allocation of the cost of natural resources to expense as the units are removed.

___A___   **10.** The allocation to expense of the cost of an intangible asset over the periods of its economic usefulness.

___O___   **11.** A method of depreciation which yields a depreciation charge that varies with the amount of asset usage.

___F___   **12.** A method of depreciation that applies a single depreciation rate to entire groups of assets.

B ___M___   **13.** Expenditures that increase operating efficiency or capacity for the remaining useful life of a plant asset.

___J___   **14.** Expenditures that increase the useful life of an asset beyond the original estimate.

___K___   **15.** A contractual agreement that conveys the right to use an asset for a stated period of time.

PART 2

Instructions: Indicate whether each of the following statements is true or false by placing a T or F in the space provided.

___T___ 1. The decline in usefulness of a plant asset because of wear from use and deterioration from the action of the elements is called functional depreciation.

___T___ 2. The method of depreciation which yields a depreciation charge that varies with the amount of asset usage is known as the units-of-production method.

___F___ 3. The method of depreciation that, each year of an asset's estimated life, applies a successively smaller fraction to the original cost less the estimated residual value is called the declining balance method.

___F___ 4. In using the declining-balance method, the asset should not be depreciated below the net book value.

___T___ 5. Accelerated depreciation methods are most appropriate for situations in which the decline in productivity or earning power of the asset is proportionately greater in the early years of its use than in later years.

___T___ 6. ACRS depreciation methods permit the use of asset lives that are often much shorter than the actual useful life.

___F___ 7. When an old plant asset is traded in for a new plant asset having a similar use, proper accounting treatment prohibits recognition of a loss.

___T___ 8. A procedure to determine depreciation for entire groups of assets by use of a single rate is called the composite-rate depreciation method.

___F___ 9. A lease which transfers ownership of the leased asset to the lessee at the end of the lease term should be classified as an operating lease.

___T___ 10. Long-lived assets that are without physical characteristics but useful in the operations of an enterprise are classified as intangible assets.

PART 3

Instructions: Circle the best answer for each of the following questions.

1. If unwanted buildings are located on land acquired for a plant site, the cost of their removal, less any salvage recovered, should be charged to the:

   a. expense accounts
   b. building account
   c. land account
   d. accumulated depreciation account

2. The depreciation method used widely in financial statements is the:

   a. straight-line method
   b. declining-balance method
   c. units-of-production method
   d. sum-of-the-years-digits method

3. The depreciation method that would provide the highest reported net income in the early years of an asset's life would be:

   a. straight-line
   b. declining-balance
   c. sum-of-the-years-digits
   d. accelerated

4. Equipment with an estimated useful life of 5 years and an estimated residual value of $800 is acquired at a cost of $12,500. Using the sum-of-the-years-digits method, what is the amount of depreciation for the first year of use of the equipment?

   a. $2,500
   b. $2,850
   c. $3,650
   d. $3,900

5. Equipment that cost $15,000 was originally estimated to have a useful life of 6 years and a residual value of $3,000. The equipment has been depreciated for 2 years using straight-line depreciation. During the third year it is estimated that the remaining useful life is 3 years (instead of 4) and that the residual value is $2,000 (instead of $3,000). The depreciation expense on the equipment in year 3 using the straight-line method would be:

   a. $2,667
   b. $3,000
   c. $3,333
   d. $3,500

6. Assume that a drill press is rebuilt during its sixth year of use so that its useful life is extended 5 years beyond the original estimate of 10 years. In this case, the cost of rebuilding the drill press should be charged to the appropriate:

   a. expense account
   b. accumulated depreciation account
   c. asset account
   d. liability account

7. Old equipment which cost $9,000 and has accumulated depreciation of $6,300 is given, along with $10,000 in cash, for the same type of new equipment with a price of $15,600. At what amount should the new equipment be recorded?

a. $15,600

b. $12,900

c. $12,700

d. $10,000

8. Assume the same facts as in No. 7, except that the old equipment and $14,000 in cash is given for the new equipment. At what amount should the new equipment be recorded for financial accounting purposes?

a. $16,700

b. $15,600

c. $14,000

d. $12,900

9. In a lease contract, the party who legally owns the asset is the:

a. contractor

b. operator

c. lessee

d. lessor

10. Which of the following items would not be considered an intangible asset?

a. lease

b. patent

c. copyright

d. goodwill

PART 4

Bellamy Inc. is planning to trade in its present truck for a new model on April 30 of the current year. The existing truck was purchased May 1 three years ago at a cost of $16,000, and accumulated depreciation is $12,000 through April 30 of the current year. The new truck has a list price of $21,800. Ralston Motors agrees to allow Bellamy $4,600 for the present truck, and Bellamy agrees to pay the balance of $17,200 in cash.

Instructions: Record the exchange according to acceptable methods of accounting for exchanges. (Omit explanation.)

	DATE	DESCRIPTION	POST. REF.	DEBIT	CREDIT	
1		TRUCK		21200		1
2		ACC. DEP.		12000		2
3		TRUCK			16000	3
4		CASH			17200	4

16000   17,200
         4,000

         21200

34800   21800

PART 5

Assume the same facts as in Part 4, except that the allowance on the present truck is $1,000 and that Bellamy agrees to pay the balance of $20,800 in cash.

Instructions:

1. Record the exchange according to acceptable methods of accounting for exchanges.

2. Record the exchange as in (1), except that the entry should be in conformity with the requirements of the Internal Revenue Code.

	DATE	DESCRIPTION	POST. REF.	DEBIT	CREDIT	
1		TRUCK		20800		1
2		ACC DEP		12000		2
3		TRK			16000	3
4		CASH			20800	4
5		LOSS OF SALE OF ASSET				5
6						6
7						7
8						8
9						9
10						10

Name _____ *1875*

PART 6

.7500

15000   4, 7500
7500   35
          32 — 30
              28

Grant Corp. has a sales representative who must travel a substantial amount. A car for this purpose was acquired January 2 four years ago at a cost of $15,000. It is estimated to have a total useful life of 4 years.   *3750 /YR*

7500

Instructions: 1. Record the annual depreciation on Grant's car at the end of the first and third years of ownership, using the straight-line method and assuming no salvage value. (Omit explanation.)

2. Record the annual depreciation on Grant's car at the end of the first and third years of ownership, *7500* using the declining-balance method at twice the straight-line rate. (Omit explanation.)

3. Record the annual depreciation on Grant's car at the end of the first and third years of ownership, *3750* using the sum-of-the-digits method and assuming no salvage value. (Omit explanation.) *7850*

	DATE	DESCRIPTION	POST. REF.	DEBIT	CREDIT	
1		DEPR EXP		3750		1
2		ACC. DEP			3750	2
3						3
4				7500		4
5		1250			7500	5
6		2500		5000		6
7		15000 50% = 7500			5000	7
8		7500 50% = 3750				8
9		3750 50% 1875.				9
10						10
11						11
12						12
13						13
14						14
15						15
16						16
17						17

PART 7

Donovan Co. uses a composite rate of 25% for the depreciation of several pieces of equipment, based on the total annual depreciation charges on these assets divided by their total cost. Assuming that the balance of the equipment account at the end of the current year is $19,000 and that all of the equipment has been in use throughout the entire year, record the depreciation of Donovan's equipment. (Omit explanation.)

	DATE	DESCRIPTION	POST. REF.	DEBIT	CREDIT	
1						1
2						2

PART 8

Big Red, Inc. uses the units-of-production method for computing the depreciation on its machines. One machine, which cost $80,800, is estimated to have a useful life of 20,000 hours and no residual value. During the first year of operation, this machine was used a total of 3,900 hours. Record the depreciation of this machine at the end of the first year. (Omit explanation.)

	DATE		DESCRIPTION	POST. REF.	DEBIT	CREDIT	
1							1
2							2

PART 9

On March 8, Todd's Book Store decides to sell for $2,000 cash some fixtures for which it paid $6,700 and on which it has taken total depreciation of $5,350 to date of sale. Record this sale. (Omit explanation.)

	DATE		DESCRIPTION	POST. REF.	DEBIT	CREDIT	
1							1
2							2
3							3
4							4

PART 10

Gran-It Co. paid $1,200,000 for some mineral rights in Utah. The deposit is estimated to contain 600,000 tons of ore of uniform grade. Record the depletion of this deposit at the end of the first year, assuming that 75,000 tons are mined during the year. (Omit explanation.)

	DATE		DESCRIPTION	POST. REF.	DEBIT	CREDIT	
1							1
2							2

PART 11

Schwartz Aerospace Corp. acquires a patent at the beginning of its calendar (fiscal) year for $85,000. Although the patent will not expire for another ten years, it is expected to be of value for only five years. Record the amortization of this patent at the end of the fiscal year. (Omit explanation.)

	DATE		DESCRIPTION	POST. REF.	DEBIT	CREDIT	
1							1
2							2

Chapter 9
Payroll, Notes Payable, and Other Current Liabilities

STUDY GOALS

After studying this chapter, you should be able to:

1. Describe and illustrate the determination of payrolls, including liabilities arising from employee earnings and deductions from earnings.

2. Describe and illustrate accounting systems for payroll and payroll taxes.

3. Describe and illustrate accounting for employee fringe benefits, including vacation pay and pensions.

4. Describe and illustrate accounting for short-term notes payable.

5. Describe and illustrate accounting for product warranties.

6. Describe and illustrate accounting for contingent liabilities.

GLOSSARY OF KEY TERMS

Contingent liabilities. Potential obligations that will materialize only if certain events take place in the future.

Discount. The interest deducted from the maturity value of a note.

Discount rate. The rate used in computing the interest to be deducted from the maturity value of a note.

Employee's earnings record. A detailed record of each employee's earnings.

FICA tax. Federal Insurance Contributions Act tax used to finance federal programs for old-age and disability benefits and health insurance for the aged.

Gross pay. The total earnings of an employee for a payroll period.

Net pay. Gross pay less payroll deductions; the amount the employer is obligated to pay the employee.

Payroll. The total amount paid to employees for a certain period.

Payroll register. A multicolumn form used to assemble and summarize payroll data at the end of each payroll period.

Proceeds. The net amount available from discounting a note.

CHAPTER OUTLINE

I. Payroll and Payroll Taxes.

A. The term payroll refers to a total amount paid to employees for a certain period.

B. Payroll expenditures are usually significant for a business enterprise for several reasons:

   1. Employees are sensitive to payroll errors or irregularities, and maintaining good employee morale requires that the payroll be paid on a timely, accurate basis.

   2. Payroll expenditures are subject to various federal and state regulations.

   3. Payroll expenditures and related payroll taxes have a significant effect on the net income of most business enterprises.

C. Salary and wage rates are determined, in general, by agreement between the employer and employees. Enterprises engaged in interstate commerce must follow the requirements of the Fair Labor Standards Act. This act requires a minimum rate of $1\frac{1}{2}$ times the regular rate for all hours worked in excess of 40 hours per week.

D. The employee earnings for a period are determined by multiplying the hours worked up to 40 hours by the regular rate, and any overtime hours by $1\frac{1}{2}$ times the regular rate.

E. Many enterprises pay their employees an annual bonus in addition to their regular salary or wage. The method used in determining the amount of a profit-sharing bonus may be expressed as a certain percentage of the following:

   1. Income before deducting the bonus and income taxes.

   2. Income after deducting the bonus but before deducting income taxes.

   3. Income before deducting the bonus but after deducting income taxes.

   4. Net income after deducting both the bonus and income taxes.

F. The total earnings of an employee for a payroll period, including bonuses and overtime pay, are often called the gross pay. From this amount is subtracted one or more deductions to arrive at net pay.

1. Most employers are required by the Federal Insurance Contributions Act (FICA) to withhold a portion of the earnings of each of their employees as a deduction.

2. Except for certain types of employment, all employers must withhold a portion of their employee's earnings for payment of the employee's liability for federal income tax.

3. Other deductions, such as union dues, employee insurance, etc. may be authorized by employees.

G. Gross earnings for a payroll period less the payroll deductions yields the amount to be paid to the employee, which is often called net pay or take-home pay.

H. Because there is a ceiling on annual earnings subject to FICA tax, when the amount of FICA tax to withhold from an employee is determined for a period, it is necessary to refer to one of the following cumulative amounts:

   1. Employee gross earnings for the year up to, but not including, the current payroll period.

   2. Employee tax withheld for the year up to, but not including, the current payroll period.

I. There is no ceiling on the amount of earnings subject to withholding for income taxes and hence no need to consider the cumulative earnings.

J. Most employers are subject to federal and state taxes based on the amount of remuneration earned by their employees. Such taxes are an operating expense of the business.

   1. Employers are required to contribute to the Federal Insurance Contributions Act (FICA) program for each employee. The tax rate and the maximum amount of employee remuneration entering into an employer's tax base are the same as those applicable to employees.

   2. Employers also are subject to federal and state unemployment compensation taxes on employee's remuneration.

K. A few states also collect a state unemployment compensation tax from employees based on the employee remuneration.

II. Accounting Systems for Payroll and Payroll Taxes.

A. Accounting systems for payroll and payroll taxes are concerned with the records and reports associated with the employer-employee relationship.

B. The major parts common to most payroll systems are the payroll register, employee's earnings record, and payroll checks.

C. A form used in assembling and summarizing the data needed at the end of each payroll period is the payroll register. A payroll register will normally include the following data for each employee:

1. Total hours worked.

2. Gross earnings, including any overtime.

3. Taxable earnings subject to unemployment compensation taxes and FICA taxes.

4. Deductions for FICA, federal and state income taxes, and other deductions.

5. The net amount of take-home pay.

6. The distribution of the employee's gross pay to the accounts to be debited for the expense of the employee's pay.

D. The payroll register serves as the basis for preparing the journal entry to record the payroll data for a period.

E. Employer payroll taxes also must be determined and the related expense and liabilities recorded each pay period.

F. Payment of the liability for payroll and payroll taxes is recorded in the same manner as payment of other liabilities.

G. It is important to note that the payroll taxes levied against employers become liabilities at the time the related remuneration is paid to employees, rather than at the time the liability to the employees is incurred.

H. Detailed payroll data must be maintained for each employee in a record called the employee's earnings record. Such a record maintains data on total hours worked, gross earnings, deductions, and net pay.

I. One of the principal outputs of most payroll systems is a series of payroll checks at the end of each pay period for distribution to employees.

1. Most employers with a large number of employees use a special bank account and payroll checks designed specifically for payroll.

2. Currency may be used as a medium of payment when payroll is paid each week or when the business location or time of payment is such that banking or check-cashing facilities are not readily available to employees.

J. Through the use of diagrams, interrelationships of principal parts of a payroll system may be shown.

1. The output of the payroll system is the payroll register, the payroll check, earnings records, and reports for tax and other purposes.

2. The basic data entering the payroll system are called the input of the system. Input data that remain relatively unchanged are characterized as constants. Those data that differ from period to period are termed variables.

K. The cash disbursement controls discussed in earlier chapters are applicable to payrolls. Thus, the use of the voucher system and the requirement that all payments be supported by vouchers are desirable.

L. Other controls include proper authorization for additions and deletions of employees and the maintenance of attendance records.

III. Liability for Employees' Fringe Benefits.

A. Many companies provide their employees a variety of benefits in addition to salary and wages earned. These benefits are called fringe benefits and include vacation pay, pensions, and stock options.

B. To properly match revenue and expense, the employer should accrue the vacation pay liability as the vacation privilege is earned, assuming that the payment is probable and can be reasonably estimated. The entry to accrue vacation pay is to debit Vacation Pay Expense and credit a liability, Vacation Pay Payable.

C. Pension plans for employees may be classified as follows:

1. A contributory plan requires the employer to withhold a portion of each

employee's earnings as a contribution to the plan.

2. A noncontributory plan requires the employer to bear the entire cost.

3. A funded plan requires the employer to set aside funds to meet future pension benefits by making payments to an independent funding agency.

4. An unfunded plan is managed entirely by the employer instead of by an independent agency.

5. A qualified plan is designed to comply with federal income tax requirements which allow the employer to deduct pension contributions for tax purposes and which exempt fund income from tax. Most pension plans are qualified.

D. The recording of pension costs involves a debit to Pension Expense. If the pension cost is fully funded, the credit is to Cash. If the pension cost is partially funded, any unfunded amount is credited to Unfunded Accrued Pension Cost.

E. When an employer first adopts or changes a pension plan, the employer must consider whether to grant employees credit for prior years service. If credit is granted for past service, a prior service cost obligation must be recognized.

F. Stock options are rights given by a corporation to its employees to purchase shares of the corporation's stock at a stated price.

G. When employees have the right to purchase the corporation's stock at a price below market value, the difference between the market price of the stock and the amount the employees are required to pay for it is recognized as an expense.

IV. Short-Term Notes Payable. $I = P \times R \times T$

A. Notes may be issued to creditors in temporary satisfaction of an account payable created earlier, or they may be issued at the time merchandise or other assets are purchased. The entries to record a note payable are:

1. Debit Accounts Payable and credit Notes Payable for the issuance of a note in temporary satisfaction of an account payable.

2. Debit Cash or other asset and credit Notes Payable for notes initially issued.

B. The entry to record payment of a note at maturity is to debit Notes Payable, debit Interest Expense, and credit Cash for the maturity amount.

C. Notes may be issued when money is borrowed from banks. Such notes may be interest-bearing or non-interest-bearing.

1. An interest-bearing note is recorded by debiting Cash and crediting Notes Payable for the face value of the note. At the due date, Notes Payable is debited for the face value of the note, Interest Expense is debited for the interest, and Cash is credited for the total due.

2. When a non-interest-bearing note is issued to a bank, the entry to record the note is to debit Cash for the proceeds, debit Interest Expense for the difference between the face value of the note and the proceeds received, and credit Notes Payable for the face value of the note. If the note is paid at maturity, Notes Payable is debited for the face value and Cash is credited.

V. Product Warranty Liability.

A. At the time of sale, a company may grant a warranty on a product. If revenues and expenses are to be matched properly, a liability to cover the warranty must be recorded in the period of the sale.

B. The entry to accrue warranty liability is to debit Product Warranty Expense and credit Product Warranty Payable.

C. When a defective product is repaired, the repair cost should be recorded by debiting Product Warranty Payable and crediting Cash, Supplies, or another appropriate account.

VI. Contingent Liabilities.

A. Contingent liabilities are potential obligations that will materialize only if certain events occur in the future.

B. If the liability is probable and the amount of the liability can be reasonably estimated, it should be recorded in the accounts.

C. If the amount cannot be reasonably estimated, the details of the contingency should be disclosed. The most common types of contingent liabilities disclosed in notes to the financial statements involve litigation, guarantees, and discounted receivables.

PART 1

Instructions: A list of terms and related statements appear below. From the list of terms, select the term that relates to each statement and print its identifying letter in the space provided.

A. Contingent liabilities	F. Gross pay	K. Unfunded plan
B. Discount	G. Noncontributory plan	L. Wages
C. Employee's earnings record	H. Payroll register	M. Stock options
D. FICA tax	I. Proceeds	
E. Funded plan	J. Salary	

J   1. Payment for managerial, administrative, or similar services, usually expressed in terms of a month or a year.

L   2. Remuneration for manual labor, computed on an hourly, weekly, or piecework basis.

F   3. The total earnings of an employee for a payroll period.

D   4. Employees' contribution to the combined federal programs for old-age and disability benefits, insurance benefits to survivors, and health insurance for the aged.

H   5. Multicolumn form used in assembling and summarizing the data needed at the end of each payroll period.

C   6. A detailed record of an employee's earnings for each payroll period and for the year.

G   7. A pension plan requiring the employer to bear the entire cost.

E   8. A pension plan requiring the employer to set aside funds to meet future pension benefits by making payments to an independent funding agency.

M   9. Rights given by a corporation to its employees to purchase shares of the corporation's stock at a stated price.

B   10. The amount of interest deducted from a future value.

I   11. The net amount available to a borrower of funds.

A   12. Potential obligations that will materialize only if certain events occur in the future.

K   13. A pension plan managed entirely by the employer instead of by an independent agency.

PART 2

Instructions: Indicate whether each of the following statements is true or false by placing a T or F in the space provided.

F   **1.** The total earnings of an employee for a payroll period are called net pay.

T   **2.** Employers are required to contribute to the Federal Insurance Contributions Act program for each employee.

F   **3.** All states require that unemployment compensation taxes be withheld from employees' pay.

T   **4.** The amounts withheld from employees' earnings have no effect on the firm's debits to the salary or wage expense accounts.

T   **5.** All payroll taxes levied against employers become liabilities at the time the related remuneration is paid to employees.

F   **6.** The recording procedures when special payroll checks are used are different from the procedures when the checks are drawn on the regular bank account.

T   **7.** Depending on when it is to be paid, vacation liability may be classified in the balance sheet as either a current liability or a long-term liability.

T   **8.** If pension cost is partially funded, the employer's contribution to a pension plan for the pension cost for a given year is recorded by a debit to Pension Expense and credits to Cash and Unfunded Accrued Pension Cost.

F   **9.** In order for revenues and expenses to be matched properly, a liability to cover the cost of a product warranty must be recorded in the period when the product is repaired.

T   **10.** If a liability is probable and its amount can be reasonably estimated, it should be recorded in the accounts.

PART 3

Instructions: Circle the best answer for each of the following questions.

1. An employee's rate of pay is $8 per hour, with time and a half for hours worked in excess of 40 during a week. If the employee works 50 hours during a week, and has FICA tax withheld at a rate of 7.5% and federal income tax withheld at a rate of 15%, the employee's net pay for the week is:
   a. $440
   b. $374
   c. $341
   d. $310

2. For good internal control, the addition or deletion of names on the payroll should be supported by written authorization from the:
   a. employee being added or deleted
   b. employee's supervisor
   c. personnel department
   d. treasurer

3. Which of the following items would not be considered a fringe benefit?
   a. vacations
   b. employee pension plans
   c. health insurance
   d. FICA benefits

4. For proper matching of revenues and expenses, the estimated cost of fringe benefits must be recognized as an expense of the period during which the:
   a. employee earns the benefit
   b. employee is paid the benefit
   c. fringe benefit contract is signed
   d. fringe benefit contract becomes effective

5. A pension plan which complies with federal income tax requirements allowing the employer to deduct contributions for tax purposes and which exempt pension fund income from tax is called a:
   a. contributory plan
   b. funded plan
   c. model plan
   d. qualified plan

PART 4

Instructions: In each of the following situations, determine the correct amount.

1. An employee of a firm operating under the Federal Wage and Hour Law worked 50 hours last week. If the hourly rate of pay is $14, what is the employee's gross earnings for the week? $_770___

2. During the current pay period, an employee earned $2,500. Prior to the current period, the employee earned (in the current year) $49,000. If the FICA tax rate is 7.5% on maximum earnings of $50,000, what is the amount to be withheld from the employee's pay this period? $_75___

3. Using the rate and maximum base as in (2), what is the amount of FICA tax withheld from the pay of an employee who has earned $10,000 but has actually received only $9,700, with the remaining $300 to be paid in the next year? $_____

75
+22.50

PART 5

The weekly gross payroll of Osborne Co. on December 7 amounts to $45,000. The following amounts are to be withheld: FICA tax $3,375; employees' income tax, $7,650; union dues, $900; and United Way, $450. The $45,000 payroll is distributed as follows: sales salaries, $34,000, and office salaries, $11,000.

Instructions: Omitting explanations, prepare journal entries to:

(1) Record the payroll.

	DATE	DESCRIPTION	POST. REF.	DEBIT	CREDIT	
1		Sales Sal Exp				1
2		Off Sal Exp				2
3		FICA Tax Pbl				3
4		Em Inc Tx				4
5		Union Dues				5
6		UW				6
7		Sal Pbl				7

(2) Record the payment of the payroll.

	DATE	DESCRIPTION	POST. REF.	DEBIT	CREDIT	
1						1
2						2

(3) Record the employer's payroll taxes. Assume that the entire payroll is subject to FICA tax at 7.5%, federal unemployment tax of .8%, and state unemployment tax at 3.0%.

	DATE	DESCRIPTION	POST. REF.	DEBIT	CREDIT	
1						1
2						2
3						3
4						4

PART 6

The president of Switzer Manufacturing Co. is to be granted an 8% profit-sharing bonus. The corporate income tax rate is 34%. The company's income before the deduction of the income tax and the bonus amounted to $500,000.

Instructions: Calculate the president's bonus under each of the following methods. (Show your work.)

(1) Bonus based on income before deducting either bonus or income tax.

$$B = .08 \times 500,000$$

(2) Bonus based on income after deducting bonus but before deducting income tax.

$$.08 (500000 - B)$$

(3) Bonus based on income before deducting bonus but after deducting income tax.

$$.08 [.34 \times 500,000]$$

(4) Bonus based on net income after deducting both bonus and income tax.

PART 7

Instructions: For each of the employees listed below, compute the taxes indicated as well as the total of each tax. Assume a 7.5% FICA tax rate on a maximum of $50,000, a state unemployment tax rate of 3.0% on a maximum of $7,000, and a federal unemployment tax rate of .8% on a maximum of $7,000.

Employee	Annual Earnings	Employee's FICA Tax	Employer's Taxes			
			FICA	State Unemployment	Federal Unemployment	Total
Johnson	$ 55,000					
Jones	$ 12,000					
Smith	$ 5,000					
Wilson	$ 52,000					
Total	$124,000					

PART 8

Instructions: Prepare the journal entries to record each of the following items for Walsh Inc. (Omit explanations.)

(1) Accrued employee vacation pay at the end of the year is $2,950.

	DATE	DESCRIPTION	POST. REF.	DEBIT	CREDIT	
1						1
2						2

(2) The estimated product warranty liability at the end of the year is 3% of sales of $125,000.

	DATE	DESCRIPTION	POST. REF.	DEBIT	CREDIT	
1		PRODUCT WARRANTY EXP				1
2		PRODUCT WARRANTY PBL				2

(3) A partially funded pension plan is maintained for employees, with an annual cost of $36,000. At the end of the year $28,000 is paid to the fund trustee and the remaining accrued pension liability is recognized.

	DATE	DESCRIPTION	POST. REF.	DEBIT	CREDIT	
1						1
2						2
3						3
4						4

Name _____

PART 9

Instructions: Prepare the journal entries to record the following transactions. (Omit explanations.)

(1) Audrey West borrowed $6,000 from the bank and gave the bank a 90-day, 11% note.

	DATE	DESCRIPTION	POST. REF.	DEBIT	CREDIT	
1						1
2						2
3						3

(2) West paid the note in (1) at maturity.

	DATE	DESCRIPTION	POST. REF.	DEBIT	CREDIT	
1						1
2						2
3						3

(3) Randy Lessman borrowed $8,000 from the bank, giving a 60-day, non-interest-bearing note which was discounted at 9%.

	DATE	DESCRIPTION	POST. REF.	DEBIT	CREDIT	
1						1
2						2
3						3

(4) Lessman paid the note recorded in (3) at maturity.

	DATE	DESCRIPTION	POST. REF.	DEBIT	CREDIT	
1						1
2						2
3						3

Chapter 10
Forms of Business Organization

STUDY GOALS

After studying this chapter, you should be able to:

1. Identify basic sole proprietorship characteristics which have accounting implications.

2. Describe the accounting for sole proprietorships.

3. Identify basic partnership characteristics which have accounting implications.

4. Describe the accounting for partnerships.

5. Identify basic corporation characteristics which have accounting implications.

6. Describe and illustrate the accounting for corporations.

7. Describe and illustrate the computation of equity per share of stock.

8. Describe and illustrate the accounting for organization costs.

GLOSSARY OF KEY TERMS

Articles of partnership. The formal written contract creating a partnership.

Capital stock. Shares of ownership of a corporation.

Cumulative preferred stock. Preferred stock that is entitled to current and past dividends before dividends may be paid on common stock.

Deficit. A debit balance in the retained earnings account.

Common stock. The basic ownership class of corporate capital stock.

Discount on stock. The excess of par value of stock over its sales price.

Equity per share. The ratio of stockholders' equity to the related number of shares of stock outstanding.

Paid-in capital. The capital acquired from stockholders.

Par. The arbitrary monetary figure printed on a stock certificate.

Participating preferred stock. Preferred stock that could receive dividends in excess of the specified amount granted by its preferential rights.

Preemptive right. The right of each shareholder to maintain the same fractional interest in the corporation by purchasing a proportionate number of shares of any additional issuances of stock.

Preferred stock. A class of stock with preferential rights over common stock.

Premium on stock. The excess of the sales price of stock over its par amount.

Retained earnings. Net income retained in a corporation.

Stated value. An amount assigned by the board of directors to each share of no-par stock.

Stockholders. The owners of a corporation.

Stockholders' equity. The equity of the shareholders in a corporation.

Stock outstanding. The stock in the hands of the stockholders.

Treasury stock. A corporation's own outstanding stock that has been reacquired.

CHAPTER OUTLINE

I. Characteristics of Sole Proprietorships.

   A. A sole proprietorship is a business enterprise owned by one individual.

   B. The sole proprietorship is a separate entity for accounting purposes, and when the owner dies or retires, the sole proprietorship ceases to exist.

   C. A primary disadvantage of a sole proprietorship may be the difficulty in raising funds. Investment in the business is limited to the owner's personal resources, plus any additional amounts that can be borrowed. The owner is also personally liable for any debts of the business.

II. Accounting for Sole Proprietorships.

   A. The transactions of the sole proprietorship must be kept separate from the personal financial affairs of the owner.

   B. One of the primary differences in accounting for a sole proprietorship compared with a corporation is the use of an owner's capital account, rather than a capital stock account, to record investments in the enterprise.

   C. The capital account, rather than a retained earnings account, is used to record changes in owner's equity from net income or net loss.

   D. Instead of a dividends account, distributions to the owner are recorded in the owner's drawing account.

III. Characteristics of Partnerships.

   A. The Uniform Partnership Act defines a partnership as "an association of two or more persons to carry on as co-owners a business for profit."

   B. Partnerships have several characteristics that have accounting implications.

      1. A partnership has a limited life. Dissolution of a partnership occurs whenever a partner ceases to be a member of the firm for any reason.

      2. Most partnerships are general partnerships, in which the partners have unlimited liability. Each partner is individually liable to creditors for debts incurred by the partnership.

      3. In some states, a limited partnership may be formed, in which the liability of some partners may be limited to the amount of their capital investment. However, a limited partnership must have at least one general partner who has unlimited liability.

      4. Partners have co-ownership of partnership property. The property invested in a partnership by a partner becomes the joint property of all the partners.

      5. The mutual agency characteristic of a partnership means that each partner is an agent of the partnership, with the authority to enter into contracts for the partnership. Thus, the acts of each partner bind the partnership and become the responsibility of all partners.

      6. A significant right of partners is participation in income of the partnership. Net income and net loss are distributed among the partners according to their agreement. In the absence of any agreement, all partners share equally.

      7. Although partnerships are nontaxable entities and therefore do not pay federal income taxes, they must file an information return with the Internal Revenue Service.

   C. A partnership is created by a voluntary contract containing all the elements essential to any other enforceable contract. This contract is known as the articles of partnership or partnership agreement.

IV. Accounting for Partnerships

   A. Most of the day-to-day accounting for a partnership is the same as the accounting for any other form of business organization. The primary differences in accounting for a partnership include the use of multiple owners' equity accounts, one for each partner, to record investments in the enterprise and to record changes in the owners' equity from net income or net loss.

   B. Distributions of assets to owners are recorded in each partner's drawing account, which is similar to the dividends account for a corporation.

V. Characteristics of a Corporation.

   A. A corporation is an artificial person, created by law and having a distinct existence separate and apart from the natural persons who are responsible for its creation and operation.

B. The most important characteristics of a corporation with accounting implications are as follows:

1. A corporation has a separate legal existence. It may acquire, own, and dispose of assets, incur liabilities, and enter into contracts according to the provisions of its charter (articles of incorporation).

2. The ownership of a corporation is divided into transferable units known as shares of stock. The stockholders (shareholders) may buy and sell shares without interfering with the activities of the corporation.

3. The stockholders of a corporation have limited liability. The financial loss that a stockholder may suffer is limited to the amount invested.

4. The stockholders exercise control over the management of corporate affairs indirectly by electing a board of directors.

5. As a separate entity, a corporation is subject to additional taxes. These taxes may include both state and federal income taxes.

C. A corporation has less freedom of action than a sole proprietorship and a partnership and may be subject to a variety of government regulations.

VI. Accounting for Corporations.

A. The owners' equity in a corporation is commonly called stockholders' equity, shareholders' equity, shareholders' investment, or capital.

B. The two main sources of stockholders' equity are:

1. Investments contributed by the stockholders, called paid-in capital or contributed capital.

2. Net income retained in the business, called retained earnings.

C. The paid-in capital contributed by the stockholders is recorded in accounts maintained for each class of stock.

D. Retained earnings result from transferring the net income to a retained earnings account at the end of a fiscal year. The dividend account, which represents distributions of earnings to stockholders, also is closed to Retained Earnings. A debit balance in Retained Earnings is termed a deficit.

E. The general term applied to the shares of ownership of a corporation is capital stock.

1. The number of shares of stock that a corporation is authorized to issue is set forth in its charter. The stock in the hands of the stockholders is called stock outstanding.

2. Shares of capital stock are often assigned an arbitrary monetary figure, known as par. The par amount is printed on the stock certificate.

3. Stock may also be issued without par, in which case it is called no-par stock. Boards of directors may assign a stated value to no-par stock.

4. State law normally requires that some specific minimum contribution by the stockholders be retained by the corporation for the protection of its creditors. This amount is called legal capital.

F. The two major classes of stock are common stock and preferred stock. The major rights that accompany ownership of a share of stock are:

1. The right to vote in matters concerning the corporation.

2. The right to share in distributions of earnings.

3. The preemptive right, which is the right to maintain the same fractional interest in the corporation by purchasing a proportionate number of shares of any additional issuances of stock.

4. The right to share in assets upon liquidation.

G. Classes of stock with various preferential rights are called preferred stock. Preferred stock may be participating or non-participating.

1. If the preferred stockholders' preferential right to dividends is limited to a certain amount, such stock is said to be non-participating.

2. Preferred stock which provides for the possibility of dividends in excess of a certain amount is said to be participating. Such preferred stock participates with common shares in dividends to varying degrees.

H. Preferred stock may be cumulative or noncumulative.

1. Preferred stock for which the preferential dividend right is assured by providing that dividends may not be paid on the common stock if any preferred dividends have been passed (said to be in arrears) is called cumulative preferred stock.

2. Preferred stock not having a cumulative right to dividends is called noncumulative.

I. Preferred stock may also be given preference in its claim to assets upon liquidation of the corporation. If the assets remaining after payment of creditors are not sufficient to return the capital contributions of both classes of stock, payment would first be made to the preferred shareholders and any balance remaining would go to the common shareholders. Preferred stock normally does not have voting rights in the corporation.

J. The entries to record investments of stockholders in a corporation are like those for investment by owners of other types of business organizations, except that the credit to stockholders' equity is to an account for each class of stock issued.

1. The capital stock accounts (Preferred Stock, Common Stock) are controlling accounts.

2. Individual stockholders accounts are kept in a subsidiary ledger known as the stockholders ledger.

K. The price at which stock is sold by a corporation is influenced by:

1. The financial condition, the earnings record, and the dividend record of the corporation.

2. Its potential earning power.

3. The availability of money for investment purposes.

4. The general business and economic conditions and prospects.

L. When capital stock is issued at a premium, cash or other assets are debited for the amount received, the stock account is credited for the par amount, and an account generally called Paid-In Capital in Excess of Par is credited for the amount of the premium.

M. When capital stock is issued at a discount, cash or other assets are debited for the amount received, the capital stock account is credited for the par amount, and a discount account is debited for the amount of the discount.

N. Premiums and discounts are reported on the balance sheet in the stockholders' equity section as either an addition to or deduction from their associated capital stock account.

O. When capital stock is issued in exchange for assets other than cash, the assets acquired should be recorded at their fair market price or at the fair market price of the stock issued, whichever is more objectively determinable.

P. In most states, both preferred and common stock may be issued without a par designation.

1. When no-par stock is issued, the entire proceeds may be credited to the capital stock account, even though the issuance price varies from time to time. In this case, the entire proceeds of the issuance of no-par stock is regarded as legal capital.

2. In some states, no-par stock may be assigned a stated value per share, and the excess of the proceeds over the stated value may be credited to Paid-In Capital in Excess of Stated Value. The accounting for no-par stock with a stated value follows the same pattern as accounting for par stock.

Q. A corporation may purchase shares of its own outstanding stock from shareholders. Such stock is called treasury stock.

R. Treasury stock should not be reported on the balance sheet as an asset. Instead, treasury stock is reported in the stockholders' equity section of the balance sheet as a deduction from total paid-in capital and retained earnings.

S. A commonly used method of accounting for treasury stock is the cost basis.

   1. When the stock is purchased by the corporation, Treasury Stock is debited for the price paid for it.

   2. When the stock is resold, Treasury Stock is credited at the price paid for it, and the difference between the price paid and the selling price is debited or credited to an account entitled Paid-In Capital from Sale of Treasury Stock.

   3. The account Paid-In Capital from Sale of Treasury Stock is reported in the paid-in capital section of the balance sheet.

VII. Equity Per Share.

A. The amount appearing on the balance sheet as total stockholders' equity may be stated in terms of equity per share or book value per share.

B. When there is only one class of stock, the equity per share is determined by dividing total stockholders' equity by the number of shares outstanding.

C. For a corporation with both preferred and common stock, it is necessary first to allocate the total equity between the two classes of stock. In making the allocation, consideration must be given to the liquidation rights of the preferred stock, including any participating and cumulative dividend features.

D. After the total is allocated to the two classes of stock, the equity per share of each class may then be determined by dividing the respective amounts by the related number of shares outstanding.

E. Equity per share is one of the many factors that are quoted in the financial press and may affect the market price of the stock.

III. Organization Costs.

A. Expenditures incurred in organizing a corporation, such as legal fees, are charged to an intangible asset account entitled Organization Costs.

B. Since organizational costs are generally small in relation to total assets and the effect on net income is ordinarily not significant, organizational costs are normally amortized over sixty months in conformity with the Internal Revenue Code.

PART 1

Instructions: A list of terms and related statements appear below. From the list of terms, select the term that relates to each statement and print its identifying letter in the space provided. Terms may be used more than once, or they may not be used at all.

A. Articles of partnership
B. Board of directors
C. Book value per share
D. Cumulative preferred stock
E. Deficit
F. General partnership

G. Equity ledger
H. Equity right
I. Limited partnership
J. Mutual agency
K. Nonpublic corporations
L. Participating preferred stock

M. Preemptive right
N. Premium
O. Public corporations
P. Stockholders ledger
Q. Treasury stock

___F___ 1. A type of partnership in which the partners have unlimited liability.

___I___ 2. A type of partnership in which the liability of some partners may be restricted to the amount of their capital investment.

___J___ 3. A characteristic of a partnership that means that each partner has the authority to enter into contracts for the partnership.

___O___ 4. Large, profit corporations whose shares of stock are widely distributed and traded in a public market.

___B___ 5. The stockholders, as owners of the corporation, exercise control over the management of corporate affairs indirectly by electing a (?).

___E___ 6. If the occurrence of net losses results in a debit balance in Retained Earnings, it is termed a (?).

___M___ ___A___ 7. The right of shareholders to maintain the same fractional interest in the corporation by purchasing a proportionate number of shares of any additional issuance of stock.

___D___ 8. Preferred stock which has the preferential dividend right that dividends may not be paid on common stock if any preferred dividends have been passed.

___P___ 9. Individual stockholders accounts are kept in the subsidiary ledger known as the (?).

___N___ 10. When stock is issued for more than par, the excess of the contract price over par is termed a (?) on stock.

___Q___ 11. Stock that has been reacquired by a corporation.

___C___ 12. Another term sometimes used in referring to the equity per share.

Name _____

PART 2

Instructions: Indicate whether each of the following statements is true or false by placing a T or F in the space provided.

___F___ 1. Corporations organized for recreational, educational, charitable, or other philanthropic purposes are usually called nonpublic corporations.

___T___ 2. The corporation charter is also called the articles of incorporation.

___F___ 3. The two main sources of corporate capital are paid-in capital and long-term debt.

___F___ 4. A generally used term for retained earnings is "earned surplus."

___T___ 5. The specified minimum stockholders' contribution that a corporation is required by law to retain for protection of its creditors is called legal capital.

___F___ 6. Preferred stock which provides for the possibility of dividends in excess of a certain amount is said to be cumulative.

___T___ 7. When par stock is issued for more than par, the excess of the contract price over par is termed a premium.

___F___ 8. When par stock is issued at a price below par, the difference is called a premium.

___F___ 9. Sales of treasury stock result in a net decrease in paid-in capital.

___F___ 10. Expenditures incurred in organizing a corporation, such as legal fees, taxes, fees paid to the state, and promotional costs, are charged to an intangible asset account entitled Goodwill.

___T___ 11. Most of the day-to-day accounting for a partnership is the same as the accounting for a sole proprietorship and a corporation.

___F___ 12. In a partnership, distributions of assets to partners are recorded in a dividends account, the same as for a corporation.

PART 3

Instructions: Circle the best answer for each of the following questions.

1. Which of the following is not a characteristic of the corporate form of organization?
   a. ownership represented by shares of stock
   b. separate legal existence
   c. unlimited liability of stockholders
   d. earnings subject to the federal income tax

2. Preferred stock whose preferential right to dividends is limited to a certain amount is termed:
   a. participating
   b. cumulative
   c. nonparticipating
   d. noncumulative

3. If a corporation has outstanding 5,000 shares of $6 cumulative preferred stock of $100 par and dividends have been passed for the preceding four years, what is the amount of preferred dividends that must be declared in the current year before a dividend can be declared on common stock?
   a. $90,000
   b. $120,000   30,000 × 5 + current yr!
   c. $150,000
   d. $180,000

4. When a corporation purchases its own stock, what account is debited for the cost of the stock?
   a. Common Stock Owned
   b. Treasury Stock
   c. Preferred Stock
   d. Common Stock Receivable

5. The excess of the proceeds from selling treasury stock over its cost should be credited to:
   a. Retained Earnings
   b. Premium on Capital Stock
   c. Gain from Sale of Treasury Stock
   d. Paid-In Capital from Sale of Treasury Stock

PART 4

Instructions: Prepare the entries (without explanation) to record each of the following unrelated transactions:

(1) Cooper Inc. issues 20,000 shares of no-par common stock for cash at $15 per share.

	DATE	DESCRIPTION	POST. REF.	DEBIT	CREDIT	
1		*CASH*				1
2		*common stock*				2

(2) Frazier Inc. issues 10,000 shares of $10 par common stock in exchange for new manufacturing equipment with a fair market price of $135,000.

	DATE	DESCRIPTION	POST. REF.	DEBIT	CREDIT	
1		*EQUIP*				1
2		*Common stock*			*100,000*	2
		PICEP			*35,000*	

(3) Mali Inc. issues 8,000 shares of $50 par preferred stock for cash at $60 per share.

	DATE	DESCRIPTION	POST. REF.	DEBIT	CREDIT	
1		*CASH*				1
2		*PICEP*				2
3		*PREF STOCK*				3
4						4

(4) Palmer Inc. issues 5,000 shares of no-par common stock for $30 per share.

	DATE	DESCRIPTION	POST. REF.	DEBIT	CREDIT	
1		*CASH*				1
2		*common stock*				2

PART 5

Price Inc. has 2,000 shares of $50 par common stock outstanding and 200 shares of $250 par 10% preferred stock outstanding. Price expects to pay annual dividends of $4,000, $6,000, $17,000, and $27,000 respectively for the next four years.

Instructions: By completing the following forms, indicate how the dividends should be distributed in each case if the preferred stock is given the rights or the restrictions indicated.

(1) The preferred stock is cumulative and nonparticipating.

Year	Total Dividends	Preferred Dividends		Common Dividends	
		Total	Per Share	Total	Per Share
1	$4,000	$4000	$20	—	—
2	6,000	$6000	$25	—	—
3	17,000	$5000	$25	12000	$6.00
4	27,000	$5000	$25	22,000	$11.00

(2) The preferred stock is cumulative and participating. The preferred stock participates in distributions of additional dividends after allowance of an $8 dividend per share on the common stock, the additional dividends to be prorated among common and preferred shares on the basis of the total par of the stock outstanding.

Year	Total Dividends	Preferred Dividends		Common Dividends	
		Total	Per Share	Total	Per Share
1	$4,000	4000	$20		
2	6,000	5000	$30		
3	17,000	5000	25	12000	6.00
4	27,000	5000	25	4000	2.00

(3) The preferred stock is noncumulative and participating. The preferred stock participates in distributions of additional dividends after allowance of a $9.50 dividend per share on the common stock, the additional dividends to be prorated among common and preferred shares on the basis of the total par of the stock outstanding.

Year	Total Dividends	Preferred Dividends		Common Dividends	
		Total	Per Share	Total	Per Share
1	$4,000	4000	20	—	—
2	6,000	5000	25	1000	1.00
3	17,000	5000	25	12000	6.00
4	27,000	6000	30	21000	10.50

9000

3000

21

1000 .33

Name _____

PART 6

The stockholders' equity section of Anderson Inc.'s balance sheet is as follows:

Stockholders' Equity

Preferred 8% stock (2,500 shares outstanding, par $40)	$100,000
Common stock (8,000 shares outstanding, par $50)	400,000
Retained earnings	500,000
Total stockholders' equity	$1,000,000

Instructions: For each of the following assumptions, determine the equity per share by making the computations and filling in the blanks.

(1) The preferred stock is noncumulative and nonparticipating. The annual 8% preferred dividend has been declared and paid prior to the preparation of the stockholders' equity section of the balance sheet for Anderson Inc.

	Par Value	+	Applicable Retained Earnings	=	Equity Per Class	+	Shares Outstanding	=	Equity Per Share
Preferred	$100,000								
Common	400,000								
Total	$500,000		$500,000		$1,000,000				

(2) The preferred stock is cumulative and nonparticipating. No dividends have been paid for the last four years, which includes the dividend year just ended.

	Par Value	+	Applicable Retained Earnings	=	Equity Per Class	+	Shares Outstanding	=	Equity Per Share
Preferred	$100,000								
Common	400,000								
Total	$500,000		$500,000		$1,000,000				

(3) The preferred stock is noncumulative and nonparticipating. No dividends have been paid for the last four years, which includes the dividend year just ended.

	Par Value	+	Applicable Retained Earnings	=	Equity Per Class	+	Shares Outstanding	=	Equity Per Share
Preferred	$100,000								
Common	400,000								
Total	$500,000		$500,000		$1,000,000				

(4) The preferred stock is cumulative and has prior claim to assets on liquidation to the extent of 120% of par. No dividends have been paid for the last five years, which includes the dividend year just ended.

	Par Value	+	Applicable Retained Earnings	=	Equity Per Class	+	Shares Outstanding	=	Equity Per Share
Preferred	$120,000*								
Common	400,000								
Total	$520,000*		$480,000*		$1,000,000*				

*Note: $20,000 of the Retained Earnings must be allocated to the liquidation value of the preferred stock.

PART 7

Instructions: Prepare the entries (without explanation) to record each of the following treasury stock transactions of Powell Inc., using the cost basis method.

(1) On October 1, Powell purchased 1,000 shares of treasury stock at $70.

	DATE	DESCRIPTION	POST. REF.	DEBIT	CREDIT	
1						1
2						2

(2) On October 31, Powell sold 500 shares of the treasury stock it purchased on October 1 at $75.

	DATE	DESCRIPTION	POST. REF.	DEBIT	CREDIT	
1						1
2						2
3						3

(3) On November 20, Powell sold 300 shares of the treasury stock it purchased on October 1 at $67.

	DATE	DESCRIPTION	POST. REF.	DEBIT	CREDIT	
1						1
2						2

Chapter 11
Stockholders' Equity, Earnings, and Dividends

STUDY GOALS

After studying this chapter, you should be able to:

1. Identify and illustrate alternative terminology used in the paid-in capital section of the balance sheet.

2. Describe and illustrate the accounting for corporate earnings and income taxes.

3. Describe and illustrate the allocation of income tax between periods.

4. Describe and illustrate the accounting for unusual items in the financial statements.

5. Describe and illustrate the computation of earnings per share.

6. Describe and illustrate the accounting for appropriations of retained earnings and the preparation of a retained earnings statement.

7. Describe and illustrate the accounting for dividends, including cash dividends, stock dividends, and liquidating dividends.

8. Describe and illustrate the accounting for stock splits.

9. Describe and illustrate the accounting for dividends and stock splits for treasury stock.

GLOSSARY OF KEY TERMS

Appropriation of retained earnings. The amount of a corporation's retained earnings that has been restricted and therefore is not available for distribution to shareholders as dividends.

Cash dividend. A cash distribution of earnings by a corporation to its shareholders.

Consistency concept. Assumption that successive financial statements of an enterprise generally should be based consistently on the same generally accepted accounting principles.

Discontinued operations. The operations of a business segment that has been disposed of.

Dividend. A distribution of earnings of a corporation to its owners (stockholders).

Earnings per share (EPS) on common stock. The profitability ratio of net income available to common shareholders to the number of common shares outstanding.

Extraordinary item. An event or transaction that is unusual and infrequent.

Funded. An appropriation of retained earnings accompanied by a segregation of cash or marketable securities.

Liquidating dividend. A distribution out of paid-in capital when a corporation permanently reduces its operations or winds up its affairs completely.

Prior period adjustment. Correction of a material error related to a prior period or periods, excluded from the determination of net income.

Stock dividend. Distribution of a company's own stock to its shareholders.

Stock split. A reduction in the par or stated value of a share of common stock and the issuance of a proportionate number of additional shares.

Taxable income. The base on which the amount of income tax is determined.

Temporary differences. Differences between income before income tax and taxable income created by items that are recognized in one period for income statement purposes and in another period for tax purposes. Such differences reverse or turn around in later years.

CHAPTER OUTLINE

I. Paid-In Capital.

    A. The main credits to paid-in capital accounts result from the issuance of stock.

        1. If par stock is issued at a price above or below par, the difference is recorded in a separate paid-in capital account.

        2. In recording the issuance of no-par stock, an account for the stated value of the no-par stock is utilized, as well as an account for any excess over stated value.

    B. Paid-in capital may also result from the sale of treasury stock.

    C. Paid-in capital may originate from donated real estate and redemptions of a corporation's own stock.

    D. Many variations in terminology and arrangement of the paid-in capital section of the balance sheet exist in practice.

        1. The details of each class of stock, including related stock premium or discount, are commonly listed first, followed by other paid-in capital accounts.

        2. Instead of describing the source of each amount in excess of par or stated value, a common practice is to combine all accounts into a single amount called "additional paid-in capital," or "capital in excess of par (or stated value) of shares."

    E. Significant changes in paid-in capital during the period should be disclosed. These changes may be disclosed in a separate paid-in capital statement or in notes to financial statements.

II. Corporate Earnings and Income Taxes.

    A. Corporations are distinct legal entities and therefore are subject to the federal income tax and, in many cases, to income taxes levied by states or other political subdivisions.

    B. Most corporations are required to estimate the amount of their federal income tax expense for the year and to make advance payments, usually in four installments. The required entry for each of the four installments is a debit to Income Tax and a credit to Cash.

    C. At year end, the actual taxable income and the actual tax are determined and an adjusting entry may be required.

    D. Because of its importance, income tax is often reported on the income statement as a special deduction from income before income tax to arrive at net income.

III. Allocation of Income Tax Between Periods.

    A. The taxable income of a corporation, determined according to the tax laws, is often different from the amount of income (before income tax) determined from the accounts and reported in the income statement. This difference may need to be allocated between periods, depending upon the nature of the items causing the differences.

    B. Temporary differences arise because some items create differences between income before income tax and taxable income because the items are recognized in one period for income statement purposes and in another period for tax purposes. Some examples of such items are as follows:

        1. Revenues or gains that are taxable after they are reported in the income statement. Example: The point of sale method is used for reporting purposes and the installment method of determining revenue is used in determining taxable income.

        2. Expenses or losses that are deducted in determining taxable income after they are reported in the income statement. Example: Product warranty expense estimated and reported in the year of the sale for reporting purposes, but is

only deductible for tax purposes when paid.

3. Revenues or gains that are taxable before they are reported in the income statement. Example: Cash received in advance for magazine subscriptions is included in taxable income of the current period when received, but included in the income statement of a future period when earned.

4. Expenses or losses that are deducted in determining taxable income before they are reported in the income statement. Example: An accelerated depreciation method is used for tax purposes, and the straight-line method is used for financial reporting purposes.

C. Temporary differences require that the amount of the tax liability be computed at the end of each year and that the proper amount of current and postponed (deferred) liability be recognized.

1. The income tax to be reported on the income statement should be the total tax based upon reported income before income tax.

2. The credit to the current liability for income tax payable should be based upon the taxable income.

3. The difference between income tax based upon reported financial statement income and the current income tax liability based upon taxable income is either debited or credited to a deferred income tax payable account.

4. The balance in the deferred income tax payable account at the end of a year will normally be a credit balance and will be reported as a liability. The amount due within one year will be classified as a current liability, and the remainder will be classified as a long-term liability or reported in a deferred credits section following the long-term liabilities section.

IV. Reporting Unusual Items in the Financial Statements.

A. Unusual items in the financial statements can be described as (1) items that affect the current year's net income and (2) items that affect a prior year's net income.

B. Three categories of unusual items affect the income statement.

1. A gain or loss resulting from the disposal of a segment of a business should be identified on the income statement as a gain or loss from discontinued operations.

a. The term segment of a business refers to a part of an enterprise whose activities represent a major line of business.

b. When an enterprise discontinues a segment of its operations, the results of continuing operations should be identified on the income statement, as well as the gain or loss on the discontinued operations.

c. In addition to the gain or loss reported on discontinued operations, details as to the identity of the segment disposed of, the disposal date, a description of the assets and liabilities involved, and the manner of disposal should be disclosed in a note to the financial statements.

2. Extraordinary gains and losses result from events and transactions that are distinguished by their unusual nature and by the infrequency of their occurrence.

a. Examples of extraordinary items include losses from floods and earthquakes, and gains and losses that result from condemnation of land or buildings for public use.

b. Gains and losses on the disposal of plant assets do not qualify as extraordinary items because they are not unusual and they recur from time to time in the ordinary course of business activities.

3. Changes in accounting principle can occur when it is believed that the use of a different principle will more fairly state net income and financial position.

a. The concept of consistency requires that the nature of the change, the justification for the change, and its effect on income be disclosed in the financial statements in the period in which the change in principle is made.

b. The generally accepted procedures for disclosing the effect on net income of a change in principle are the reporting of the cumulative effect of the change on net income of prior periods as a special item on the income statement, and the reporting of the effect of the change on net income of the current period.

c. If an extraordinary item or items are reported on the income statement, the amount related to the change in principle should follow the extraordinary items.

d. Special procedures exist for reporting the effect of changes in accounting principle from the lifo assumption for inventory costing and in the method of accounting for long-term construction contracts.

4. The amount reported as a gain or loss from discontinued operations, an extraordinary item, or the cumulative effect of a change in accounting principle should be net of the related income tax. The related income tax may be reported on the face of the financial statement or in an accompanying note.

5. Although many variations in terminology and format are possible, unusual items should be reported on the income statement in the following order: loss on discontinued operations, extraordinary items, cumulative effects of changes in accounting principles.

C. Unusual items that affect the retained earnings statement include errors discovered in the determination of a prior period's net income.

D. Material errors that are not discovered within the same fiscal period in which they occurred are called prior period adjustments.

1. Prior period adjustments should not be included in the determination of net income for the current period.

2. Prior period adjustments should be reported as an adjustment of the Retained Earnings balance at the beginning of the period in which the correction is made.

3. An example of a prior period adjustment is the correction of a material error in computing depreciation expense for a prior period.

4. Prior period adjustments are reported net of their related income tax.

5. The effect of prior period adjustments on the net income of prior years should be disclosed in the current period's financial statements.

6. Prior period adjustments are rare in modern financial accounting.

V. Earnings Per Common Share.

A. The term earnings per share refers to the net income per share of common stock outstanding during a given period. Earnings per share is often useful in comparing financial statements of different business entities.

1. If a company has only common stock outstanding, the earnings per share of common stock is determined by dividing net income by the number of common shares outstanding.

2. If preferred stock is outstanding, the net income must be reduced by the amount of any preferred dividend requirements before dividing by the number of common shares outstanding.

B. The effect of nonrecurring additions to or deductions (unusual items) from income of a period should be considered in computing earnings per share.

C. If there are nonrecurring items on the income statement, the earnings per share amounts should be reported for: income from continuing operations, income before extraordinary items and the cumulative effect of a change in accounting principle, the cumulative effect of a change in accounting principle, and net income. Presentation of earnings per share amounts is optional for the gain or loss on discontinued operations and for extraordinary items.

VI. Appropriation of Retained Earnings.

A. The amount of a corporation's retained earnings available for distribution to its shareholders may be limited by action of the board of directors. The amount restricted, which is called an appropriation or a reserve, remains a part of retained earnings and should be so classified in the financial statements.

B. An appropriation can be effected by transferring the desired amount from Retained Earnings to a special account designating its purpose, such as Appropriation for Plant Expansion.

C. Appropriations may be initiated by the board of directors, or they may be required by law or contract.

D. When a part or all of an appropriation is no longer needed, the amount should be transferred back to the retained earnings account. The entry transferring the appropriation back to retained earnings is the reverse of the entry used to establish the appropriation.

E. An appropriation account is not directly related to any certain group of asset accounts, and its existence does not imply that there is an equivalent amount of cash or other assets set aside in a special fund.

F. Appropriations of retained earnings may be accompanied by a segregation of cash or marketable securities, in which case the appropriations are said to be funded.

G. The details of retained earnings disclosing appropriated and unappropriated amounts should be set forth either on the face of the balance sheet or in an accompanying note.

VII. Nature of Dividends.

A. A dividend is a distribution by a corporation to its shareholders.

B. A distribution of cash by a corporation to its shareholders is called a cash dividend. Cash dividends are the most usual form of dividend.

C. The three prerequisites to paying a cash dividend include sufficient unappropriated retained earnings, sufficient cash, and formal action by the board of directors.

D. Three dates are important in the distribution of dividends.

1. The date of declaration is the date the directors take formal action declaring the dividend.

2. The date of record is the date as of which ownership of shares is determined for the distribution of the dividend to shareholders.

3. The date of payment is the date the actual distribution of cash will be made to shareholders.

E. The liability for a cash dividend is recorded on the declaration date by debiting Cash Dividends and crediting Cash Dividends Payable.

F. On the date of payment the cash dividends are distributed and recorded in the accounting records by debiting Cash Dividends Payable and crediting Cash.

G. Dividends on cumulative preferred stock do not become a liability until they are declared by formal action by the corporation's board of directors. However, dividends in arrears at a balance sheet date should be disclosed in the financial statements.

H. A pro rata distribution of shares of stock of a company to the stockholders, accompanied by a transfer of retained earnings to paid-in capital accounts, is called a stock dividend. Such distributions are usually in common stock and are issued to holders of common stock.

I. Stock dividends are unlike cash dividends in that there is no distribution of cash or other corporate assets to the stockholders.

J. The effect of a stock dividend on the capital structure of the issuing corporation is to transfer accumulated retained earnings to paid-in capital. The amount transferred to the paid-in capital accounts is normally based upon the fair market value of the shares distributed.

K. The entry to record a stock dividend in which the fair market value of the stock exceeds the par value is to debit Stock Dividends, credit Stock Dividends Distributable, and credit Premium on Common Stock.

L. On the date of issuance of the stock certificates the accounting entry is recorded by debiting Stock Dividends Distributable and crediting Common Stock for the par or stated value of the stock distributed.

M. A stock dividend has no effect on the total amount of assets, liabilities, or stockholders' equity of the corporation.

N. The issuance of a stock dividend does not affect the total amount of a stockholder's equity and proportionate interest in the corporation.

O. Stock dividends are normally used by corporations that "plow back" (retain) earnings for use in expanding operations and wish to recognize a commitment to their shareholders.

P. The term liquidating dividend is applied to a distribution to stockholders from paid-in capital. Liquidating dividends are usually paid when a corporation permanently reduces its operations or winds up its affairs completely.

VIII. Stock Splits.

A. Corporations sometimes reduce the par or stated value of their common stock and issue a proportionate number of additional shares. Such a procedure is called a stock split or stock split-up.

B. The primary purpose of a stock split is to bring about a reduction in the market price per share and thus to encourage more investors to enter the market for the company's shares.

C. A stock split does not change any balances of any of the corporation's accounts, and therefore no entry is required to record the stock split. Only the number of shares and the par value per share are changed and should be notated in the accounting records.

D. Each shareholder in a corporation whose stock is split owns the same total par amount of stock before and after the stock split.

IX. Dividends and Stock Splits for Treasury Stock.

A. Cash or property dividends are not paid on treasury stock.

B. When a corporation holding treasury stock declares a stock dividend, the number of shares to be issued may be based on either the number of shares outstanding or the number of shares issued. In practice, small differences result and either method may be utilized.

C. In the case of a stock split, the reduction in par or stated value should apply to all shares of stock including unissued, issued, and treasury shares.

PART 1

Instructions: A list of terms and related statements appear below. From the list of terms, select the term that relates to each statement and print its identifying letter in the space provided. Terms may be used more than once, or they may not be used at all.

A. Appropriated	G. Funded	M. Reported income before income tax
B. Change in accounting principle	H. Gain or loss from discontinued operations	N. Stock dividend
C. Dividend	I. Liquidating dividend	O. Stock split
D. Earnings per share	J. Other income or loss	P. Taxable income
E. Equity per share	K. Permanent	Q. Temporary
F. Extraordinary items	L. Prior period adjustments	R. Unusual items

_____ 1. This amount is determined by dividing net income by the number of common shares outstanding.

_____ 2. A distribution by a corporation to its shareholders.

_____ 3. Use of accelerated depreciation for tax purposes and straight-line depreciation for financial reporting purposes is an example of a (?) difference between taxable income and the amount of income before tax reported on the income statement.

_____ 4. The income tax to be reported on the income statement should be the total tax based upon (?).

_____ 5. A gain or loss resulting from the disposal of a segment of the business.

_____ 6. A switch to the use of an accelerated depreciation method from straight-line depreciation is an example of (?).

_____ 7. A distribution to stockholders from paid-in capital.

_____ 8. A pro rata distribution of shares of stock from a company to its stockholders, accompanied by a transfer of retained earnings to paid-in capital accounts.

_____ 9. Events and transactions that are distinguished by their unusual nature and by their infrequency of occurrence.

_____ 10. Material errors that are not discovered within the same fiscal period in which they occurred.

PART 2

Instructions: Indicate whether each of the following statements is true or false by placing a T or F in the space provided.

_____ T **1.** The amount reported as a gain or loss from discontinued operations on the income statement should be reported net of related income tax.

_____ F **2.** Appropriations of retained earnings are normally associated with a particular group of assets.

_____ F **3.** Cash or property dividends are normally paid on treasury stock.

_____ T **4.** Paid-in capital and retained earnings are two major subdivisions of stockholders' equity.

_____ T **5.** Income tax should be allocated to the fiscal year in which the related income is reported and earned.

_____ T **6.** To be classified as an extraordinary item, an item must be unusual in nature and infrequent in occurrence.

F _____ F **7.** When a corporation borrows money by issuing bonds, retained earnings must be appropriated to cover the indebtedness.

_____ F **8.** A liability for a dividend is normally recorded in the accounting records on the date of record.

_____ F **9.** A gain or loss resulting from the disposal of a segment of the business should be identified on the income statement as an extraordinary item.

_____ T **10.** An accounting entry is required to record a stock dividend.

PART 3

Instructions: Circle the best answer for each of the following questions.

1. The income tax to be reported on the income statement should be the total tax based upon:

    a. taxable income reported on the tax return

    b. income before income tax reported on the financial statements

    c. income from continuing operations

    d. income resulting from permanent differences between the tax return and reported income

2. The account Deferred Income Tax is normally classified in the financial statements as:

    a. expense

    b. liability

    c. revenue

    d. paid-in capital

3. During its first year of operations, a corporation elected to use the straight-line method of depreciation for financial reporting purposes and the sum-of-the-years-digits method for reporting taxable income. If the income tax is 40% and the amount of depreciation expense is $200,000 under the straight-line method and $350,000 under the sum-of-the-years-digits method, what is the amount of income tax deferred to future years?

    a. $20,000

    b. $60,000

    c. $80,000

    d. $140,000

4. Which of the following would appear as an extraordinary item on the income statement?

    a. Correction of an error in the prior year's financial statements

    b. Gain resulting from the sale of plant assets

    c. Loss on sale of temporary investments

    d. Loss on condemnation of land

5. A company with 20,000 authorized shares of $50 par common stock issued 12,000 shares at $60. Subsequently, the company declared a 5% stock dividend on a date when the market price was $65 per share. What is the amount transferred from the retained earnings account to paid-in capital accounts as a result of the stock dividend?

    a. $30,000

    b. $36,000

    c. $39,000

    d. $65,000

PART 4

(1) Judd Inc. reported $450,000 income before tax on its income statement for the year. Because of temporary differences in accounting and tax methods, taxable income for the year is $320,000. Assuming an income tax rate of 40%, prepare the journal entry to record the income tax expense, liability, and deferred liability of Judd Inc.

	DATE	DESCRIPTION	POST. REF.	DEBIT	CREDIT	
1						1
2						2
3						3

(2) In the following year, Judd Inc. reported $500,000 income before income tax. Because of temporary differences in accounting and tax methods, taxable income for this year is $550,000. Assuming an income tax rate of 40%, prepare the journal entry to record the income tax expense, liability, and reduction of the deferred liability of Judd Inc.

	DATE	DESCRIPTION	POST. REF.	DEBIT	CREDIT	
1						1
2						2
3						3

PART 5

Myers Inc. estimates its income tax expense for the year to be $240,000. At the end of the year, Myers Inc. determines that its actual income tax for the year is $260,000.

Instructions:

(1) Prepare the entry to record one of the four estimated income tax payments.

	DATE	DESCRIPTION	POST. REF.	DEBIT	CREDIT	
1						1
2						2

(2) Prepare the entry to record the additional income tax liability for the year.

	DATE	DESCRIPTION	POST. REF.	DEBIT	CREDIT	
1						1
2						2

PART 6

Berg Inc. issued $15,000,000 worth of 30-year bonds. The corporation agreed to restrict the distribution of earnings during the life of the bonds by making annual transfers of $500,000 to an appropriation account.

Instructions:

(1) Prepare the entry to record one of the 30 equal annual transfers.

	DATE	DESCRIPTION	POST. REF.	DEBIT	CREDIT	
1						1
2						2

(2) Prepare the entry to eliminate the appropriation after the bonds have been retired.

	DATE	DESCRIPTION	POST. REF.	DEBIT	CREDIT	
1						1
2						2

PART 7

Instructions: Journalize the following transactions of Cowell Inc. (Omit explanations.)

(1) February 20. Declared an $80,000 cash dividend.

	DATE	DESCRIPTION	POST. REF.	DEBIT	CREDIT	
1						1
2						2

(2) March 22. Paid the cash dividend declared on February 20.

	DATE	DESCRIPTION	POST. REF.	DEBIT	CREDIT	
1						1
2						2

(3) December 15. Declared a 4% stock dividend on 180,000 shares of $20 par value common stock with a market value of $28 per share.

	DATE	DESCRIPTION	POST. REF.	DEBIT	CREDIT	
1						1
2						2
3						3

(4) January 14. Issued the stock certificates for the stock dividend declared on December 15.

	DATE	DESCRIPTION	POST. REF.	DEBIT	CREDIT	
1						1
2						2

PART 8

The stockholders' equity of Santana Inc. consists of 200,000 shares of $25 par stock, paid-in capital of $2,000,000 and retained earnings of $6,440,000. Theodore Rafael owns 1,000 of the outstanding shares.

Instructions:

(1) In Column A below, fill in the blanks with the appropriate figures based on the data given.

(2) In Column B, fill in the blanks with the appropriate figures based on the data given, but after a $1.80 per share cash dividend has been declared and paid.

(3) In Column C, fill in the blanks with the appropriate figures based on the data given, but after a 5% stock dividend has been declared and paid. The market value of Santana Inc.'s stock is $30. (Ignore the instructions in (2) when making these calculations.)

	Column A Before Any Dividend	Column B After Cash Dividend	Column C After Stock Dividend
a. Total number of shares outstanding			
b. Total par value of shares outstanding			
c. Total paid-in capital			
d. Total retained earnings			
e. Total stockholders' equity			
f. Equity per share			
g. Amount required to pay a $1.80 per share cash dividend next year. (Assume no further changes in the capital structure.) . . .			
h. Percentage of total stock owned by Rafael			
i. Total number of shares owned by Rafael			
j. Total par value of Rafael's shares			
k. Total equity of Rafael's shares			

PART 9

Summary data for Watley Inc. for the current fiscal year ended March 31 are as follows:

Cost of merchandise sold	$1,400,000
Cumulative effect on prior years of changing to a different depreciation method	80,000
Loss on disposal of a segment of the business	64,000
Income taxes:	
Applicable to a change in depreciation method	18,000
Reduction applicable to loss on disposal of segment	14,000
Applicable to ordinary income	176,000
Reduction applicable to loss from earthquake	48,000
Loss from earthquake	240,000
Operating expenses	96,000
Sales	2,000,000

Instructions: On the form on the next page, prepare an income statement for Watley Inc., including a section for earnings per share in the form illustrated in this chapter. There were 50,000 shares of common stock outstanding throughout the year and the effect of the change in depreciation method was to increase income.

Name _____

Watley Inc.
Income Statement
For Year Ended March 31, 19—

Chapter 12
Long-Term Liabilities and Investments in Bonds

STUDY GOALS

After studying this chapter, you should be able to:

1. Describe and illustrate the impact of borrowing on a long-term basis as a means of financing corporations.

2. Describe the characteristics of bonds.

3. Describe the present value concept.

4. Describe and illustrate the present value concept for bonds payable.

5. Describe and illustrate the accounting for bonds payable.

6. Describe and illustrate the use of and accounting for bond sinking funds.

7. Describe and illustrate the accounting for an appropriation for bonded indebtedness.

8. Describe and illustrate the accounting for bond redemption.

9. Describe the balance sheet presentation of bonds payable.

10. Describe and illustrate the accounting for long-term investments in bonds.

GLOSSARY OF KEY TERMS

Annuity. A series of fixed payments at fixed intervals.

Bond. A form of interest-bearing note employed by corporations to borrow on a long-term basis.

Bond discount. The excess of the face value of bonds over their issue price.

Bond indenture. The contract between a corporation issuing bonds and the bondholders.

Bond premium. The excess of the issue price of bonds over their face value.

Carrying amount. The amount at which a temporary or a long-term investment or a long-term liability is reported on the balance sheet; also called basis or book value.

Contract rate of interest. The interest rate specified on a bond.

Debt security. A bond or a note payable.

Effective rate of interest. The market rate of interest at the time bonds are issued.

Future value. The amount that will accumulate at some future date as a result of an investment or a series of investments.

Long-term investment. An investment that is not intended to be a ready source of cash in the normal operations of a business and that is listed in the "investments" section of the balance sheet.

Present value. The estimated present worth of an amount of cash to be received (or paid) in the future.

Sinking fund. Assets set aside in a special fund to be used for a specific purpose.

CHAPTER OUTLINE

I. Financing Corporations.

  A. Many factors influence the board of directors of a corporation in deciding upon the best means of obtaining funds.

  B. When funds are borrowed for the issuance of bonds, there is a definite commitment to pay interest and to repay the principal at a stated future date.

  C. Bondholders are creditors of the issuing corporation and their claims for interest and repayment of principal rank ahead of claims of stockholders.

  D. The issuance of bonds, preferred stock, and common stock have a direct influence on the earnings per share available for common stockholders. Depending upon the results of operations, more or less earnings per share for common shareholders may be made available by the issuance of bonds or preferred stock.

II. Characteristics of Bonds.

  A. When a corporation issues bonds, it executes a contract with the bondholders known as a bond indenture or trust indenture.

  B. The principal amount of each bond is called its face value.

  C. Registered bonds may be transferred from one owner to another only by endorsement on the bond certificate, and the issuing corporation must maintain a record of the name and address of each bondholder.

  D. Title to bearer bonds, which are also called coupon bonds, is transferred merely by delivery, and the issuing corporation does not know the identity of the bondholders.

  E. When all bonds of an issue mature at the same time, they are called term bonds.

  F. If the maturities of a bond issue are spread over several dates, they are called serial bonds.

  G. Bonds that may be exchanged for other securities under certain conditions are called convertible bonds.

  H. Bonds issued by a corporation that reserves the right to redeem them before maturity are referred to as callable bonds.

  I. A secured bond is one that gives the bondholder a claim on specific assets in case the issuing corporation fails to meet its obligations on the bonds.

  J. Unsecured bonds issued on the basis of the general credit of the corporation are called debenture bonds.

III. Present Value Concepts.

  A. The concept of present value is that an amount of cash to be received at some date in the future is not the equivalent of the same amount of cash held at an earlier date. In other words, a sum of cash to be received in the future is not as valuable as the same sum on hand today, because cash on hand today can be invested to earn income.

  B. An example of the present value concept is that $100 on hand today will be more valuable than $100 to be received a year from today. If $100 cash on hand today can be invested to earn 10% per year, the $100 will accumulate to $110 one year from today.

IV. Present Value Concepts for Bonds Payable.

  A. When a corporation issues bonds, present value concepts may be used to determine the value of the bonds at the issuance date.

  B. The present value of the face amount of bonds at the maturity date is the value today of the promise to pay the face amount at some future date.

  C. The present value of the periodic interest payments on bonds is the value today of the promise to pay a fixed amount of interest at the end of each of a number of periods. Such a series of fixed payments at fixed intervals is called an annuity.

V. Accounting for Bonds Payable.

  A. The interest rate specified in the bond indenture is called the contract or coupon rate.

  B. The rate prevailing in the market at the time the bonds are issued is the market or effective rate.

  C. The bonds issued by a corporation will sell at an amount equal to, less than, or more than their face amount, depending upon the relationship between the contract rate of interest and the market rate of interest.

D. If the contract rate of interest on bonds is equal to the market rate of interest at the time the bonds are issued, the bonds will sell for their face amount.

   1. Using the tables for present value of $1 and the present value of an annuity of $1, the present value of a bond issue (the amount for which the bonds will sell) may be determined.

   2. The entry to record the issuance of bonds at their face amount is to debit Cash and credit Bonds Payable for the face amount of the bonds.

E. If the market rate of interest is greater than the contract rate of interest, a bond issue will sell at a discount.

   1. The discount on a bond issue is equal to the difference between the face amount of the bonds and the total present value of the bonds as of the date of issuance.

   2. The entry to record the issuance of bonds at a discount is to debit Cash for the present value of the bonds, debit Discount on Bonds Payable for the amount of the discount, and credit Bonds Payable for the face amount of the bonds.

   3. A discount on bonds payable must be amortized over the life of the bond issue.

   4. Discount on bonds payable may be amortized by the straight-line or interest methods on either an annual or semiannual basis.

   5. The straight-line method of bond discount amortization provides for a constant amount of interest expense over the life of the bond issue.

   6. The interest method of bond discount amortization provides for a constant rate of interest on the carrying amount (book value) of the bond issue.

   7. The entry to record the amortization of bond discount is to debit Interest Expense and credit Discount on Bonds Payable for the amount of the amortization.

   8. Bond discount may be amortized at the end of the year, or at the time the semiannual interest payments are made. If the amortization is recorded at the time of the semiannual interest payments, normally a compound journal entry is prepared recording both the amortization and the semiannual payment of interest.

F. If the market rate of interest is less than the contract rate of interest on a bond issuance, the bonds will sell at a premium.

   1. The amount of the premium on the bond issue is the difference between the total present value of the bonds and the face amount of the bonds.

   2. The entry to record the issuance of bonds at a premium is to debit Cash for the total present value of the bonds, credit Bonds Payable for the face amount of the bonds, and credit Premium on Bonds Payable for the amount of premium.

   3. A premium on bonds payable must be amortized over the life of the bond issue.

   4. Bond premiums may be amortized by using either the straight-line method or the interest method of amortization similar to that used for amortizing discount on bonds payable.

   5. The entry to record the amortization of bond premium is to debit Premium on Bonds Payable and credit Interest Expense for the amount of the amortization.

   6. Bond premium may be amortized at the end of the year, or at the time the semiannual interest payments are made. If the amortization is recorded at the time of the semiannual interest payments, normally a compound journal entry is prepared recording both the amortization and the semiannual payment of interest.

G. Zero-coupon bonds provide for only the payment of the face amount of the bonds at the maturity date. Because the bonds do not provide for periodic interest payments, they sell at a large discount. The accounting for zero-coupon bonds is similar to that for interest-bearing bonds that have been sold at a discount.

VI. Bond Sinking Fund.

A. The bond indenture may provide that funds for the payment of bonds at maturity be accumulated over the life of the issue. The amounts set aside are kept separate from other assets in a special fund called a sinking fund.

B. Future value is the amount that will accumulate at some future date as a result of an investment or a series of investments.

   1. The future value of an investment can be determined by using a table of future values to find the future value of $1 for the appropriate number of periods, and then multiplying the amount of the investment by this future value factor.

   2. The future value of a series of investments can be determined by using a table of future values to find the future value of an annuity of $1 for the appropriate number of periods, and then multiplying the amount of the investment by the future value factor.

C. The concept of future value can be used to determine the amount of periodic deposits in a sinking fund using the following formula:

$$\text{Annual Deposit} = \frac{\text{Maturity Value of Bonds}}{\text{Future Value of Annuity of \$1 for n Periods at i\%}}$$

D. When cash is transferred to the sinking fund, an account called Sinking Fund Cash is debited and Cash is credited.

E. The purchase of investments is recorded by a debit to Sinking Fund Investments and a credit to Sinking Fund Cash.

F. As interest or dividends are received, the cash is debited to Sinking Fund Cash and Sinking Fund Income is credited.

G. At the maturity date of the bonds, all sinking fund investments are sold and the proceeds are debited to Sinking Fund Cash.

H. The payment of the bonds at maturity is recorded by debiting Bonds Payable and crediting Sinking Fund Cash.

I. If the balance in the Sinking Fund Cash account is insufficient to pay for the bonds at maturity, any shortage of cash is taken from the regular cash account. Likewise, any excess cash in the sinking fund cash account after payment of the bonds at maturity is transferred to the regular cash account.

J. Sinking fund income represents earnings of the corporation and is reported in the income statement as Other income.

K. The cash and the securities making up the sinking fund are classified in the balance sheet as Investments, which usually appears immediately below the current assets section.

VII. Appropriation for Bonded Indebtedness.

A. The restriction of dividends during the life of a bond issue is one means of increasing the assurance that the bond obligation will be paid at maturity.

B. One means of restricting dividends during the life of the bond issuance is to appropriate retained earnings for bonded indebtedness.

C. The entry to record the appropriation of retained earnings for bonded indebtedness is to debit Retained Earnings and credit Appropriation for Bonded Indebtedness for the amount of the appropriation.

D. When there is both a fund and an appropriation for bonded indebtedness, the appropriation may be said to be funded.

VIII. Bond Redemption.

A. Callable bonds are redeemable by the issuing corporation within the period of time and at the price stated in the bond indenture.

B. A corporation may also redeem all or a portion of its bonds before maturity by purchasing them on the open market.

C. When a corporation redeems bonds at a price below their carrying amount (book value), the corporation realizes a gain. If the price is in excess of the carrying amount, a loss is incurred.

D. The redemption of a bond issue is recorded by debiting Bonds Payable for the face amount of the bonds, debiting Premium on Bonds Payable (or crediting Discount on Bonds Payable) for the balance of the premium (or discount) account, crediting Cash for the amount of cash used to redeem the bonds, and debiting Loss on Redemption of Bonds or crediting Gain on Redemption of Bonds for the amount to balance the entry.

E. Gains and losses on redemption of bonds are recorded as extraordinary items on the income statement.

IX. Balance Sheet Presentation of Bonds Payable.

   A. Bonds payable are usually reported on the balance sheet as long-term liabilities.

   B. When the balance sheet date is within one year of the bond maturity date, the bonds should be transferred to the current liability classification if they are to be paid out of current assets.

   C. If the bonds are to be paid with funds that have been set aside or if they are to be replaced with another bond issue, they should remain in the noncurrent category and their anticipated liquidation disclosed in an explanatory note to the financial statements.

   D. The balance in a discount account should be reported in the balance sheet as a deduction from the related bonds payable.

   E. The balance in a premium account should be reported in the balance sheet as an addition to the related bonds payable.

   F. In the financial statements or in accompanying notes, a description of the bonds (terms, security, due date, effective interest rate, maturities, and sinking fund requirements) should be disclosed.

X. Investments in Bonds.

   A. Investments in debt securities not intended as a ready source of cash in the normal operations of the business are classified as long-term investments.

   B. A business may make long-term investments because it has excess cash, or it plans to maintain business relations with the issuing company.

   C. Long-term investments in debt securities are customarily carried at cost. The cost of bonds purchased includes the amount paid to the seller plus other costs related to the purchase, such as the broker's commission.

   D. When bonds are purchased between interest dates, the buyer pays the seller the interest accrued from the last interest payment date to the date of purchase. The amount of the interest paid should be debited to Interest Income, since it is an offset against the interest that will be received at the next interest date.

   E. When bonds held as long-term investments are purchased at a price other than the face amount, the discount or premium should be amortized over the remaining life of the bonds. However, a separate discount or premium account is not maintained for long-term investments.

   F. The amortization of discount or premium may be computed using either the straight-line method or the interest method.

   G. The amortization of discount is recorded by debiting Investment in Bonds and crediting Interest Income.

   H. The amortization of premium is recorded by debiting Interest Income and crediting Investment in Bonds.

   I. The interest received on bond investments is recorded by a debit to Cash and a credit to Interest Income.

   J. At the end of a fiscal year, the interest accrued should be recorded by a debit to Interest Receivable and a credit to Interest Income. The amortization of premium or discount on bond investments may be recorded at the fiscal year-end or semiannually when the interest is received. If the bond premium and discount amortization is recorded when the interest is received, normally a compound entry is recorded recognizing the receipt of the cash for the interest, the amortization of the premium or discount, and the effect on interest income.

   K. When bonds held as long-term investments are sold, the seller will receive the sales price (less commissions and other selling costs) plus the interest accrued since the last payment date.

   L. Before recording the proceeds, the seller should record the appropriate amount of the amortization of discount or premium for the current period, up to the date of sale.

   M. In recording the proceeds, any gain or loss incurred on the sale should be recognized.

PART 1

Instructions: A list of terms and related statements appear below. From the list of terms, select the term that relates to each statement and print its identifying letter in the space provided. Terms may be used more than once, or they may not be used at all.

A. Bearer bonds	**F.** Future value	**K.** Registered bonds
B. Bond indenture	**G.** Interest method	**L.** Secured bonds
C. Bonds	**H.** Long-term investments	**M.** Serial bonds
D. Contract rate	**I.** Market rate	**N.** Straight-line method
E. Debenture bonds	**J.** Present value	**O.** Term bonds

_____ **1.** Bonds whose title is transferred by mere delivery.

_____ **2.** When all bonds of an issue mature at the same time, the bonds are called (?).

_____ **3.** The interest rate specified in the bond indenture.

_____ **4.** Investments that are not intended as a ready source of cash in the normal operations of the business.

_____ **5.** A form of interest-bearing note issued by corporations on a long-term basis.

_____ **6.** Unsecured bonds issued on the basis of the general credit of the corporation.

_____ **7.** A contract with bondholders.

_____ **8.** This concept states that the amount of cash to be received at some date in the future is not the equivalent of the same amount of cash held at an earlier date.

_____ **9.** The amount that will accumulate at some future date as a result of an investment or a series of investments.

_____ **10.** The method of amortization of bond premium and discount which provides for a constant rate of interest.

Name _____

PART 2

Instructions: Indicate whether each of the following statements is true or false by placing a T or F in the space provided.

_____ 1. The interest rate specified on the bond indenture is called the contract rate or effective rate.

_____ 2. If the market rate is lower than the contract rate, the bonds will sell at a discount.

_____ 3. When the maturities of bonds are spread over several dates, the bonds are called term bonds.

_____ 4. The principal of each bond is also called the face value.

_____ 5. Bonds that give the bondholder a claim on particular assets in the event that the issuing corporation fails to meet its obligations on the bonds are called debenture bonds.

_____ 6. The straight-line method of allocating bond discount provides for a constant amount of interest expense each period.

_____ 7. Bonds that may be exchanged for other securities under specified conditions are called coupon bonds.

_____ 8. The interest method of allocating bond premium provides for a constant rate of interest on the carrying amount of the bonds at the beginning of each period.

_____ 9. If the market rate is lower than the contract rate, the bonds will sell at a premium.

_____ 10. A special fund accumulated over the life of the bond issue and kept separate from other assets in order to provide for payment of bonds at maturity is called a sinking fund.

PART 3

Instructions: Circle the best answer for each of the following questions.

1. A bond that gives the bondholder a claim on specific assets in case the issuing corporation fails to meet its obligations is called a:
   a. secured bond
   b. registered bond
   c. term bond
   d. convertible bond

2. What is the present value of $1,000 to be paid in one year if the current interest rate is 8%?
   a. $920
   b. $926
   c. $1,000
   d. $1,080

3. The entry to record the amortization of a discount on bonds payable is:
   a. debit Bonds Payable; credit Interest Expense
   b. debit Interest Expense; credit Discount on Bonds Payable
   c. debit Discount on Bonds Payable; credit Interest Expense
   d. debit Discount on Bonds Payable; credit Bonds Payable

4. Under the interest method of bond discount amortization, as a bond payable approaches maturity, the total yearly amount of interest expense will:
   a. increase
   b. decrease
   c. remain the same
   d. both increase and decrease

5. On May 1, $50,000 of bonds were purchased as a long-term investment at 104 and $800 was paid as the brokerage commission. If the bonds bear interest at 9%, which is paid semiannually on January 1 and July 1, what is the total cost to be debited to the investment account?
   a. $50,000
   b. $52,000
   c. $52,800
   d. $54,300

PART 4

Johnson Inc. issued $8,000,000, 10-year, 12% bonds with interest payable semiannually.

Instructions:

(1) Compute **(a)** the cash proceeds and **(b)** the amount of premium or discount from the sale of the bonds if the effective interest rate is 12%.

(2) Compute **(a)** the cash proceeds and **(b)** the amount of premium or discount from the sale of the bonds if the effective interest rate is 13%.

(3) Compute **(a)** the cash proceeds and **(b)** the amount of premium or discount from the sale of the bonds if the effective interest rate is 11%.

PART 5

On December 31 of the current fiscal year, Pascal Inc. issued $1,000,000 of 12%, 10-year bonds. The bonds were dated December 31 of the same year. Interest on the bonds is payable on June 30 and December 31 of each year.

Instructions: Record the following transactions. (Omit explanations and round to the nearest dollar).

(a) The bonds were sold for $1,059,724 on December 31 of the current year. The market rate of interest on this date was 11%.

(b) Interest was paid on June 30, and the related amount of bond premium was amortized, based on the interest method.

(c) Interest was paid on December 31, and the related amount of bond premium was amortized, based on the interest method.

(d) On December 31 (bonds are one year old) one half of the bonds were redeemed at 103.

JOURNAL

	DATE		DESCRIPTION	POST. REF.	DEBIT	CREDIT	
1							1
2							2
3							3
4							4
5							5
6							6
7							7
8							8
9							9
10							10
11							11
12							12
13							13
14							14
15							15
16							16

Name _____

PART 6

Instructions: Assuming the same facts as in Part 5, except that bond premium amortization is based on the straight-line method, record transactions (b), (c), and (d).

JOURNAL

	DATE		DESCRIPTION	POST. REF.	DEBIT	CREDIT	
1							1
2							2
3							3
4							4
5							5
6							6
7							7
8							8
9							9
10							10
11							11
12							12

PART 7

Gowdy Co. issued $5,000,000 of 20-year bonds on January 1 of the current year. The bond indenture requires that equal deposits be made in a bond sinking fund at the end of each of the 20 years. The fund is expected to be invested in securities that will yield 6% per year compounded annually.

Instructions:

(1) Determine the amount of each of the 20 deposits to be made in the sinking fund.

	DATE	DESCRIPTION	POST. REF.	DEBIT	CREDIT	
1						1
2						2
3						3

(2) Prepare the entry to record the first deposit made in the sinking fund.

	DATE	DESCRIPTION	POST. REF.	DEBIT	CREDIT	
1						1
2						2

PART 8

Kreese Inc. issued $20,000,000 of 8%, 10-year bonds, interest payable June 30 and December 31. The bond indenture required that a bond sinking fund be established with annual contributions of $275,000 and that annual transfers of $2,000,000 be made to an appropriation for bonded indebtedness.

Instructions: Record the following transactions. (Omit explanations.)

(a) The bonds were sold for $17,507,760 on January 1, the date of the bonds. The market rate of interest on this date was 10%.

	DATE	DESCRIPTION	POST. REF.	DEBIT	CREDIT	
1						1
2						2
3						3

(b) The interest was paid on June 30 and the related amount of bond discount was amortized, based on the interest method.

	DATE	DESCRIPTION	POST. REF.	DEBIT	CREDIT	
1						1
2						2
3						3

(c) The annual addition to the bond sinking fund was made on December 31.

	DATE	DESCRIPTION	POST. REF.	DEBIT	CREDIT	
1						1
2						2

(d) The annual addition to the appropriation for bonded indebtedness was made on December 31.

	DATE	DESCRIPTION	POST. REF.	DEBIT	CREDIT	
1						1
2						2

continued

(e) The bonds were paid off at maturity on December 31. (All proper entries for the ten-year period have been made to date, and it is assumed that there was an excess of $18,200 in the sinking fund.)

	DATE		DESCRIPTION	POST. REF.	DEBIT	CREDIT	
1							1
2							2
3							3

(f) The appropriation for bonded indebtedness was returned in full to retained earnings on December 31.

	DATE		DESCRIPTION	POST. REF.	DEBIT	CREDIT	
1							1
2							2

PART 9

Instructions: Record the following transactions. (Omit explanations.)

(a) On October 1, 1990, purchased for cash, as a long-term investment, $100,000 of Edy Inc. 15% bonds at 99 plus accrued interest of $3,750.

(b) On December 31, 1990, received first semiannual interest.

(c) On December 31, 1990, amortized $30 discount on the bond investment.

(d) On December 31, 1992, sold the bonds at 102 plus accrued interest of $6,250. The carrying amount of the bonds was $99,260 at the time of sale.

JOURNAL

	DATE		DESCRIPTION	POST. REF.	DEBIT	CREDIT	
1							1
2							2
3							3
4							4
5							5
6							6
7							7
8							8
9							9
10							10
11							11
12							12
13							13
14							14

PART 10

Instructions: Record the following transactions, which were the only entries affecting a sinking fund. (Omit explanations.)

(a) On January 3, $75,000 was transferred from the general cash account to the sinking fund cash account.

(b) On January 6, $60,000 of sinking fund cash was used to purchase sinking fund investments.

(c) On December 31, cash income of $6,150 was received on the sinking fund investments.

(d) On December 31, the sinking fund investments were sold for $69,300.

(e) On December 31, bonds for which the sinking fund was established matured and were retired at their face value of $90,000.

JOURNAL

	DATE	DESCRIPTION	POST. REF.	DEBIT	CREDIT	
1						1
2						2
3						3
4						4
5						5
6						6
7						7
8						8
9						9
10						10
11						11
12						12
13						13
14						14
15						15
16						16

Chapter 13
Investments in Stocks; Consolidated Statements; International Operations

STUDY GOALS

After studying this chapter, you should be able to:

1. Describe investments in stocks.

2. Describe and illustrate the accounting for long-term investments.

3. Describe alternative methods of combining businesses.

4. Describe the accounting for parent-subsidiary affiliations.

5. Describe and illustrate the basic principles of consolidation of financial statements.

6. Illustrate a corporate balance sheet for a parent company and its subsidiaries.

7. Describe and illustrate the accounting for international operations.

GLOSSARY OF KEY TERMS

Consolidated statement. A financial statement resulting from combining parent and subsidiary company statements.

Consolidation. The creation of a new corporation by the transfer of assets and liabilities from two or more existing corporations.

Cost method. A method of accounting for an investment in stock, by which the investor recognizes as income its share of cash dividends of the investee.

Equity method. A method of accounting for investments in common stock, by which the investment account is adjusted for the investor's share of periodic net income and property dividends of the investee.

Equity security. Preferred or common stock.

Exchange rate. The rate at which one unit of currency can be converted into another currency.

Merger. The fusion of two corporations by the acquisition of the properties of one corporation by

another, with the dissolution of one of the corporations.

Minority interest. The portion of a subsidiary corporation's capital stock that is not owned by the parent corporation.

Parent company. The company owning all or a majority of the voting stock of another corporation.

Pooling of interests method. A method of accounting for an affiliation of two corporations resulting from an exchange of voting stock of one corporation for substantially all of the voting stock of the other corporation.

Purchase method. The accounting method employed when a parent company acquires a controlling share of the voting stock of a subsidiary other than by the exchange of voting common stock.

Subsidiary company. The corporation that is controlled by a parent company.

CHAPTER OUTLINE

I. Investments in Stocks.

   A. A business may make long-term investments in equity securities (preferred and common shares), simply because it has excess cash not needed for normal operations.

   B. A corporation may purchase stocks as a means of establishing or maintaining business relations with the issuing company.

   C. A corporation may acquire all or a large part of the voting stock of another corporation in order to control its activities.

   D. Investments in stocks may be purchased directly from the issuing corporation or from other investors on organized stock exchanges.

   E. Investments in equity securities not intended as a ready source of cash in the normal operations of the business are reported in the balance sheet under the caption "Investments" and are listed as a noncurrent asset.

II. Accounting for Long-Term Investments in Stock.

   A. There are two methods of accounting for long-term investments in stock: the cost method and the equity method.

   B. The method used depends upon whether the investor owns enough of the voting stock of the investee (company whose stock is owned by the investor) to have a significant influence over its operating and financing policies.

     1. If the investor does not have a significant influence, the cost method (with the lower of cost or market rule) must be used.

     2. If the investor can exercise significant influence, the equity method must be used.

   C. The cost of stocks purchased includes not only the amount paid to the seller but also other costs related to the purchase, such as the broker's commission and postage charges for delivery.

   D. Since dividends do not accrue from day to day, stocks purchased between dividend dates do not contain a separate charge for the pro rata amount of the dividend.

   E. The total cost of stocks purchased should be debited to an investment account.

   F. Under the cost method, cash dividends on capital stock held as an investment are recorded as an increase in the appropriate asset account (cash) and income account (dividend income).

   G. A dividend in the form of additional shares of stock (a stock dividend) is not considered income and therefore no entry is needed beyond a notation as to the additional shares of stock acquired.

   H. Under the cost method, long-term investments in stock are subject to the lower of cost or market rule.

     1. In applying the rule, it is the lower of the total cost or total market price of the portfolio of equity securities at the balance sheet date which is used.

     2. Any market value changes below cost are not included in net income, but are reported as a separate item in the stockholders' equity section of the balance sheet.

     3. If the decline in market value is other than temporary, the cost basis of the individual securities is written down and the amount of write-down is accounted for as a realized loss. After the write-down, the carrying amount of the individual security cannot be changed for subsequent recoveries in market value.

   I. When the equity method of accounting is used, a stock purchase is recorded at cost as under the cost method. However, the equity method is distinguished from the cost method in the following ways:

     1. The investor records its share of the periodic net income of the investee as an increase in the investment account and as revenue of the period. Conversely, the investor's share of the investee's periodic loss is recorded as a decrease in the investment and a loss of the period.

     2. The investor records its share of cash or property dividends on the stock as a decrease in the investment account and an increase in the appropriate asset accounts.

J. When shares of stock held as a long-term investment are sold, the investment account is credited for the carrying amount of the shares sold and the cash or appropriate receivable account is debited for the proceeds (sales price less commission and other selling costs).

K. Any difference between the proceeds and the carrying amount is recorded as a gain or loss on the sale.

III. Business Combinations.

A. When one corporation acquires the properties of another corporation and the latter then dissolves, the joining of the two enterprises is called a merger.

B. When two or more corporations transfer their assets and liabilities to a corporation which has been created for purposes of a takeover, the combination is called a consolidation.

C. A common means of achieving a business combination is by one corporation owning a controlling share of the outstanding voting stock of one or more other corporations. When this method is used, none of the participants dissolves. All continue as separate legal entities.

1. The corporation owning all or a majority of the voting stock of another corporation is known as the parent company.

2. The corporation that is controlled is known as the subsidiary company.

3. Two or more corporations closely related through stock ownership are sometimes called affiliated or associated companies.

D. The relationship of a parent and a subsidiary company may be established by "purchase" or by a "pooling of interests."

1. When a corporation acquires a controlling share of the voting common stock of another corporation in exchange for cash, other assets, issuance of notes or other debt obligations, or by a combination of these items, the transaction is treated as a purchase. It is then accounted for by the purchase method.

2. When two corporations become affiliated by means of an exchange of voting common stock of one corporation (the parent) for substantially all (at least 90%) of the voting common stock of the other corporation (the subsidiary), the transaction is termed a pooling of interests. It is accounted for by the pooling of interests method.

IV. Accounting for Parent-Subsidiary Affiliations.

A. Although the corporations that make up a parent-subsidiary affiliation may operate as a single economic unit, they continue to maintain separate accounting records and prepare their own periodic financial statements.

B. The parent corporation uses the equity method of accounting for its investment in the stock of a subsidiary.

C. Because of the central managerial control factor and the intertwining of relationships, it is usually desirable to present the results of operations and the financial position of a parent company and its subsidiaries as if the group were a single company with one or more branches or divisions. Such statements are generally called consolidated statements.

V. Basic Principles of Consolidation of Financial Statements.

A. When the data on the financial statements of the parent corporation and its subsidiaries are combined to form the consolidated statements, special attention should be given to the relationships between the separate corporations.

1. Intercompany items, which are called reciprocals, must be eliminated from the statements that are to be consolidated.

2. An example of a reciprocal intercompany item is a note representing a loan by the parent corporation to its subsidiary, which would appear as a Note Receivable in the parent's balance sheet and a Note Payable in the subsidiary's balance sheet. When the two balance sheets are combined, the Note Receivable and Note Payable would be eliminated because the consolidated balance sheet is prepared as if the parent and the subsidiary were one operating unit.

B. When a parent-subsidiary affiliation is effected as a purchase, the parent corporation is deemed to have purchased all or a major part of the subsidiary corporation's net assets. Accordingly, the principles of accounting for a sale-purchase transaction are applied to the consolidation of the parent and the subsidiary.

1. At the date of acquisition, the assets of the subsidiary should be reported on the consolidated balance sheet at their cost to the parent.

2. In the subsidiary's ledger, the reciprocal of the investment account of the parent at the date of acquisition is the composite of all of the subsidiary's stockholders' equity accounts.

3. When the balance sheets of the two corporations are consolidated, the reciprocal accounts (Investment in Subsidiary) and stockholders' equity accounts of the subsidiary (Common Stock, Retained Earnings) are offset against each other, or eliminated.

4. If the subsidiary's stock's total cost to the parent exceeds the book value of the subsidiary's stock, the difference must be assessed to determine why the parent paid more than the book equity for the subsidiary's stock.

5. When the amount paid above book equity is due to an excess of fair market value over book value of the subsidiary's assets, the values of the appropriate assets should be revised upward.

6. When the parent paid more for the subsidiary's stock because the subsidiary has prospects for high future earnings, the difference should be reported on the consolidated balance sheet under a description such as "Goodwill" or "Excess of cost of business acquired over related net assets."

7. When the amount paid above book equity is due to an excess of fair market value over both book value of assets and high future earnings prospects, the excess of cost over book equity should be allocated accordingly.

8. If the stock of a subsidiary corporation is acquired from the stockholders at a cost that is less than book equity, the difference is treated in the reverse fashion as in that situation in which the acquisition price is higher than book equity.

9. When a parent corporation does not acquire all of the outstanding stock of the subsidiary corporation, the remaining stock is owned by outsiders who are called collectively the minority interest.

10. Minority interest of the subsidiaries is normally reported in the long-term liability section of the consolidated financial statements.

11. Subsequent to acquisition of a subsidiary, the parent company must use the equity method to account for its investment in the subsidiary. Consequently, the amount to be eliminated for the reciprocal accounts of Investment in Subsidiary and the subsidiary's stockholders' equity accounts will change each year subsequent to acquisition.

12. If the consolidation process becomes complex or the amount of data to be processed is substantial, all of the relevant data for the consolidated statements may be assembled on work sheets. Whether or not a work sheet is used, the basic concepts and the consolidated balance sheet would not be affected.

C. When a parent-subsidiary affiliation is effected as a pooling of interests, the ownership of the two companies is joined together in the parent corporation.

1. In a pooling of interests, the amount the parent company debits to its investment in subsidiary account will equal the amount of the subsidiary's net assets (stockholders' equity accounts).

2. Any difference that may exist between the carrying amount of the subsidiary's net assets and the fair market value of the subsidiary's assets is not recorded by the parent in the consolidation process.

3. Since the parent's investment in the subsidiary is equal to the carrying amount of the subsidiary's net assets, no change is needed in the amounts at which the subsidiary's assets should be included in the consolidated balance sheet prepared at the date of affiliation.

4. According to the concept of continuity of ownership interests under the pooling of interests method, subsidiary earnings accumulated prior to the affiliation should be combined with those of the parent on the consolidated balance sheet. It is as though there had been a single economic unit from the time the enterprises began operations.

5. The equity method is used by the parent corporation in recording changes in its investment account subsequent to the acquisition. Thus, the account is increased by the parent's share of the subsidiary's earnings and decreased by its share of dividends.

6. Because the equity method is used by the parent corporation in accounting for the subsidiary, the amount eliminated for the reciprocal account Investment in Subsidiary and the subsidiary's stockholders' equity accounts will change each year after the date of acquisition.

7. As under the purchase method, a work sheet may be used to assemble data for preparation of the consolidated balance sheet under the pooling of interests method.

D. The principles used in the consolidation of income statements of a parent and subsidiaries are the same as those used in the preparation of consolidated balance sheets.

   1. These principles are the same regardless of whether the affiliation is deemed to be a purchase or a pooling of interests.

   2. When consolidated income statements are prepared, all amounts resulting from intercompany transactions, such as management fees or interest on loans charged by one affiliate to another, must be eliminated.

VI. Corporation Financial Statements.

   A. Examples of retained earnings statements and sections of income statements affected by the corporate form of organization have been presented in preceding chapters of the text.

   B. A complete balance sheet of a corporation, containing items discussed in Chapter 13 and preceding chapters, is illustrated on pages 622 and 623 of the text.

VII. Accounting for International Operations.

   A. If transactions with foreign companies are executed in dollars, no special accounting problems arise. Such transactions will be recorded as illustrated previously in the text.

   B. When a U.S. company executes a transaction with a company in a foreign country using a currency other than the dollar, one currency needs to be converted to another to settle the transaction.

   1. For example, a U.S. company purchasing merchandise from a British company may require payment in British pounds to settle the transaction.

   2. The exchange of one currency into another involves the use of an exchange rate.

   C. Special accounting problems arise when the exchange rate fluctuates between the date of the original transaction and the settlement of that transaction in cash in the foreign currency.

   1. In such cases, a foreign exchange gain or loss may arise.

   2. The foreign exchange gain or loss is recognized at the time the transaction is settled.

   3. The transaction settlement is recorded in the normal manner except that an exchange gain or loss will be recorded as either a debit or credit to balance the transaction.

   D. If financial statements are prepared between the date of the original transaction and the date of cash receipt or payment, and the exchange rate has changed since the original transaction, an unrealized gain or loss must be recognized in the financial statements.

   1. The exchange gain or loss is recognized at the end of the fiscal period by debiting or crediting the associated account receivable or account payable.

   2. A balance in the exchange gain or loss account at the end of a fiscal period should be reported in the other income or expense section of the income statement.

E. Before the financial statements of domestic and foreign companies are consolidated, the amounts shown on the statements for the foreign companies must be converted to U.S. dollars.

1. Asset and liability amounts are normally converted to U.S. dollars by using the exchange rates as of the balance sheet date.

2. Revenues and expenses are normally converted by using the exchange rates that were in effect when those transactions were executed. For practical purposes, averages for the period are normally used for revenues and expenses.

3. The adjustments (gains or losses) resulting from the conversion are reported as a separate item in the stockholders' equity section of the balance sheets of the foreign companies.

4. After the foreign company statements have been converted to U.S. dollars, the financial statements of U.S. and foreign subsidiaries are consolidated in the normal manner as described previously in this chapter.

PART 1

Instructions: A list of terms and related statements appear below. From the list of terms, select the term that relates to each statement and print its identifying letter in the space provided. Terms may be used more than once, or they may not be used at all.

A. Affiliation   **G.** Equity   **L.** Parent company
B. Affiliated statements   **H.** Equity method   **M.** Pooling of interests method
C. Consolidated statements   **I.** Exchange rate   **N.** Purchase method
D. Consolidation   **J.** Merger   **O.** Reciprocals
E. Cost   **K.** Minority interest   **P.** Subsidiary company
F. Cost method

_____ 1. This method of accounting for long-term investments in stock must be used when less than 20% ownership of voting stock is held by the investor, who does not have a significant influence over operating and financing policies of the investee.

_____ 2. Under this method of accounting for long-term investments in stock, the receipt of dividends is recorded as a debit to Cash and a credit to Dividend Income.

_____ 3. The financial statements resulting from the combining of parent and subsidiary statements are called (?).

_____ 4. The corporation owning all or a majority of the voting stock of another corporation.

_____ 5. Preferred and common shares are termed (?) securities.

_____ 6. This method of accounting for long-term investments in stock must be used when the investor can exercise a significant influence over the operating and financing policies of the investee; generally the investor in this circumstance will hold more than 20% of the voting stock of the investee.

_____ 7. When a corporation acquires a controlling share of the voting stock of another corporation in exchange for cash, other assets, issuance of notes or other debt obligations, or a combination of these items, the business combination must be accounted for under this method.

_____ 8. When one corporation acquires the properties of another corporation and the latter then dissolves, the joining of the two enterprises is called a (?).

_____ 9. Stock that is not held by the parent company but held by outsiders.

_____ 10. The rate at which one unit of currency can be converted into another currency.

_____ 11. Intercompany items which must be eliminated from the statements that are to be consolidated are called (?)

_____ 12. When two corporations become affiliated by means of an exchange of voting common stock of one corporation for substantially all of the voting common stock of the other corporation, the transaction must be accounted for under this method.

PART 2

Instructions: Indicate whether each of the following statements is true or false by placing a T or F in the space provided.

_____ 1. Under the equity method of accounting for investments in stocks, the investor records its share of cash dividends as a decrease in the investment account and an increase in the cash account.

_____ 2. A corporation that is controlled by another corporation is known as a subsidiary.

_____ 3. Under the pooling of interests method, earnings of a subsidiary accumulated prior to the date of the parent-subsidiary affiliation must be excluded from the consolidated statements.

_____ 4. The two methods of accounting for investments in stock are the pooling of interests method and the equity method.

_____ 5. When two or more corporations transfer their assets and liabilities to a corporation which has been created for the purpose of the takeover, the combination is called a merger.

_____ 6. When two or more corporations become affiliated by means of an exchange of the voting stock of one corporation (the parent) for substantially all of the voting common stock of another corporation (the subsidiary), the transaction is termed a purchase.

_____ 7. Subsequent to acquisition of a subsidiary, a parent company's investment account should be increased periodically for its share of the subsidiary's income.

_____ 8. A note representing a loan by a parent corporation to its subsidiary would appear as a note receivable in the parent's balance sheet and a note payable in the subsidiary's balance sheet.

_____ 9. If a U.S. company purchases goods on account from a British company when the exchange rate is $1.90 per British pound, and settles the account when the exchange rate is $2.00 per British pound, the U.S. company would incur an exchange gain.

_____ 10. If transactions with foreign companies are executed in dollars, no exchange gain or loss will be incurred.

PART 3

Instructions: Circle the best answer for each of the following questions.

1. Under this method of accounting for long-term investments in stock, receipt of dividends from an investee is recorded as a debit to Cash and a credit to the dividend income account.
   a. Cost method
   b. Equity method
   c. Rate of return method
   d. Lifo method

2. Under what section of the Parent's balance sheet would the balance of the account Investment in Subsidiary appear?
   a. Current assets
   b. Temporary investments
   c. Investments
   d. Stockholders' equity

3. The acquisition of a subsidiary at a cost above the subsidiary's book equity may be caused by which of the following?
   a. The book value of the subsidiary's land account is overstated.
   b. The book value of the subsidiary's plant and equipment is overvalued.
   c. The subsidiary's temporary investment account is overvalued.
   d. The subsidiary's plant and equipment accounts are undervalued.

4. During the year in which Parent Company owned 90% of the outstanding common stock of Subsidiary Company, the Subsidiary reported net income of $100,000 and dividends declared and paid of $30,000. What is the amount of net increase in the Investment in Subsidiary account for the year?
   a. $30,000
   b. $63,000
   c. $70,000
   d. $90,000

5. On August 10, 1991, a sale on account for $5,000 to a Mexican company was billed for 12,500,000 pesos. The exchange rate was $.0004 per peso on August 10 and $.0003 per peso on September 9, 1991 when the cash was received on account. Which of the following statements identifies the exchange gain or loss for the fiscal year ended December 31, 1991?
   a. Realized exchange loss, $1,250
   b. Realized exchange gain, $1,250
   c. Unrealized exchange loss, $1,250
   d. Unrealized exchange gain, $1,250

PART 4

Instructions: Record the following transactions for Richards Inc.

(a) As a long-term investment, Richards Inc. acquires 40,000 shares of Norris Inc. common stock at a cost of $600,000. Richards Inc. uses the equity method of accounting for this investment because it represents 25% of the voting stock of Norris Inc.

(b) On May 18, a cash dividend of $.75 per share is paid by Norris Inc.

(c) Norris Inc. reports net income of $900,000 for the year.

JOURNAL

	DATE		DESCRIPTION	POST. REF.	DEBIT	CREDIT	
1							1
2							2
3							3
4							4
5							5
6							6
7							7
8							8

PART 5

Instructions: In each of the following cases involving a parent-subsidiary relationship, fill in the blanks for the proper amount for each case.

(a) Parent creates a subsidiary, transferring to it $750,000 of assets and $150,000 of liabilities, and taking in exchange 150,000 share of $4 par common stock of the subsidiary.

	Assets	Stockholders' Equity
Parent:		
Investment in subsidiary, 150,000 shares	$	
Subsidiary:		
Net assets	$	
Common stock, 150,000 shares, $4 par		$

(b) Parent acquires for $800,000 all of the outstanding stock of Subsidiary from Subsidiary's stockholders. Subsidiary stockholders' equity is composed of 30,000 shares of $18 par common stock and retained earnings of $120,000.

	Assets	Stockholders' Equity
Parent:		
Investment in subsidiary, 30,000 shares	$	
Eliminate 100% of Subsidiary stock		
Eliminate 100% of Subsidiary retained earnings		
Excess of cost over book equity of Subsidiary interest .		$
Subsidiary:		
Net assets	$	
Common stock, 30,000 shares, $18 par		$
Retained earnings		

(c) Parent acquires for $350,000 all of the outstanding stock of Subsidiary from Subsidiary's stockholders. Subsidiary stockholders' equity is composed of 20,000 shares of $12 par common stock and retained earning of $200,000.

	Assets	Stockholders' Equity
Parent:		
Investment in subsidiary, 20,000 shares	$	
Eliminate 100% of Subsidiary stock		
Eliminate 100% of Subsidiary retained earnings		
Excess of cost over book equity of Subsidiary interest .		$
Subsidiary:		
Net assets	$	
Common stock, 20,000 shares, $12 par		$
Retained earnings		

(d) Parent acquires 90% of the 100,000 shares of common stock of Subsidiary for $1,350,000. Subsidiary's stockholders' equity consists of 100,000 shares of $8 par common stock and $400,000 of retained earnings.

Parent:	Assets	Stockholders' Equity
Investment in subsidiary	$ _____	
Eliminate 90% of Subsidiary stock	_____	
Eliminate 90% of Subsidiary retained earnings	_____	
Excess of cost over book equity of Subsidiary interest .		$ _____
Subsidiary:		
Common stock	$ _____	
Eliminate 90% of Subsidiary stock	_____	
Remainder		$ _____
Retained earnings	$ _____	
Eliminate 90% of Subsidiary retained earnings	_____	
Remainder		_____
Minority interest		$ _____

(e) Subsidiary in (d) earns net income of $150,000 and pays dividends of $50,000 during the year subsequent to Parent's 90% acquisition of its stock. Complete the following entries:

Investment in Subsidiary	_____	
Income of Subsidiary		_____
Cash	_____	
Investment in Subsidiary		_____

continued

The balance in Subsidiary's retained earnings account has now increased to $500,000 ($400,000 + $150,000 - $50,000). The balance in Parent's investment in subsidiary account has now increased to $1,440,000 ($1,350,000 + $135,000 - $45,000).

	Assets	Stockholders' Equity
Parent:		
Investment in subsidiary	$ _____	
Eliminate 90% of Subsidiary stock	_____	
Eliminate 90% of Subsidiary retained earnings	_____	
Excess of cost over book equity of Subsidiary interest .		$ _____
Subsidiary:		
Common stock	$ _____	
Eliminate 90% of Subsidiary stock	_____	
Remainder		$ _____
Retained earnings	$ _____	
Eliminate 90% of Subsidiary retained earnings	_____	
Remainder		
Minority interest		$ _____

(f) Net assets of Subsidiary are $1,200,000, consisting of 50,000 shares of $15 par common stock and retained earnings of $450,000. To effect a pooling of interests, Parent agrees to issue 7,500 shares of its own $100 par common stock in exchange for all of Subsidiary's stock. Parent's net assets prior to the acquisition consist of 100,000 shares of common stock ($10,000,000 at par) and $2,780,000 of retained earnings.

	Assets	Stockholders' Equity
Parent:		
Investment in subsidiary, 50,000 shares	$ _____	
Other net assets	_____	
Common stock, 107,500 shares, $100 par		$ _____
Retained earnings		_____
Subsidiary:		
Net assets	$ _____	
Common stock, 50,000 shares, $15 par		$ _____
Retained earnings		_____

PART 6

On December 31 of the current year, Pasteur Inc. purchased 85% of the stock of Stertz Inc. for $350,000. The data reported on their separate balance sheets immediately after the acquisition appear in the Pasteur Inc. and Stertz Inc. columns of the following work sheet.

| | Pasteur Inc. | Stertz Inc. | Eliminations | | Consolidated |
			Debit	Credit	Balance Sheet
Investment in Subsidiary	350,000				
Land	100,000	50,000			
Other asstes	450,000	350,000			
	900,000	400,000			
Liabilities	200,000	30,000			
Common stock:					
Pasteur Inc.	400,000				
Stertz Inc.		250,000			
Retained earnings:					
Pasteur Inc	300,000				
Stertz Inc.		120,000			
	900,000	400,000			

Instructions:

1. Complete the work sheet by entering appropriate eliminations from the reciprocal accounts in the Eliminations columns and extending appropriate amounts to the Consolidated Balance Sheet column. The excess of cost over book equity should be attributed to the land.

2. Based on the data in the Consolidated Balance Sheet column of the work sheet, determine the correct amount for each of the following items:

   (a) Excess of cost over book equity $ _____

   (b) Minority interest $ _____

   (c) On the following page, prepare a consolidated balance sheet as of December 31, in report form.

Name _____

PART 7

Hepp Company makes sales on account to British companies, which it bills in British pounds. Record the following transactions of Hepp Company (omit explanations).

Mar. 12   Sold goods on account, £20,000; exchange rate, $1.80 per pound.

Apr. 19   Received cash from sale of March 12, £20,000; exchange rate, $1.75 per pound.

	DATE		DESCRIPTION	POST. REF.	DEBIT	CREDIT	
1							1
2							2
3							3
4							4
5							5
6							6

PART 8

Bremar Company makes purchases on account from a Japanese company that requires payment in yen. Record the following transactions and year-end adjustments of Bremar Company (omit explanations).

Nov. 8   Purchased goods on account, ¥200,000; exchange rate, $.004 per yen.

Nov. 20   Purchased goods on account, ¥300,000; exchange rate, $.005 per yen.

Dec. 7   Paid invoice of Nov. 8; exchange rate, $.005 per yen.

Dec. 31   Exchange rate at year end, $.006 per yen. Recognize the change in exchange rate in Bremar Company accounts.

	DATE		DESCRIPTION	POST. REF.	DEBIT	CREDIT	
1							1
2							2
3							3
4							4
5							5
6							6
7							7
8							8
9							9
10							10
11							11
12							12

Chapter 14
Statement of Cash Flows

STUDY GOALS

After studying this chapter, you should be able to:

1. Describe the nature of the statement of cash flows.

2. Describe and illustrate the reporting of cash flow activities, including:

> Cash flows from operating activities
> Cash flows from investing activities
> Cash flows from financing activities

3. Describe and illustrate the preparation of the statement of cash flows.

GLOSSARY OF KEY TERMS

Cash flows from financing activities. Cash receipts from the issuance of equity and debt securities; and cash payments for dividends, repurchase of equity securities, and redemption of debt securities.

Cash flows from investing activities. Cash receipts from the sale of investments and plant assets and other noncurrent assets; and cash payments for the acquisition of investments and plant assets and other noncurrent assets.

Cash flows from operating activities. Cash receipts and payments that enter into the determination of net income.

Direct method. The method of reporting cash flows from operating activities in which the major classes of operating cash receipts and operating cash payments are reported.

Indirect method. The method of reporting cash flows from operating activities in which the effect of all deferrals of past cash receipts and payments and all accruals of expected future cash receipts and payments are removed from the net income reported on the income statement.

Statement of cash flows. A financial statement that provides a summary of the major cash receipts and cash payments for a specific period of time.

CHAPTER OUTLINE

I. Nature of the Statement of Cash Flows.

  A. The statement of cash flows reports a firm's major sources of cash receipts and major uses of cash payments for a period.

  B. The statement of cash flows provides useful information about a firm's activities in generating cash from operations, maintaining and expanding operating capacity, meeting its financial obligations and paying dividends.

II. Reporting Cash Flows.

  A. The statement of cash flows classifies cash receipts and cash payments by three types of activities:

    1. Cash flows from operating activities, which include cash transactions that enter into the determination of net income.

2. Cash flows from investing activities, which include receipts from the sale of investments and plant assets and other noncurrent assets; and payments for the acquisition of investments and plant assets and other noncurrent assets.

3. Cash flows from financing activities, which include receipts from the issuance of equity and debt securities; and payments for dividends, repurchase of equity securities, and redemption of debt securities.

B. By grouping cash flows by operating, investing, and financing activities, significant relationships within and among the activities can be evaluated.

C. The most frequent and often the most important cash flows relate to operating activities entered into for the purpose of earning net income.

   1. One method of reporting cash flows from operating activities is the direct method, which reports the major classes of operating cash receipts and operating cash payments.

      a. Under the direct method, the difference between operating cash receipts and cash payments will be reported as net cash flow from operating activities.

      b. The principal advantage of the direct method is that it reports the major categories of cash receipts and cash payments.

      c. The principal disadvantage of the direct method is that the necessary data are often costly to accumulate.

   2. Another method of reporting cash flows from operating activities is the indirect method.

      a. Under the indirect method, the effects of all deferrals and past cash receipts and payments and all accruals and expected future cash receipts and payments are removed from net income reported on the income statement. This is done by adjusting the amount of reported net income upward or downward to determine the net amount of cash flows from operating activities.

      b. One of the major advantages of the indirect method is that it will focus on the differences between net income and cash flows from operating activities.

      c. Another advantage of the indirect method is that the data needed are generally more available and less costly to obtain than the data needed for the direct method.

D. Cash flows from investing activities are classified into cash inflows and outflows.

   1. Cash inflows from investing activities generally arise from the sale of investments, plant assets, and intangible assets.

   2. Cash outflows generally include payments to acquire investments, plant assets, and intangible assets.

   3. In reporting cash flows from investing activities, the cash inflows are usually reported first, followed by the cash outflows.

   4. The net cash flow from investing activities can be described as either "net cash flow provided by investing activities" or "net cash flow used for investing activities."

E. Cash flows from financing activities are classified into cash inflows and outflows.

   1. Cash inflows from financing activities include proceeds from the issuance of equity securities, bonds, mortgage notes payable, and other long-term and short-term borrowings.

   2. Cash outflows from financing activities include the payment of cash dividends, the acquisition of treasury stock, and the repayment of amounts borrowed.

   3. In reporting cash flows from financing activities, the cash inflows are usually reported first, followed by the cash outflows.

   4. The net cash flow can be described as "net cash flow provided by financing activities" or "net cash flow used for financing activities."

F. The statement of cash flows is divided into three sections: cash flows from operating activities, cash flows from investing activities, and cash flows from financing activities.

   1. The cash flows from operating activities is presented first, followed by

the cash flows from investing activities and the cash flows from financing activities.

2. The total of the net cash flow from these activities is the net increase or decrease in cash for the period.

3. The cash balance at the beginning of the period is added to the net increase or decrease in cash for the period to arrive at the cash balance at the end of the period.

4. In the remainder of this chapter, the indirect method of reporting cash flows from operating activities will be used because it is used more frequently than the direct method.

G. Investing and financing activities may be affected by transactions that do not involve cash. Such transactions should be reported in a separate schedule to accompany the statement of cash flows.

1. For example, the issuance of common stock in liquidation of long-term debt has no effect on cash.

2. Other transactions involving noncash investing and financing activities include the issuance of bonds or capital stock in exchange for plant assets, and the issuance of common stock in exchange for convertible preferred stock.

H. The term cash flow per share is sometimes reported in the financial press.

1. The reporting of cash flow per share might mislead readers into thinking that cash flow is equivalent to or perhaps superior to earnings per share in appraising the relative success of operations.

2. The financial statements, including the statement of cash flows, should not report a cash flow per share amount.

III. Assembling Data and Preparing the Statement of Cash Flows.

A. The indirect method is generally the more efficient method of assembling data for preparation of the statement of cash flows.

B. Under the indirect method, the noncash balance sheet accounts are examined to determine the type of cash flow activity that has led to changes in these accounts during the period.

C. Although there is no order in which the noncash balance sheet accounts must be analyzed, time can be saved and greater accuracy can be achieved by selecting the accounts in the reverse order in which they appear on the balance sheet. Thus, the retained earnings account is normally the starting point for the analysis.

D. To determine the amount of cash flows from operating activities, the accrual basis net income, as reported on the income statement, must be converted to the cash basis. The conversion can be summarized as follows:

Net income, per income statement
Add: Depreciation of plant assets
        Amortization of bond discount
            and intangible assets
        Decreases in current assets
            (receivables, inventories,
            prepaid expenses)
        Increases in current liabilities
            (accounts and notes payable,
            accrued liabilities)
        Losses on disposal of assets and
            retirement of debt
Deduct: Amortization of bond premium
        Increases in current assets
            (receivables, inventories,
            prepaid expenses)
        Decreases in current liabilities
            (accounts and notes payable,
            accrued liabilities)
        Gains on disposal of assets and
            retirement of debt
Net cash flow from operating activities

E. The amount of cash flows from investing activities can be determined by analyzing the equipment, building, land, and investments accounts.

1. Increases in the equipment, building, land, and investments accounts representing acquisitions for cash should be treated as cash flows from investing activities. If the acquisition is in exchange for stock or bonds, it should be treated as a noncash financing and investing activity.

2. Increases or decreases in the investments account reflect the acquisition of or sale of investments, respectively. These represent cash flows from investing activities.

F. To determine the amount of cash flows from financing activities, dividends, equity and bond transactions must be examined.

1. Cash paid for dividends is determined by analyzing the retained earnings and dividends payable accounts. The amount of dividends declared during the period must be adjusted for increases or decreases in the dividends payable account.

2. An increase in the common stock or preferred stock account would reflect the issuance of additional stock. If the stock is issued for cash, this should be treated as a cash flow from financing activities. If the stock is issued for noncash assets, this should be treated as a noncash financing and investing activity.

3. An increase or decrease in the bonds payable account would reflect the issuance of additional bonds or the retirement of bonds, respectively. The issuance or retirement of bonds for cash should be treated as a cash flow from financing activities.

PART 1

Instructions: A list of terms and related statements appear below. From the list of terms, select the term that relates to each statement and print its identifying letter in the space provided. Terms may be used more than once, or they may not be used at all.

A. Accounting Principles Board
B. Bonds payable
C. Cash flow per share
D. Common stock
E. Depreciation of plant assets
F. Direct method
G. Financial Accounting Standards Board

H. Financing activity
I. Governmental Accounting Standards Board
J. Increase in inventories
K. Indirect method
L. Investing activity
M. Gain on disposal of assets

N. Noncash investing and financing activities
O. Operating activity
P. Plant assets
Q. Retained earnings
R. Statement of cash flows
S. Statement of changes in financial position

_____ 1. The financial statement which reports a firm's major source of cash receipts and major uses of cash payments for a period.

_____ 2. The method of analyzing cash flows from operating activities that begins by reporting net income and adjustments to the net income for accruals and deferrals.

_____ 3. The method of analyzing operating cash flows that reports the major classes of operating cash receipts and of operating cash payments.

_____ 4. Proceeds from the sale of plant assets would be classified as a cash inflow from this type of activity.

_____ 5. Proceeds from the issuance of equity securities would be classified as a cash inflow from this type of activity.

_____ 6. Transactions involving these types of activities are reported in a separate schedule to accompany the statement of cash flows.

_____ 7. Under the indirect method, this item would be added to reported net income in arriving at cash flows from operating activities.

_____ 8. Under the indirect method, this noncash balance sheet account is normally analyzed first.

_____ 9. This term should not be reported in the financial statements, since it could mislead readers.

_____ 10. Issued *Statement of Financial Accounting Standards No. 95,* which requires the inclusion of a statement of cash flows as part of the basic set of financial statements.

PART 2

Instructions: Indicate whether each of the following statements is true or false by placing a T or F in the space provided.

_____ 1. The statement of cash flows is required as part of the basic set of financial statements.

_____ 2. Cash outflows from the payment of cash dividends is a type of financing activity.

_____ 3. There are two acceptable methods of reporting cash flows from operating activities in the statement of cash flows.

_____ 4. Under the indirect method, the effects of all deferrals of past cash receipts and payments and all accruals and expected future cash receipts and payments are removed from the net income reported on the income statement.

_____ 5. Cash receipts from the sale of plant assets would be classified as a cash flow from investing activities.

_____ 6. Under the indirect method, depreciation is the first noncash account balance analyzed.

_____ 7. Cash flow per share is normally reported as part of the income statement.

_____ 8. Cash flows resulting from the redemption of debt securities will be classified in the statement of cash flows as related to financing activities.

_____ 9. Under the indirect method, increases in current liabilities are deducted from net income reported on the income statement in determining cash flows from operating activities.

_____ 10. Noncash investing and financing activities that may have a significant effect on future cash flows should be included in a separate schedule to the statement of cash flows.

_____ 11. One of the major advantages of the direct method of reporting cash flows from operating activities is that it focuses on the differences between net income and cash flows from operating activities.

_____ 12. One of the major advantages of the indirect method of reporting cash flows from operating activities is that the data needed are generally more readily available and less costly to obtain than the data needed for the direct method.

_____ 13. The issuance of long-term notes or bonds represents a cash inflow from investing activities.

_____ 14. Transfers between the retained earnings account and appropriations accounts should not be reported on the statement of cash flows.

PART 3

Instructions: Circle the best answer for each of the following questions.

1. Which of the following is *not* one of the major types of cash flow activities that is reported on the statement of cash flows?
   a. Cash flows from financing activities
   b. Cash flows from selling activities
   c. Cash flows from operating activities
   d. Cash flows from investing activities

2. Cash dividends would be reported on the statement of cash flows as which type of cash flow activity?
   a. Cash flows from selling activities
   b. Cash flows from operating activities
   c. Cash flows from financing activities
   d. Cash flows from investing activities

3. Noncash investing and financing activities which may have a significant effect on future cash flows are reported:
   a. In the statement of cash flows
   b. In a separate schedule to accompany the statement of cash flows
   c. In the retained earnings statement
   d. In a footnote accompanying the balance sheet

4. Under the indirect method, which of the following items must be deducted from reported net income to determine net cash flow from operating activities?
   a. Depreciation of plant assets
   b. Decreases in current assets
   c. Decreases in current liabilities
   d. Amortization of bond discount

5. During the past year Lockhart Inc. declared $40,000 in cash dividends. If the beginning and ending balance of the dividends payable account was $12,000 and $10,000 respectively, what amount of cash paid for dividends will appear in the cash flows from financing activities section of the statement of cash flows?
   a. $30,000
   b. $38,000
   c. $40,000
   d. $42,000

6. In preparing the statement of cash flows, which of the following items is a cash flow from an investing activity?
   a. Retirement of long-term debt
   b. Acquisition of treasury stock
   c. Payment of dividends
   d. Purchases of plant assets

7. If an enterprise sold land that cost $50,000 for $80,000 (a gain of $30,000), the amount that should be reported in the cash flows from investing activities section of the statement of cash flows is
   a. $30,000
   b. $50,000
   c. $80,000
   d. $1·10,000

PART 4

Instructions: Listed in the first column below are selected transactions, and account balance changes of McHugh Inc. for the current year. Indicate by placing a check mark in the appropriate column(s) how each of the items would be reported in the statement of cash flows.

Item	Cash Flows From			Schedule of Noncash Investing and Financing Activities
	Operating Activities	Investing Activities	Financing Activities	
1. Decrease in prepaid expenses				
2. Retirement of bonds				
3. Proceeds from sale of investments				
4. Increase in inventories				
5. Issuance of preferred stock				
6. Purchase of equipment				
7. Cash dividends paid				
8. Acquisition of land in exchange for common stock				
9. Amortization of patents				
10. Amortization of discount on bonds payable .				

184

PART 5

The net income reported on the income statement of Reynolds Inc. for the current year was $120,000. Depreciation recorded on equipment and building amounted to $36,000 for the year. Balances of the current asset and current liability accounts at the beginning and end of the year are as follows:

	End of Year	Beginning of Year
Cash	$34,300	$29,000
Trade receivables (net)	118,000	110,000
Inventories	87,500	75,000
Prepaid expenses	7,400	9,500
Accounts payable (merchandise creditors)	45,600	32,000
Salaries payable	6,100	8,500

Instructions: Prepare the cash flows from operating activities section of the statement of cash flows.

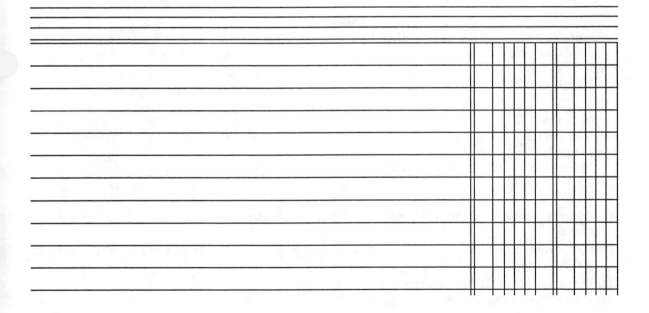

PART 6

The comparative balance sheet of Strauss Inc. at December 31, 1991, appears below.

Strauss Inc.
Comparative Balance Sheet
December 31, 1991 and 1990

The following additional data were taken from the records of Strauss Inc.:

	1991	1990	Increase Decrease*
Assets			
Cash	$ 70,000	$ 55,000	$ 15,000
Trade receivables (net)	130,000	120,000	10,000
Inventories	250,000	255,000	5,000 *
Prepaid expenses	10,000	12,000	2,000 *
Land	50,000	80,000	30,000 *
Building	300,000	300,000	—
Accumulated depreciation—building	(100,000)	(76,000)	(24,000)
Equipment	150,000	85,000	65,000
Accumulated depreciation—equipment	(60,000)	(59,000)	(1,000)
Total assets	$ 800,000	$ 772,000	$ 28,000
Liabilities			
Accounts payable (merchandise creditors)	$ 180,000	$ 174,000	$ 6,000
Dividends payable	20,000	18,000	2,000
Bonds payable	200,000	250,000	50,000 *
Total liabilities	$ 400,000	$ 442,000	$ 42,000 *
Stockholders' Equity			
Common stock	$ 100,000	$ 100,000	—
Retained earnings	300,000	230,000	$ 70,000
Total stockholders' equity	$ 400,000	$ 330,000	$ 70,000
Total liabilities and stockholders' equity	$ 800,000	$ 772,000	$ 28,000

(a) Equipment costing $80,000 was purchased, and fully depreciated equipment costing $15,000 was discarded.

(b) Net income, including gain on sale of land, was $95,000. Depreciation expense on equipment was $16,000; on building, $24,000.

(c) Bonds payable of $50,000 were retired at face value.

(d) A cash dividend of $25,000 was declared.

(e) Land costing $30,000 was sold for $45,000, resulting in a $15,000 gain on the sale.

continued

Name _____

Instructions: Complete the following statement of cash flows.

Strauss Inc.
Statement of Cash Flows
For Year Ended December 31, 1991

Cash flows from operating activities:

    Net income, per income statement . . . . $ _____

    Add: Depreciation . . . . $ _____

             Decrease in prepaid expenses . . . . _____

             Increase in accounts payable . . . . _____ $ _____

    Deduct: Increase in trade receivables . . . . $ _____

             Gain on sale of land . . . . _____ _____

    Net cash flow provided by operating activities . . . . . . $ _____

Cash flows from investing activities:

    Cash received from land sold . . . . $ _____

    Less cash paid for purchase of equipment . . . . _____

    Net cash flow used by investing activities . . . .   _____

Cash flows from financing activities:

    Cash used to retire bonds payable . . . . $ _____

    Cash paid for dividends . . . . _____

    Net cash flow used by financing activities . . . .   _____

Increase in cash . . . . $ _____

Cash, January 1, 1991 . . . .   _____

Cash, December 31, 1991 . . . . $ _____

Chapter 15
Financial Statement Analysis and Annual Reports

STUDY GOALS

After studying this chapter, you should be able to:

1. Describe basic financial statement analytical procedures.

2. Describe the focus of financial statement analysis.

3. Describe and illustrate the application of financial statement analysis in assessing solvency.

4. Describe and illustrate the application of financial statement analysis in assessing profitability.

5. Summarize and describe how analytical measures can be used in appraising the present performance of an enterprise and in forecasting its future.

6. Identify and illustrate the content of corporate annual reports.

7. Describe the content of interim financial reports.

GLOSSARY OF KEY TERMS

Accounts receivable turnover. The relationship between credit sales and accounts receivable, computed by dividing net sales on account by the average net accounts receivable.

Acid-test ratio. The ratio of the sum of cash, receivables, and marketable securities to current liabilities.

Common-size statement. A financial statement in which all items are expressed only in relative terms.

Constant dollar. Historical costs that have been converted to constant dollars through the use of a price-level index.

Current cost. The amount of cash that would have to be paid currently to acquire assets of the same age and in the same condition as existing assets.

Current ratio. The ratio of current assets to current liabilities.

Earnings per share (EPS) on common stock. The profitability ratio of net income available to common shareholders to the number of common shares outstanding.

Horizontal analysis. The percentage of increases and decreases in corresponding items in comparative financial statements.

Inventory turnover. The relationship between the volume of goods sold and inventory, computed by dividing the cost of goods sold by the average inventory.

Leverage. The tendency of the rate earned on stockholders' equity to vary from the rate earned on total assets because the amount earned on assets acquired through the use of funds provided by creditors varies from the interest paid to these creditors.

Number of days' sales in inventory. The relationship between the volume of sales and inventory, computed by dividing the inventory at the end of the year by the average daily cost of goods sold.

Number of days' sales in receivables. The relationship between credit sales and accounts receivable, computed by dividing the net accounts receivable at the end of the year by the average daily sales on account.

Price-earnings (P/E) ratio. The ratio of the market price per share of common stock, at a specific date, to the annual earnings per share.

Price-level index. The ratio of the total cost of a group of commodities prevailing at a particular time to the total cost of the same group of commodities at an earlier base time.

Profitability. The ability of a firm to earn income.

Quick assets. The sum of cash, receivables, and marketable securities.

Rate earned on common stockholders' equity. A measure of profitability computed by dividing net income, reduced by preferred dividend requirements, by common stockholders' equity.

Rate earned on stockholders' equity. A measure of profitability computed by dividing net income by total stockholders' equity.

Rate earned on total assets. A measure of the profitability of assets, without regard to the equity of creditors and stockholders in the assets.

Solvency. The ability of a firm to pay its debts as they come due.

Vertical analysis. The percentage analysis of component parts in relation to the total of the parts in a single financial statement.

Working capital. The excess of total current assets over total current liabilities at some point in time.

CHAPTER OUTLINE

I. Basic Analytical Procedures

  A. The percentage analysis of increases and decreases in corresponding items in comparative financial statements is called horizontal analysis.

    1. The amount of each item on the most recent statement is compared with a corresponding item on one or more earlier statements.

    2. The increase or decrease in the amount of an item is listed, together with the percent of increase or decrease.

    3. When the comparison is made between two statements, the earlier statement is used as the base.

  B. Percentage analysis may be used to show the relationship of the component parts to the total in a single statement. This type of analysis is called vertical analysis.

    1. In vertical analysis of the balance sheet, each asset item is stated as a percent of total assets and each liability and stockholders' equity item is stated as a percent of total liabilities and stockholders' equity.

    2. In vertical analysis of the income statement, each item is stated as a percent of net sales.

  C. In common-size statements, all items are expressed only in relative terms.

    1. Common-size statements may be prepared in order to compare percentages of a current period with past periods.

    2. Common-size statements may also be prepared to compare individual businesses or to compare one business with industry percentages.

  D. Other analytical measures that may be useful in financial statement analysis include a variety of ratios which may be evaluated in terms of solvency and profitability.

II. Focus of Financial Statement Analyses.

  A. Users of financial statements are interested in the ability of a business to pay its debts as they come due and to earn a reasonable amount of income. These two aspects of the status of an enterprise are called factors of solvency and profitability.

  B. In analyzing financial statements, it is important to recognize that analyses of historical data are useful in assessing past performance and in forecasting future performance.

III. Solvency Analysis.

  A. Solvency is the ability of a business to meet its financial obligations as they come due.

B. The use of ratios showing the ability to liquidate current liabilities is called current position analysis.

1. Working capital is the excess of current assets of an enterprise over its current liabilities at a specific moment of time.

2. The current ratio (sometimes called the working capital ratio or bankers' ratio) is computed by dividing the total current assets by the total current liabilities.

3. A ratio that measures "instant" debt-paying ability of the company is the acid-test ratio (or quick ratio). This is the ratio of the total of the quick assets (cash, marketable securities, and receivables) to the total current liabilities.

C. Accounts receivable analysis assesses whether accounts receivable are being maintained at an optimal level.

1. The relationship between credit sales and accounts receivable is stated as the accounts receivable turnover. This ratio is computed by dividing net sales on account by the average net accounts receivable. An increase in the accounts receivable turnover indicates an acceleration in the collection of receivables.

2. The number of days' sales in receivables is determined by dividing the net accounts receivable at the end of the year by the average daily sales on account (net sales on account divided by 365). The number of days' sales in receivables gives a rough measure of the length of time the accounts receivable have been outstanding.

D. Inventory analysis assesses whether the levels of inventory are being maintained at optimal levels.

1. The relationship of the volume of goods (merchandise) sold and inventory may be stated as the inventory turnover. This ratio is computed by dividing the cost of goods sold by the average inventory. An increasing inventory turnover is usually an indication of the efficient management of inventories.

2. The number of days' sales in inventory is determined by dividing the inven-

tories at the year end by the average daily cost of goods sold (cost of goods sold divided by 365). The number of days' sales in inventory gives a rough measure of the length of time it takes to acquire, sell, and then replace the average inventory.

E. The ratio of total plant assets to long-term liabilities provides a solvency measure that shows the margin of safety of the noteholders or bondholders.

1. This ratio is computed by dividing total plant assets by total long-term liabilities.

2. This ratio gives an indication of the potential ability of the enterprise to borrow additional funds on a long-term basis.

F. The ratio of stockholders' equity to liabilities provides a solvency measure that indicates the margin of safety for the creditors and the ability of the enterprise to withstand adverse business conditions.

1. This ratio is computed by dividing total stockholders' equity by total liabilities.

2. The larger this ratio the greater the ability of the enterprise to withstand adverse business conditions.

G. The number of times interest charges are earned during the year is a solvency measure that shows the relative risk of the debtholders.

1. This ratio is computed by dividing income before tax plus interest charges by the amount of interest charges.

2. This ratio provides an indication of the general financial strength of the enterprise.

3. A similar analysis can be applied to dividends on preferred stock.

IV. Profitability Analysis.

A. Profitability is the ability of an entity to earn income.

B. The ratio of net sales to assets is a profitability measure that shows how effectively a firm utilizes its assets.

1. This ratio is computed by dividing net sales by the total average assets (excluding long-term investments) for the period.

2. The higher this ratio the more effectively an enterprise is utilizing its assets.

C. The rate earned on total assets is a measure of the profitability of the assets, without regard to the equity of creditors and stockholders in the assets.

1. This ratio is computed by dividing net income plus interest expense by the total average assets for the period.

2. In computing this ratio it is preferable to exclude unusual items such as extraordinary items and cumulative effects of accounting changes.

D. The rate earned on stockholders' equity emphasizes the income yield in relationship to the amount invested by the stockholders.

1. This ratio is computed by dividing net income by the average stockholders' equity for the period.

2. The tendency of the rate on stockholders' equity to be greater than the rate on total assets is called financial leverage.

E. The rate earned on common stockholders' equity is the net income less preferred dividend requirements for the period, stated as a percentage of the average equity of the common stockholders.

1. This ratio is computed by subtracting preferred dividends from net income and dividing by the average common stockholders' equity.

2. The rate earned on common stockholders' equity may differ from the rates earned on total assets and total stockholders' equity because of financial leverage.

F. Earnings per share on common stock is the most commonly quoted profitability measure in the financial press.

1. This ratio is computed by subtracting preferred dividends from net income and dividing by the number of shares of stock outstanding.

2. Any changes in the number of shares outstanding during the year, such as would result from stock dividends or stock splits, should be disclosed in quoting earnings per share on common stock.

G. The price-earnings (P/E) ratio is commonly quoted by the financial press.

1. This ratio is computed by dividing the market price per share of common stock by the earnings per share on common stock.

2. This ratio is used as an indicator of the firm's future earnings prospects.

H. The dividend yield on common stock is a profitability measure that shows the rate of return to common stockholders in terms of cash dividend distributions.

1. This ratio is computed by dividing the dividends per share on common stock by the market price per share on common stock.

2. The dividend yield is of special interest to investors whose main investment objective is to receive a current return on the investment rather than an increase in the market price of the investment.

V. Summary of Analytical Measures.

A. The table on the next page summarizes the methods of computation and uses of the analytical measures discussed in this chapter.

B. The analytical measures discussed in this chapter are not a substitute for sound judgment, nor do they provide definitive guides to action. In selecting and interpreting analytical measures, proper consideration should be given to any conditions peculiar to the enterprises or to the industry of which the enterprise is a part.

VI. Corporate Annual Reports.

A. Although there are many differences in the form and sequence of the major sections of annual reports, in addition to the financial statements (including the accompanying notes), most annual reports include a section on financial highlights, a letter from the president, the independent auditors' report, the management report, and an historical summary.

B. The financial highlights section typically summarizes the major financial results for the last year or two.

C. The president's letter normally summarizes the results of operations and the prospects for future earnings.

	Method of Computation	Use
Solvency measures		
Working capital	Current assets - current liabilities	To indicate the ability to meet currently maturing obligations
Current ratio	$\dfrac{\text{Current assets}}{\text{Current liabilities}}$	
Acid-test ratio	$\dfrac{\text{Quick assets}}{\text{Current liabilities}}$	To indicate instant debt-paying ability
Accounts receivable turnover	$\dfrac{\text{Net sales on account}}{\text{Average accounts receivable}}$	To assess the efficiency in collecting receivables and in the management of credit.
Number of days' sales in receivables	$\dfrac{\text{Accounts receivable, end of year}}{\text{Average daily sales on account}}$	
Inventory turnover	$\dfrac{\text{Cost of goods sold}}{\text{Average inventory}}$	To assess the efficiency in the management of inventory
Number of days' sales in inventory	$\dfrac{\text{Inventory, end of year}}{\text{Average daily cost of goods sold}}$	
Ratio of plant asstes to long-term liabilities	$\dfrac{\text{Plant assets (net)}}{\text{Long-term liabilities}}$	To indicate the margin of safety to long-term creditiors
Ratio of stockholders' equity to liabilities	$\dfrac{\text{Total stockholders' equity}}{\text{Total liabilities}}$	To indicate the margin of safety to creditors
Number of times interest charges earned	$\dfrac{\text{Income before income tax + interest expense}}{\text{Interest expense}}$	To assess the risk to debtholders in terms of number of times interest charges were earned
Profitability measures		
Ratio of net sales to assets	$\dfrac{\text{Net sales}}{\text{Average total assets (excluding long-term investments)}}$	To assess effectiveness in the use of assets
Rate earned on total assets	$\dfrac{\text{Net income + interest expense}}{\text{Average total assets}}$	To assess the profitability of the assets
Rate earned on stockholders' equity	$\dfrac{\text{Net income}}{\text{Average stockholders' equity}}$	To assess the profitability of the investment by stockholders
Rate earned on common stockholders' equity	$\dfrac{\text{Net income - preferred dividends}}{\text{Average common stockholders' equity}}$	To assess the profitability of the investment by common stockholders
Earnings per share on common stock	$\dfrac{\text{Net income - preferred dividends}}{\text{Shares of common stock outstanding}}$	
Dividends per share of common stock	$\dfrac{\text{Dividends}}{\text{Shares of common stock outstanding}}$	To indicate the extent to which earnings are being distributed to common stockholders
Price-earnings ratio	$\dfrac{\text{Market price per share of common stock}}{\text{Earnings per share on common stock}}$	To indicate future earnings prospects, based on the relationship between market value of common stock and earnings
Dividend yield	$\dfrac{\text{Dividends per common share}}{\text{Market price per common share}}$	To indicate the rate of return to common stockholders in terms of dividends

D. All publicly held corporations are required to engage an independent public accountant (CPA) to conduct an examination of the financial statements.

   1. Upon completion of the examination, an independent auditors' report is prepared and reported in the financial statements.

   2. The independent auditors' report generally includes three paragraphs: an introductory paragraph identifying the financial statements being audited, a "scope" paragraph describing the nature of the audit, and an "opinion" paragraph presenting the auditor's opinion as to the fairness of the financial statements.

E. The management report generally includes a statement from the chief financial officer or other representative of management concerning the preparation of the financial statements in conformity with generally accepted accounting principles, an assessment of the company's internal accounting control system, and any other comments on pertinent matters related to the accounting system, financial statements, and the examination by the independent auditor.

F. The historical summary section of the corporate annual report normally includes selected financial and operating data for five or ten years.

G. To help financial statement users in assessing past performance and future potential of diversified companies, financial statements should disclose information on the segments of a business, such as the amounts of business in different industries, its foreign markets, and its major customers.

H. Financial statements are expressed in terms of money. Because money changes in value as prices change, changing price levels affect financial reporting. There are two main possibilities for supplementing conventional statements to disclose the effects of changing prices: (1) current cost data, and (2) constant dollar data.

I. Current cost is the amount of cash that would have to be paid currently to acquire assets of the same age and same condition as existing assets.

   1. The use of current costs permits the identification of gains and losses that result from holding assets during periods of changes in price levels.

   2. The major disadvantage in the use of current costs is the absence of established standards and procedures for determining such costs.

J. Constant dollar data are historical costs that have been converted to constant dollars through the use of a price-level index.

   1. A price-level index is the ratio of the total cost of a group of commodities prevailing at a particular time to the total cost of the same group of commodities at an earlier base time.

   2. A general price-level index may be used to determine the effect of changes in price levels on certain financial statement items by computing constant dollar equivalents.

K. There is currently no requirement that companies disclose supplemental current cost/constant dollar information, but companies are encouraged to experiment with different methods of providing such information.

L. Other information may be included in corporate annual reports, such as forecasts of financial plans and expectations.

VII. Corporate Interim Reports

Corporations customarily issue interim financial reports to their stockholders. Interim reports should disclose such information as gross revenue, costs and expenses, provision for income taxes, extraordinarily or infrequently occurring items, net income, earnings per share, continuing items, and significant changes in financial position.

PART 1

Instructions: A list of terms and related statements appear below. From the list of terms, select the term that relates to each statement and print its identifying letter in the space provided. Terms may be used more than once, or they may not be used at all.

A. Acid-test ratio	**G.** Earnings per share on	**L.** Profitability
B. Common-size statements	common stock	**M.** Ratio of net sales to assets
C. Current cost data	**H.** General price-level data	**N.** Ratio of total plant assets
D. Current position analysis	**I.** Horizontal analysis	to long-term liabilities
E. Current ratio	**J.** Independent auditors' report	**O.** Solvency
F. Dividend yield	**K.** Management report	**P.** Vertical analysis

_____ **1.** Percentage analysis used to show the relationship of the component parts to the total in a single statement.

_____ **2.** The percentage analysis of increases and decreases in corresponding items in comparative financial statements.

_____ **3.** The ability of an entity to earn income.

_____ **4.** The use of ratios showing the ability to liquidate current liabilities.

_____ **5.** The ability of a business to meet its financial obligations as they come due.

_____ **6.** Statements prepared in order to compare percentages of the current period with past periods, to compare individual businesses, or to compare one business with industry percentages published by trade associations and financial information services.

_____ **7.** The ratio of current assets to current liabilities.

_____ **8.** A profitability measure that shows the rate of return to common stockholders in terms of cash dividend distributions.

_____ **9.** A profitability measure that shows how effectively a firm utilizes its assets.

_____ **10.** A report describing the results of an independent examination of the financial statements.

_____ **11.** Data indicating the amount of cash that would have to be paid currently to acquire assets of the same age and in the same condition as existing assets.

_____ **12.** Data indicating historical cost amounts that have been converted to constant dollars.

PART 2

Instructions: Indicate whether each of the following statements is true or false by placing a T or F in the space provided.

_____ 1. All items in common-size statements are expressed only in relative terms.

_____ 2. In horizontal analysis of the income statement, each item is stated as a percentage of total sales.

_____ 3. Solvency is the ability of a business to meet its financial obligations as they come due.

_____ 4. The ratio of (net sales to assets) provides a solvency measure that shows the margin of safety of the debtholders.

_____ 5. The acid-test ratio or quick ratio is the ratio of the sum of cash, receivables, and marketable securities to current liabilities.

_____ 6. Net sales on account divided by the average net accounts receivable gives the accounts receivable turnover.

_____ 7. Net income minus the amount required for preferred dividends divided by the average common stockholders' equity gives the rate earned on common stockholders' equity.

_____ 8. The rate earned on total assets is calculated by adding preferred dividends to net income and dividing this sum by the average total assets.

_____ 9. The tendency of the rate earned on stockholders' equity to vary disproportionately from the rate earned on total assets is called financial leverage.

_____ 10. In the management report, the chief financial officer or other representative of management presents an assessment of the company's internal accounting control system, states that the financial statements are management's responsibility, and comments on other pertinent matters.

_____ 11. The accounting principles used on an annual basis are usually followed in preparing interim statements.

_____ 12. The major disadvantage in the use of current costs is the absence of established standards and procedures for determining such costs.

_____ 13. Corporate enterprises are required to disclose both current and constant dollar information annually as supplemental data.

PART 3

Instructions: Circle the best answer to each of the following questions.

1. Statements in which all items are expressed only in relative terms (percentages of a common base) are:
   a. Relative statements
   b. Horizontal statements
   c. Vertical statements
   d. Common size statements

2. Which one of the following measures is a solvency measure?
   a. Rate earned on total assets
   b. Price-earnings ratio
   c. Accounts receivable turnover
   d. Ratio of net sales to assets

3. Based on the following data for the current year, what is the inventory turnover?
   Net sales, $8,000,000   Inventory, end of year, $600,000
   Cost of goods sold, $4,800,000   Accounts receivable, beginning of year, $250,000
   Inventory, beginning of year, $400,000   Accounts receivable, end of year, $390,000
   a. 8
   b. 9.6
   c. 12
   d. 16

4. Based on the following data for the current year, what is the accounts receivable turnover?
   Net sales on account, $8,000,000   Inventory, end of year, $600,000
   Cost of goods sold, $4,800,000   Accounts receivable, beginning of year, $250,000
   Inventory, beginning of year, $400,000   Accounts receivable, end of year, $390,000
   a. 15
   b. 20.5
   c. 25
   d. 32

5. Which of the following sections of corporate annual reports normally includes a statement concerning an assessment of a company's internal accounting control system?
   a. Financial highlights section
   b. President's letter
   c. Independent auditors' report
   d. Management report

6. For each significant reporting segment of a business, an enterprise is required to disclose each of the following except
   a. identifiable assets associated with the segment
   b. identifiable liabilities associated with the segment
   c. revenue
   d. income from operations

PART 4

Instructions: Using the information in the statement below and on the following page, perform a horizontal analysis for Bellamy Inc. by filling in the *Amount* and *Percent* columns which are provided (one decimal place).

Bellamy Inc.
Comparative Income Statement
For Years Ended December 31, 1991 and 1990

	1991	1990	Increase (Decrease*) Amount	Percent
Sales	$984,500	$830,000		
Sales returns and allowances	33,000	30,000		
Net sales	$921,500	$800,000		
Cost of goods sold	585,600	480,000		
Gross profit	$335,900	$320,000		
Selling expenses	$78,400	$80,000		
Administrative expenses	60,000	60,000		
Total operating expenses	$138,400	$140,000		
Operating income	$197,500	$180,000		
Other income	17,000	20,000		
	$214,500	$200,000		
Other expense	75,600	70,000		
Income before income tax	$138,900	$130,000		
Income tax	54,600	52,000		
Net income	$84,300	$78,000		

Name _____

Bellamy Inc.
Comparative Balance Sheet
December 31, 1991 and 1990

	1991	1990	Increase (Decrease*) Amount	Percent
Assets				
Cash	$ 88,000	$ 80,000		
Marketable securities	120,000	150,000		
Accounts receivable (net)	219,300	215,000		
Inventory	480,000	400,000		
Prepaid expenses	31,800	30,000		
Long-term investments	50,000	50,000		
Plant assets (net)	910,000	875,000		
Intangible assets	20,000	25,000		
Total assets	$ 1,919,100	$ 1,825,000		
Liabilities				
Current liabilities	$ 143,600	$ 120,000		
Long-term liabilities	480,000	500,000		
Total liabilities	$ 623,600	620,000		
Stockholders' Equity				
Preferred 3% stock, $100 par	$ 110,000	$ 100,000		
Common stock, $50 par	520,000	500,000		
Retained earnings	665,500	605,000		
Total stockholders' equity	$ 1,295,500	$ 1,205,000		
Total liabilities and stockholders' equity	$ 1,919,100	$ 1,825,000		

PART 5

Instructions: Using the information below and on the following page, perform a vertical analysis for Pinnella Inc. by filling in the *Percent* columns on the statements provided.

Pinnella Inc.
Comparative Balance Sheet
December 31, 1991 and 1990

	1991		1990	
	Amount	Percent	Amount	Percent
Assets				
Cash	$ 450,000		$ 375,000	
Marketable securities	150,000		135,000	
Accounts receivable (net)	630,000		525,000	
Inventory	810,000		690,000	
Prepaid expenses	54,000		45,000	
Long-term investments	400,000		360,000	
Plant assets (net)	6,506,000		5,370,000	
Total assets	$ 9,000,000	100.0%	$ 7,500,000	100.0%
Liabilities				
Current liabilities	$ 1,040,000		$ 1,000,000	
Long-term liabilities	2,100,000		2,000,000	
Total liabilities	3,140,000		3,000,000	
Stockholders' Equity				
Preferred 5% stock, $200 par	$ 300,000		$ 300,000	
Common stock, $50 par	2,500,000		2,500,000	
Retained earnings	3,060,000		1,700,000	
Total stockholders' equity	$ 5,860,000		$ 4,500,000	
Total liabilities and stockholders' equity	$ 9,000,000	100.0%	$ 7,500,000	100.0%

Name _____

Pinnella Inc.
Income Statement
For Year Ended December 31, 1991

	Amount	Percent
Sales	$ 12,750,000	
Sales returns and allowances	250,000	
Net sales	$ 12,500,000	100.0%
Cost of goods sold	7,500,000	
Gross profit	$ 5,000,000	
Selling expenses	$ 1,500,000	
Administrative Expenses	750,000	
Total operating expenses	$ 2,250,000	
Operating income	$ 2,750,000	
Other income	75,000	
	$ 2,825,000	
Other expense (Interest)	100,000	
Income before income tax	$ 2,725,000	
Income tax	1,100,000	
Net income	$ 1,625,000	

PART 6

Pinnella Inc. declared $250,000 of common stock dividends during 1991, and the price of Pinnella's common stock on December 31, 1991, is $32.20.

Instructions: Using the data for Pinnella Inc. from Part 5, determine the following amounts and ratios for 1991. Round all ratios to one decimal point.

a. Working capital . . . . _____

b. Current ratio . . . . _____

c. Acid-test ratio . . . . _____

d. Accounts receivable turnover . . . . _____

e. Number of days' sales in receivables . . . . _____

f. Inventory turnover . . . . _____

g. Number of days' sales in inventory . . . . _____

h. Ratio of plant assets to long-term liabilities . . . . _____

i. Ratio of stockholders' equity to liabilities . . . . _____

j. Number of times interest charges earned . . . . _____

k. Number of times preferred dividends earned . . . . _____

l. Ratio of net sales to assets . . . . _____

m. Rate earned on total assets . . . . _____

n. Rate earned on stockholders' equity . . . . _____

o. Rate earned on common stockholders' equity . . . . _____

p. Earnings per share on common stock . . . . _____

q. Price-earnings ratio . . . . _____

r. Dividend yield . . . . _____

Chapter 16
Accounting for Not-for-Profit Organizations

STUDY GOALS

After studying this chapter, you should be able to:

1. Describe the characteristics of not-for-profit organizations.

2. Describe and illustrate the accounting for not-for-profit organizations, including fund accounting.

3. Describe and illustrate the flow of data through an accounting system for a not-for-profit organization.

GLOSSARY OF KEY TERMS

Appropriation. A designated use of revenues for which a potential liability is recognized by not-for-profit organizations.

Encumbrances. A commitment by a not-for-profit organization to incur expenditures in the future.

Fund. In accounting for not-for-profit organizations, an accounting entity with accounts maintained for recording assets, liabilities, fund equity, revenues, and expenditures for a particular purpose.

Fund equity. The excess of assets over liabilities in a not-for-profit organization.

Statement of revenues, expenditures, and changes in fund balance. The statement for a not-for-profit enterprise that provides a comparison of budgeted and actual revenues and expenditures along with the effect of operations on the unreserved fund balance.

Zero-base budgeting. A concept of budgeting that requires all levels of management to start from zero and estimate budget data as if there had been no previous activities in their unit.

CHAPTER OUTLINE

I. Characteristics of Not-for-Profit Organizations.

    A. The distinguishing characteristics of not-for-profit organizations are the following:

        1. There is neither a conscious profit motive nor an expectation of earning net income.

        2. No part of any excess of revenues over expenditures is distributed to those who contributed support through taxes or voluntary donations.

        3. Any excess of revenues over expenditures that results from operations in the short run is ordinarily used in later years to further the purposes of the organization.

    B. Most not-for-profit organizations are established to provide a service to society without levying against the user a direct charge equal to the full cost of the service.

II. Accounting for Not-for-Profit Organizations.

A. The Governmental Accounting Standards Board (GASB) is responsible for establishing accounting standards for state and governmental units.

B. The accounting systems for all not-for-profit organizations must provide financial data to internal management for use in planning and controlling operations and to external parties, such as taxpayers and donors, for use in determining the effectiveness of operations.

1. The basic double-entry system of accounting is appropriate for use in accounting for not-for-profit organizations.

2. Accounting systems for not-for-profit organizations should include mechanisms to ensure that management observes the restrictions imposed upon it by law, etc. and provides reports to taxpayers and donors that such restrictions have been met.

C. In accounting for not-for-profit organizations, a fund is defined as an accounting entity with accounts maintained for recording assets, liabilities, fund equity, revenues, and expenditures for a particular purpose according to specified restrictions and limitations.

1. Funds may be established by law, provisions of a charter, administrative action, or by a special contribution to a charitable organization.

2. A "General Fund" is used by not-for-profit organizations for recording transactions related to many community services and other activities rather than for a special purpose. Additional funds may be maintained for various special purposes.

D. Budgeting is the process of developing plans for the future expressed in financial terms. Budgeting is an important part of an accounting system for not-for-profit organizations and is incorporated into fund accounting.

1. Estimated revenues of a not-for-profit organization may be viewed as potential assets.

2. Appropriations may be viewed as potential liabilities.

3. The concept of zero-base budgeting for not-for-profit organizations requires all levels of management to start from zero and estimate revenues and appropriations as if there had been no previous activities in their unit.

4. The approval of a budget is recorded as a debit to Estimated Revenues, a credit to Appropriations, and either a credit or debit to Fund Balance for the difference.

5. Subsidiary ledgers are maintained for the estimated revenues and appropriations controlling accounts.

E. The realization of revenues is recorded by debiting an asset account (such as Cash) and crediting Revenues.

F. Regularly recurring expenditures, such as payrolls, are recorded by debiting Expenditures and crediting the appropriate liability accounts or Cash.

G. Encumbrances are legally binding commitments to pay money for future expenditures.

1. Encumbrances are recorded by debiting Encumbrances and crediting Fund Balance Reserved for Encumbrances.

2. When orders are filled or contracts are completed for amounts encumbered, the entry that recorded the encumbrance is reversed and the expenditure is recorded in the normal fashion.

3. When encumbrances are recorded, the balance of the accounts Encumbrances and Expenditures can be viewed as offsets to the account Appropriations. The difference obtained by subtracting the balances of Encumbrances and Expenditures from the balance of Appropriations is the amount of commitments that can still be made.

H. Appropriations, Encumbrances, and Expenditures are controlling accounts for which a subsidiary ledger exists. This single subsidiary ledger is called the expenditure ledger.

I. When long-lived assets are purchased, they are usually recorded as debits to the account Expenditures in the same manner as supplies and other ordinary expenses. A separate record of individual assets can be maintained for the purpose of assigning responsibility for the custody and the use of long-lived assets.

J. A not-for-profit organization should prepare interim statements comparing actual revenues and expenditures with related budgeted amounts.

K. At the end of a fiscal year, closing entries are recorded and the operating data are summarized and reported.

1. The entry to close revenues and estimated revenues accounts is to debit Revenues for its balance, credit Estimated Revenues for its balance, and debit or credit Fund Balance for the difference.

2. The entry to close the appropriations and expenditures accounts is to debit Appropriations for its balance, credit Expenditures for its balance, and debit or credit Fund Balance for the difference.

3. The entry to close the encumbrances account, which represents the commitments outstanding at the end of the year, is to debit Fund Balance for the balance of the encumbrances account, and credit Encumbrances.

4. The account Fund Balance Reserved for Encumbrances is not closed and is included in the fund equity section of the year-end balance sheet. When the orders are filled in the next year, Fund Balance Reserved for Encumbrances will be debited and Accounts Payable credited.

L. Financial statements for each fund and combined financial statements for all funds should be prepared periodically.

M. The principal financial statements prepared at the end of the fiscal year are the following:

1. A balance sheet, which is similar to a commercial enterprise balance.

2. A statement of revenues, expenditures, and changes in fund balance.

N. The objective of the statement of revenues, expenditures, and changes in fund balance is to provide users with information on a not-for-profit entity's operating performance for a period.

1. The first part of the statement presents a comparison of the budgeted and actual revenues and expenditures, but not a net income amount.

2. The second part presents the effects of operations and encumbrances on the unreserved fund balance.

III. Illustration of Not-for-Profit Accounting.

A. An illustration of the journal entries for transactions completed during the year for the General Fund of the City of Lewiston is presented in the text.

B. In addition, the trial balance, balance sheet, and statement of revenues, expenditures, and changes in fund balance are presented.

PART 1

Instructions: A list of terms and related statements appear below. From the list of terms, select the term that relates to each statement and print its identifying letter in the space provided. Terms may be used more than once, or they may not be used at all.

A. Appropriations
B. Balance sheet
C. Budget
D. Encumbrances
E. Endowment fund
F. Estimated revenues

G. Expenditure ledger
H. Financial Accounting
   Standards Board
I. Fund
J. Fund equity
K. Governmental Accounting
   Standards Board

L. Net assets
M. Revenue ledger
N. Statement of revenues,
   expenditures, and changes
   in fund balance
O. Zero-base budgeting

_____ 1. In accounting for a not-for-profit organization, (?) may be viewed as potential assets.

_____ 2. The financial statement for a not-for-profit organization which shows the total assets, total liabilities, and total fund equities.

_____ 3. The body responsible for establishing accounting standards for state and local governmental units.

_____ 4. An accounting entity with accounts maintained for recording assets, liabilities, fund equity, revenues, and expenditure for a not-for-profit organization.

_____ 5. A special fund from which only the income may be spent.

_____ 6. A concept that requires all levels of management to estimate revenues and appropriations as if there had been no previous activities in their unit.

_____ 7. The excess of assets over liabilities of a fund.

_____ 8. A subsidiary ledger containing accounts used for recording estimated revenues and actual revenues.

_____ 9. In accounting for a not-for-profit organization, (?) may be viewed as potential liabilities.

_____ 10. Legally binding commitments to pay money in the future for expenditures.

_____ 11. The subsidiary ledger for appropriations, encumbrances, and expenditures.

_____ 12. The financial statement for a not-for-profit organization which presents the effects of operations and encumbrances on the unreserved fund balance.

PART 2

Instructions: Indicate whether each of the following statements is true or false by placing a T or F in the space provided.

_____ **1.** In closing the accounts at the end of the fiscal year, if revenues exceed estimated revenues, the difference is credited to Fund Surplus.

_____ **2.** The statement of revenues, expenditures, and changes in fund balance does not present a net income amount.

_____ **3.** One of the distinguishing characteristics of not-for-profit organizations is that there is neither a conscious profit motive nor an expectation of earning net income.

_____ **4.** Because of the nature of the accounting issues, the basic double-entry system is not appropriate for not-for-profit organizations.

_____ **5.** In a budget for a not-for-profit organization, the appropriations may be viewed as potential assets.

_____ **6.** Any difference between the estimated revenues and appropriations is recorded in the fund equity account, Fund Balance.

_____ **7.** When the budget shows an excess of estimated revenues over appropriations, Fund Balance is debited.

_____ **8.** Each subsidiary account in the revenue ledger is used for recording the estimated revenues and the actual revenues.

_____ **9.** In fund accounting, legally binding commitments to pay money are called encumbrances.

_____ **10.** When encumbrances are recorded, the sum of the balances of the accounts Encumbrances and Expenditures can be viewed as an offset to the account Appropriations.

_____ **11.** When encumbrances are recorded, the total balance of the encumbrances accounts can be viewed as an offset to the account Fund Balance.

_____ **12.** When long-lived assets are purchased, they are usually recorded as debits to the appropriate fixed asset accounts.

PART 3

Instructions: Circle the best answer for each of the following questions.

1. If a charitable organization has funds from which only the income may be spent, these funds may be called
   a. income funds
   b. revenue funds
   c. restricted funds
   d. endowment funds

2. The accounts that are maintained in a profit-making corporation but not in a not-for-profit organization are
   a. assets
   b. liabilities
   c. stockholders' equity
   d. revenues

3. If appropriations of $600,000 were approved when the budget was adopted, $400,000 of expenditures were recorded during the year to date, and encumbrances outstanding total $50,000, what is the amount available for commitment by the not-for-profit entity during the remainder of the year?
   a. $150,000
   b. $250,000
   c. $300,000
   d. $400,000

4. In preparing the entry to close the appropriations and expenditures accounts, to what account is the difference between the two accounts recorded?
   a. Encumbrances
   b. Fund Balance Reserved for Encumbrances
   c. Fund Balance
   d. Income Summary

5. When long-lived assets are purchased, they are usually recorded as debits to
   a. Expenditures
   b. Supplies
   c. Encumbrances
   d. Operating plant

6. The principal financial statements for a not-for-profit organization are a statement of revenues, expenses, and changes in fund balance, and a (an)
   a. trial balance
   b. income statement
   c. fund statement
   d. balance sheet

PART 4

Instructions: Prepare entries to record the following transactions for the General Fund of Kenton County.

(a) The budget approved for the fiscal year indicated appropriations of $5,450,000 and estimated revenues of $5,700,000.

(b) Received $970,000 in revenues from property taxes.

(c) Entered into a contract with Moore Construction Co. to pave Blue Avenue for $700,000.

(d) Received a bill for initial payment on contract with Moore, $50,000.

(e) Made payment of $50,000 on contract with Moore.

JOURNAL

	DATE	DESCRIPTION	POST. REF.	DEBIT	CREDIT	
1						1
2						2
3						3
4						4
5						5
6						6
7						7
8						8
9						9
10						10
11						11
12						12
13						13
14						14
15						15
16						16
17						17
18						18
19						19
20						20
21						21

PART 5

Selected account balances from the summer grant fund ledger of the Huskie Foundation at the end of the current fiscal year are as follows:

Appropriations	$545,000	Fund Balance	$113,600
Encumbrances	14,000	Fund Balance Reserved for Encumbrances .	14,000
Estimated Revenues	548,000	Revenues	553,000
Expenditures	530,000		

Instructions: Prepare closing entries.

JOURNAL

	DATE	DESCRIPTION	POST. REF.	DEBIT	CREDIT	
1						1
2						2
3						3
4						4
5						5
6						6
7						7
8						8
9						9
10						10
11						11

Name _____

PART 6

The partially completed statement of revenues, expenditures, and changes in the fund balance for the general fund of the City of Bolton for the year ended June 30, 1991, is given below. In addition, the accounts in the general fund ledger had the following balances as of June 30, 1991:

Cash	$290,000
Savings accounts	397,600
Property taxes receivable	79,300
Accounts payable	73,700
Wages payable	27,500
Fund balance reserved for encumbrances	17,400

Instructions:

1. Complete the statement of revenues, expenditures, and changes in fund balance for the year ended June 30, 1991. The fund balance account had a balance of $645,700 on July 1, 1990, the beginning of the current fiscal year.

2. Prepare a balance sheet as of June 30, 1991.

City of Bolton - General Fund
Statement of Revenues, Expenditures, and Changes in Fund Balance
For Year Ended June 30, 1991

	Budget	Actual	Over	Under
Revenues:				
General property taxes	$3,135,000	$3,125,000		
Sales taxes	1,017,000	1,059,000		
Motor vehicle licenses	184,000	190,000		
Interest on savings accounts	30,000	26,000		
Miscellaneous	20,000	18,000		
Total revenues	$4,386,000	$4,418,000		
Expendutures:				
General government	$1,772,000	$1,783,000		
Police department	897,000	880,000		
Fire department	500,000	495,000		
Streets and roads	450,000	485,000		
Sanitation	400,000	415,000		
Public welfare	350,000	340,000		
Total expenditures	$4,369,000	$4,398,000		
Excess of revenues over expenditures ..	$ 17,000	$ 20,000		
Fund balance, July 1, 1990				
Less encumbrances				
Fund balance, June 30, 1991				

City of Bolton - General Fund
Balance Sheet
June 30, 1991

SOLUTIONS

CHAPTER 1

PART 1

1. H	2. E	3. I	4. N
5. P	6. D	7. B	8. Q
9. S	10. C	11. J	12. F
13. K	14. R	15. O	16. A
17. M	18. L	19. G	20. T

PART 2

1. F	2. T	3. F	4. T
5. T	6. T	7. F	8. T
9. T	10. F	11. T	12. F
13. T	14. F	15. T	

PART 3

1. d	2. c	3. b	4. d
5. a			

PART 4

	A	L	OE
1.	+	0	+
2.	+	+	0
3.	+	0	+
4.	+	0	+
5.	-	0	-
6.	+ -	0	0
7.	+ -	0	0
8.	-	-	0
9.	-	-	0
10.	-	0	-

PART 5

	Assets				Liabilities		Owners Equity
	Cash	+	Supplies	+	Land	=	Accts. Payable	+	Capital Stock
1.	$30,000								$30,000S
2.			+3,000				+3,000		
Bal.	$30,000		$3,000				$3,000		$30,000
3.	-14,000				+14,000				
Bal.	$16,000		$3,000		$14,000		$3,000		$30,000
4.	-1,800						-1,800		
Bal.	$14,200		$3,000		$14,000		$1,200		$30,000
5.	-2,000								-2,000D
Bal.	$12,200		$3,000		$14,000		$1,200		$28,000
6.	-2,800								-2,800E
Bal.	$9,400		$3,000		$14,000		$1,200		$25,200
7.							+900		-900E
Bal.	$9,400		$3,000		$14,000		$2,100		$24,300
8.	+12,000								+12,000S
Bal.	$21,400		$3,000		$14,000		$2,100		$36,300
9.	+340								+340R
Bal.	$21,740		$3,000		$14,000		$2,100		$36,640
10.			-600						-600E
Bal.	$21,740		$2,400		$14,000		$2,100		$36,040

PART 6

1. Cash	30,000	
Capital Stock		30,000
2. Supplies	3,000	
Accounts Payable		3,000
3. Land	14,000	
Cash		14,000
4. Accounts Payable	1,800	
Cash		1,800
5. Dividends	2,000	
Cash		2,000
6. Rent Expense	2,800	
Cash		2,800
7. Miscellaneous Expense	900	
Accounts Payable		900
8. Cash	12,000	
Capital Stock		12,000
9. Cash	340	
Repair Fees Earned		340
10. Supplies Expense	600	
Supplies		600

PART 7

1.

Beyers Company
Income Statement
For Year Ended December 31, 1991

Sales		$50,940
Operating expenses:		
Rent expense	$10,320	
Advertising expense	7,650	
Utilities expense	6,000	
Supplies expense	2,940	
Miscellaneous expense	1,350	28,260
Net income		$22,680

2.

Beyers Company
Retained Earnings Statement
For Year Ended December 31, 1991

Retained earnings, January 1, 1991		$12,120
Net income for the year	$22,680	
Less dividends	14,760	
Increase in retained earnings		7,920
Retained earnings, December 31, 1991		$20,040

3.

Beyers Company
Balance Sheet
December 31, 1991

Assets

Cash	$19,200
Accounts receivable	9,300
Supplies	2,700
Land	21,600
Total assets	$52,800

Liabilities

Accounts payable	$ 2,760

Stockholders' Equity

Capital stock	$30,000
Retained earnings	20,040
Total stockholders' equity	$50,040
Total liabilities and stockholders' equity	$52,800

4.

Beyers Company
Statement of Cash Flows
For Year Ended December 31, 1991

Cash flows from operating activities:		
Cash received from customers	$47,110	
Deduct cash payments for expenses and payments to creditors	30,010	
Net cash flow from operating activities		$17,100
Cash flows from financing activities:		
Cash dividends		14,760
Increase in cash		$ 2,340
Cash balance, January 1, 1991		16,860
Cash balance, December 31, 1991		$19,200

CHAPTER 2

PART 1

1. A	**2.** G	**3.** C	**4.** B
5. I	**6.** E	**7.** D	**8.** F
9. H	**10.** J		

PART 3

1. b	**2.** c	**3.** a	**4.** c
5. a	**6.** d	**7.** d	

PART 2

1. T	**2.** F	**3.** F	**4.** T
5. F	**6.** T	**7.** T	**8.** F
9. F	**10.** F		

PART 4

1.	Purchases	5,000	
	Accounts Payable		5,000
2.	Accounts Payable	5,000	
	Cash		4,900
	Purchases Discounts		100
3.	Purchases	3,500	
	Transportation In	80	
	Accounts Payable		3,580
4.	Accounts Payable	750	
	Purchases Returns and Allowances		750
5.	Accounts Payable	2,830	
	Cash		2,775
	Purchases Discounts		55

PART 5

1.	Accounts Receivable	3,150	
	Sales		3,150
2.	Cash	2,850	
	Sales		2,850
3.	Cash	3,025	
	Credit Card Collection Expense	125	
	Accounts Receivable		3,150
4.	Accounts Receivable	4,500	
	Sales		4,500
	Accounts Receivable	150	
	Cash		150
5.	Sales Returns and Allowances	350	
	Accounts Receivable		350
6.	Cash	4,217	
	Sales Discounts	83	
	Accounts Receivable		4,300

PART 6

1.

Apr.	3	Cash	11	30,000	
		Capital Stock	31		30,000
	10	Equipment	18	10,600	
		Accounts Payable	21		10,600
	14	Purchases	51	6,900	
		Accounts Payable	21		6,900
	22	Equipment	18	5,100	
		Accounts Payable	21		5,100
	29	Accounts Payable	21	2,400	
		Cash	11		2,400

2.

Account	Cash						Account No. 11

Date	Item	Post. Ref.	Debit	Credit	Balance Debit	Balance Credit
19—						
Apr. 3	....	1	30,000		30,000	
29	....	1		2,400	27,600	

Account	Equipment					Account No. 18

Date	Item	Post. Ref.	Debit	Credit	Balance Debit	Balance Credit
19—						
Apr. 10	....	1	10,600		10,600	
22	....	1	5,100		15,700	

Account	Accounts Payable					Account No. 21

Date	Item	Post. Ref.	Debit	Credit	Balance Debit	Balance Credit
19—						
Apr. 10	....	1		10,600		10,600
14	....	1		6,900		17,500
22	....	1		5,100		22,600
29	....	1	2,400			20,200

Account	Capital Stock					Account No. 31

Date	Item	Post. Ref.	Debit	Credit	Balance Debit	Balance Credit
19—						
Apr. 3	....	1		30,000		30,000

Account	Purchases					Account No. 51

Date	Item	Post. Ref.	Debit	Credit	Balance Debit	Balance Credit
19—						
Apr. 14	....	1	6,900		6,900	

3.

Momper Co.
Trial Balance
April 30, 19—

	Debit	Credit
Cash	27,600	
Equipment	15,700	
Accounts Payable		20,200
Capital Stock		30,000
Purchases	6,900	
	50,200	50,200

CHAPTER 3

PART 1

1. A	2. E	3. G	4. C
5. F	6. D	7. B	8. H
9. K	10. I	11. L	12. J

PART 3

1. b	2. c	3. d	4. a
5. b	6. c	7. b	8. d
9. d	10. a		

PART 2

1. F	2. F	3. T	4. T
5. T	6. T	7. F	8. T
9. T	10. F	11. F	12. T

PART 4

1.

Cash		Prepaid Insurance		Insurance Expense	
May 1	5,400	May 1 5,400	Dec. 31 1,200	Dec. 31 1,200	

2. Unexpired insurance $4,200
3. Insurance expense $1,200

PART 5

| Dec. 31 | Unearned Rent . . . . | 3,000 | |
| | Rent Income . . . . | | 3,000 |

PART 6

1. Dec. 31	Salary Expense	1,250	
	Salaries Payable		1,250
2. 31	Interest Receivable	260	
	Interest Income		260

PART 7

| Dec. 31 | Delivery Service Receivable . . . . | 700 | |
| | Delivery Service Income . . . . | | 700 |

Delivery Service Receivable		Delivery Service Income	
Dec. 31	700	Dec. 31	3,200
		31	700

PART 8

1. Dec. 31   Depreciation Expense—Equipment   4,100
                 Accumulated Depreciation—Equipment   4,100

Equipment	Accumulated Depreciation - Equipment	Depreciation Expense - Equipment
Dec. 31 62,000	Dec. 31 4,100	Dec. 31 4,100

2.   (a) Understated   (b) Overstated   (c) Overstated   (d) Overstated   (e) Overstated

CHAPTER 4

PART 1

1. G	**2.** M	**3.** E	**4.** L
5. B	**6.** F	**7.** I	**8.** A
9. K	**10.** J	**11.** C	**12.** D
13. H			

PART 3

1. b	**2.** a	**3.** d	**4.** a
5. b	**6.** d	**7.** c	**8.** d

PART 2

1. F	**2.** F	**3.** T	**4.** T
5. T	**6.** T	**7.** F	**8.** F
9. F	**10.** F	**11.** F	**12.** T
13. T	**14.** T	**15.** T	

PART 4

19—
1. Dec. 31 Salary Expense   611   230
                Salaries Payable   213   230
2.   31 Income Summary   313   44,730
                Salary Expense   611   44,730
3. Jan.   1 Salaries Payable   213   230
                Salary Expense   611   230
4.   4 Salary Expense   611   1,250
                Cash   111   1,250

ACCOUNT   Cash   ACCOUNT NO. 111

Date	Item	Post. Ref.	Debit	Credit	Balance Debit	Balance Credit
19—						
Jan. 1	Balance	✓			90,000	
4	. . . .	23		1,250	88,750	

ACCOUNT   Salaries Payable   ACCOUNT NO. 213

Date	Item	Post. Ref.	Debit	Credit	Balance Debit	Balance Credit
19—						
Dec. 31	. . . .	23		230		230
Jan. 1	. . . .	23	230			-0-

ACCOUNT   Income Summary   ACCOUNT NO. 313

Date	Item	Post. Ref.	Debit	Credit	Balance Debit	Balance Credit
19—						
Dec. 31	. . . .	23	44,730		44,730	

ACCOUNT   Salary Expense   ACCOUNT NO. 611

Date	Item	Post. Ref.	Debit	Credit	Balance Debit	Balance Credit
19—						
Dec. 31	Balance	✓			44,500	
31	. . . .	23	230		44,730	
31	. . . .	23		44,730	-0-	
19—						
Jan. 1	. . . .	23		230		230
4	. . . .	23	1,250		1,020	

PART 5

Cost of merchandise sold:

Merchandise inventory, July 1, 1990			$130,000
Purchases		$435,000	
Less: Purchases returns and allowances	$3,780		
Purchases discounts	4,590	8,370	
Net purchases		$426,630	
Add transportation in		2,970	
Cost of merchandise purchased			429,600
Merchandise available for sale			$559,600
Less merchandise inventory, June 30, 1991			155,000
Cost of merchandise sold			$404,600

PART 6
Halsey Corporation
Work Sheet
For Month Ended March 31, 19 —

ACCOUNT TITLE	TRIAL BALANCE Debit	TRIAL BALANCE Credit	ADJUSTMENTS Debit	ADJUSTMENTS Credit	INCOME STATEMENT Debit	INCOME STATEMENT Credit	BALANCE SHEET Debit	BALANCE SHEET Credit
Cash	7 310 00						7 310 00	
Accounts Receivable	11 400 00						11 400 00	
Merchandise Inventory	16 039 00				16 039 00	11 580 00	11 580 00	
Office Supplies	1 035 00			(a) 910 00			125 00	
Prepaid Insurance	2 474 00			(b) 1 398 00			1 076 00	
Delivery Equipment	6 015 00						6 015 00	
Accum. Dep. - Deliv. Equip.		1 390 00		(c) 905 00				2 295 00
Accounts Payable		7 530 00						7 530 00
Salaries Payable				(d) 200 00				200 00
Capital Stock		12 800 00						12 800 00
Retained Earnings		7 565 00						7 565 00
Income Summary								
Sales		105 670 00				105 670 00		
Sales Returns & Allow.	1 301 00				1 301 00			
Purchases	69 290 00				69 290 00			
Purchases Discounts		643 00				643 00		
Sales Salaries Expense	7 712 00		(d) 113 00		7 825 00			
Advertising Expense	1 309 00				1 309 00			
Delivery Expense	4 210 00				4 210 00			
Dep. Expense - Deliv. Equip.			(c) 905 00		905 00			
Misc. Selling Expense	1 395 00				1 395 00			
Office Salaries Expense	5 493 00		(d) 87 00		5 580 00			
Office Supplies Expense			(a) 910 00		910 00			
Insurance Expense			(b) 1 398 00		1 398 00			
Misc. Administrative Expense	687 00				687 00			
Interest Income		72 00				72 00		
	135 670 00	135 670 00	3 413 00	3 413 00	110 849 00	117 965 00	37 506 00	30 390 00
Net Income					7 116 00			7 116 00
					117 965 00	117 965 00	37 506 00	37 506 00

1. Adjusting Entries

19—

(a) Mar. 31	Office Supplies Expense	. . . .	9,100	
	Office Supplies	. . . .		9,100
(b) 31	Insurance Expense	. . . .	13,980	
	Prepaid Insurance	. . . .		13,980
(c) 31	Depreciation Expense—Delivery Equipment	. . . .	9,050	
	Accumulated Depreciation—Delivery Equipment	. . . . . .		9,050
(d) 31	Sales Salaries Expense	. . . .	1,130	
	Office Salaries Expense	. . . .	870	
	Salaries Payable	. . . .		2,000

2. Closing Entries

19—

Mar. 31	Merchandise Inventory	. . . .	115,800	
	Sales	. . . .	1,056,700	
	Purchases Discounts	. . . .	6,430	
	Interest Income	. . . .	720	
	Income Summary	. . . .		1,179,650
31	Income Summary	. . . .	1,108,490	
	Merchandise Inventory	. . . .		160,390
	Sales Returns and Allowances	. . . .		13,010
	Purchases	. . . .		692,900
	Sales Salaries Expense	. . . .		78,250
	Advertising Expense	. . . .		13,090
	Delivery Expense	. . . .		42,100
	Depreciation Expense-Delivery Equipment	. . . .		9,050
	Miscellaneous Selling Expense	. . . .		13,950
	Office Salaries Expense	. . . .		55,800
	Office Supplies Expense	. . . .		9,100
	Insurance Expense	. . . .		13,980
	Miscellaneous Administrative Expense	. . . .		6,870
31	Income Summary	. . . .	71,160	
	Retained Earnings	. . . .		71,160

PART 8

Halsey Corporation
Income Statement
For Year Ended March 31, 19—

Revenue from sales:			
Sales		$1,056,700	
Less: Sales returns and allowances		13,010	
Net sales			$1,043,690
Cost of merchandise sold:			
Merchandise inventory, April 1, 19—		$ 160,390	
Purchases	$692,900		
Less: Purchases discounts	6,430		
Net purchases		686,470	
Merchandise available for sale		$ 846,860	
Less: Merchandise inventory, March 31, 19— . . .		115,800	
Cost of merchandise sold			731,060
Gross profit			$ 312,630
Operating expenses:			
Selling expenses:			
Sales salaries expense	$78,250		
Advertising expense	13,090		
Delivery expense	42,100		
Depreciation expense—delivery equipment . . .	9,050		
Miscellaneous selling expense	13,950		
Total selling expenses		$ 156,440	
Administrative expenses:			
Office salaries expense	$55,800		
Office supplies expense	9,100		
Insurance expense	13,980		
Miscellaneous administrative expense	6,870		
Total administrative expenses		85,750	
Total operating expenses			242,190
Income from operations			$ 70,440
Other income:			
Interest income			720
Net income			$ 71,160

PART 9

Halsey Corporation
Balance Sheet
March 31, 19—

Assets

Cash		$73,100
Accounts receivable		114,000
Merchandise inventory		115,800
Office supplies		1,250
Prepaid insurance		10,760
Delivery equipment	$60,150	
Less: Accumulated depreciation	22,950	37,200
Total assets		$352,110

Liabilities

Accounts payable	$75,300	
Salaries payable	2,000	
Total liabilities		$77,300

Stockholders' Equity

Capital stock	$128,000	
Retained earnings	146,810	
Total stockholders' equity		274,810
Total liabilities and stockholders' equity		$352,110

PART 10

Halsey Corporation
Retained Earnings Statement
For Year Ended March 31, 19—

Retained earnings, April 1, 19—	$ 75,650
Net income for the year	71,160
Retained earnings, March 31, 19—	$146,810

CHAPTER 5

PART 1

1. F	2. C	3. D	4. B
5. H	6. A	7. J	8. I
9. G	10. E		

PART 3

1. d	2. b	3. b	4. a
5. d	6. c		

PART 2

1. T	2. F	3. F	4. T
5. T	6. T	7. F	8. T
9. T	10. F	11. F	12. F
13. T	14. T	15. F	

PART 4

1.

Lambert Inc.
Bank Reconciliation
June 30, 19—

Balance according to bank statement		$8,510
Add deposit not recorded		1,820
		$10,330
Deduct outstanding checks:		
No. 1255	$285	
No. 1280	150	
No. 1295	715	1,150
Adjusted balance		$ 9,180
Balance according to depositor's records		$ 7,795
Add: Error in recording Check No. 1289	$270	
Error in deposit	450	
Note and interest collected by bank	680	1,400
		$ 9,195
Deduct bank service charge		15
Adjusted balance		$ 9,180

2.

June 30	Cash in Bank		1,385	
	Miscellaneous Administrative Expense		15	
	Vouchers Payable			270
	Accounts Receivable			450
	Notes Receivable			600
	Interest Income			80

PART 5

Sept.	8	Purchases	6,272	
		Accounts Payable		6,272
	10	Purchases	9,999	
		Accounts Payable		9,999
	20	Accounts Payable	9,999	
		Cash in Bank		9,999
Oct.	9	Accounts Payable	6,272	
		Discounts Lost	128	
		Cash in Bank		6,400

(5) (6)

PART 6

1.	Petty Cash	500.00	
	Accounts Payable		500.00
2.	Accounts Payable	500.00	
	Cash in Bank		500.00
3.	Office Supplies	91.15	
	Miscellaneous Selling Expense	128.27	
	Miscellaneous Administrative Expense	59.16	
	Cash Short and Over		2.98
	Accounts Payable		275.60
4.	Accounts Payable	275.60	
	Cash in Bank		275.60

CHAPTER 6

PART 1				PART 2			
1. I	**2.** E	**3.** H	**4.** C	**1.** T	**2.** T	**3.** F	**4.** F
5. F	**6.** B	**7.** D	**8.** G	**5.** T	**6.** T	**7.** F	**8.** T
9. A	**10.** J			**9.** F	**10.** T		

PART 3				PART 4		
1. c	**2.** d	**3.** b	**4.** a	**1.** $60.00	**2.** $25.00	**3.** $30.00
5. b	**6.** a	**7.** c		**4.** $60.00	**5.** $25.00	**6.** $180.00
				7. $180.00		

PART 5

1.	Face value	$5,000.00
	Interest on face value	150.00
	Maturity value	5,150.00
	Discount on maturity value	130.18
	Proceeds	$5,019.82
2.	Face value	$9,000.00
	Interest on face value	240.00
	Maturity value	9,240.00
	Discount on maturity value	256.67
	Proceeds	$8,983.33

PART 6

(a)	Notes Receivable	6,500.00	
	Accounts Receivable-Bev Davidson		6,500.00
(b)	Cash	6,574.75	
	Interest Income		74.75
	Notes Receivable		6,500.00
(c)	Accounts Receivable-Bev Davidson	6,630.00	
	Cash		6,630.00
(d)	Cash	6,650.26	
	Interest Income		20.26
	Accounts Receivable-Bev Davidson		6,630.00
(e)	Notes Receivable	1,000.00	
	Accounts Receivable-Mary Douglass		1,000.00
(f)	Accounts Receivable-Mary Douglass	1,025.00	
	Interest Income		25.00
	Notes Receivable		1,000.00

PART 7

(a)	Uncollectible Accounts Expense	16,500	
	Allowance for Doubtful Accounts		16,500
(b)	Uncollectible Accounts Expense	4,945	
	Allowance for Doubtful Accounts		4,945
(c)	Allowance for Doubtful Accounts	4,300	
	Accounts Receivable-Milton, Inc.		4,300
(d)	Accounts Receivable-Gordon Co.	1,625	
	Allowance for Doubtful Accounts		1,625
	Cash	1,625	
	Accounts Receivable-Gordon Co.		1,625

PART 8

1.	July 31	Uncollectible Accounts Expense	210	
		Accounts Receivable-D.Moore		210
2.	Sept. 8	Accounts Receivable-D.Moore	210	
		Uncollectible Accounts Expense		210
	8	Cash	210	
		Accounts Receivable-D.Moore		210

PART 9

Carrying amount of securities	$67,000

CHAPTER 7

<table>
<tr><td colspan="2">PART 1</td><td colspan="4"></td><td colspan="2">PART 3</td></tr>
</table>

PART 1

1.	G	**2.**	I	**3.**	J	**4.**	C
5.	E	**6.**	A	**7.**	F	**8.**	H
9.	K	**10.**	D	**11.**	L	**12.**	B

PART 3

1. b 2. a 3. b 4. d 5. c

PART 2

1.	F	**2.**	F	**3.**	T	**4.**	T
5.	T	**6.**	T	**7.**	F	**8.**	F
9.	T	**10.**	T				

PART 4

1. Average unit cost: $\dfrac{\$11{,}415}{210} = \$54.36$

   20 units in the inventory @ $54.36 = <u>$1,087.20</u>

2. Date Purchased	Units	Price	Total Cost
November 1	<u>20</u>	$57	<u>$ 1,140</u>
Total	20		$ 1,140
3. January 10	15	$48	$ 720
May 15	<u>5</u>	54	<u>270</u>
Total	20		$ 990
4. January 10	5	$48	$ 240
November 1	<u>15</u>	57	<u>855</u>
Total	20		$ 1,095

PART 5

	(1) Fifo	(2) Lifo	(3) Average Cost
Sales	$1,950,000	$1,950,000	$1,950,000
Ending inventory	352,600	250,000	297,300
Cost of merchandise sold	1,431,300	1,533,900	1,486,600
Gross profit	518,700	416,100	463,400

COMPUTATION OF ENDING INVENTORY

	Date of Purchase	Units	Unit Price	Total Cost
FIFO:	Nov. 1	3,100	$69	$213,900
	Dec. 1	1,900	73	138,700
	Total	5,000		$352,600
LIFO:	Jan. 1	5,000	50	$250,000

AVERAGE COST:

$$\text{Average Unit Cost:} \quad \frac{\$1,783,900}{30,000} = \$59.46$$

$$\$59.46 \times 5,000 = \underline{\$297,300}$$

PART 6

	Cost	Total Lower of Cost or Market
Commodity A	$3,750	$3,600
Commodity B	3,150	3,150
Commodity C	1,260	1,155
Commodity D	1,440	1,290
Total	$9,600	$9,195

PART 7

1.

	Cost	Retail
Merchandise inventory, May 1	$121,300	$170,000
Purchases in May (net)	265,400	474,500
Merchandise available for sale	$386,700	$644,500

Ratio of cost to retail:

$$\frac{\$386,700}{\$644,500} = 60\%$$

Sales in May (net)		482,900
Merchandise inventory; May 31, at retail		$161,600
Merchandise inventory; May 31, at estimated cost ($161,600 x 60%)		$ 96,960

229

2.

Merchandise inventory; May 1	$121,300
Purchases in May (net)	265,400
Merchandise available for sale	$386,700
Sales in May (net) $482,900	
Less estimated gross profit ($482,900 x 40%) 193,160	
Estimated cost of merchandise sold	289,740
Estimated merchandise inventory; May 31	$ 96,960

PART 8

(1)$2,040,000   (2) $1,430,000   (3)$610,000

CHAPTER 8

PART 1

1. I	2. L	3. N	4. G
5. E	6. M	7. C	8. D
9. H	10. A	11. O	12. F
13. B	14. J	15. K	

PART 3

1. c	2. a	3. a	4. d
5. b	6. b	7. c	8. b
9. d	10. a		

PART 2

1. F	2. T	3. F	4. F
5. T	6. T	7. F	8. T
9. F	10. T		

PART 4

Apr. 30	Accumulated Depreciation—Truck	12,000	
	Truck	21,200	
	Truck		16,000
	Cash		17,200

PART 5

1. Apr. 30	Accumulated Depreciation—Truck	12,000	
	Truck	21,800	
	Loss on Disposal of Plant Assets	3,000	
	Truck		16,000
	Cash		20,800
2. Apr. 30	Accumulated Depreciation—Truck	12,000	
	Truck	24,800	
	Truck		16,000
	Cash		20,800

PART 6

1. Dec.	31	Depreciation Expense—Automobile	3,750	
		Accumulated Depreciation—Automobile		3,750
Dec.	31	Depreciation Expense—Automobile	3,750	
		Accumulated Depreciation—Automobile		3,750
2. Dec.	31	Depreciation Expense—Automobile	7,500	
		Accumulated Depreciation—Automobile		7,500
Dec.	31	Depreciation Expense—Automobile	1,875	
		Accumulated Depreciation—Automobile		1,875
3. Dec.	31	Depreciation Expense—Automobile	6,000	
		Accumulated Depreciation—Automobile		6,000
Dec.	31	Depreciation Expense—Automobile	3,000	
		Accumulated Depreciation—Automobile		3,000

PART 7

Dec.	31	Depreciation Expense—Equipment	4,750	
		Accumulated Depreciation—Equipment		4,750

PART 8

Dec.	31	Depreciation Expense—Equipment	15,756	
		Accumulated Depreciation—Equipment		15,756

PART 9

Mar.	8	Accumulated Depreciation—Fixtures	5,350	
		Cash	2,000	
		Fixtures		6,700
		Gain on Disposal of Assets		650

PART 10

Dec.	31	Depletion Expense	150,000	
		Accumulated Depletion—Mineral Rights		150,000

PART 11

Dec.	31	Amortization Expense—Patents	17,000	
		Patents		17,000

CHAPTER 9

PART 1

1. J	2. L	3. F	4. D
5. H	6. C	7. G	8. E
9. M	10. B	11. I	12. A
13. K			

PART 3

1. c	2. c	3. d	4. a
5. d			

PART 4

1. $770	2. $75	3. $727.50

PART 2

1. F	2. T	3. F	4. T
5. T	6. F	7. T	8. T
9. F	10. T		

PART 5

(1) Dec.	7	Sales Salaries Expense	34,000	
		Office Salaries Expense	11,000	
		FICA Tax Payable		3,375
		Employees Income Tax Payable		7,650
		Union Dues Payable		900
		United Way Payable		450
		Salaries Payable		32,625
(2) Dec.	7	Salaries Payable	32,625	
		Cash		32,625
(3) Dec.	7	Payroll Taxes Expense	5,085	
		FICA Tax Payable		3,375
		State Unemployment Tax Payable		1,350
		Federal Unemployment Tax Payable		360

PART 6

(1)
$$B = .08(\$500,000)$$
$$B = \$40,000$$

(2)
$$B = .08(\$500,000 - B)$$
$$B = \$40,000 - .08B$$
$$1.08B = \$40,000$$
$$B = \$37,037.04$$

(3)
$$B = .08(\$500,000 - T)$$
$$T = .34(\$500,000 - B)$$
$$B = .08[\$500,000 - .34(\$500,000 - B)]$$
$$B = .08(\$500,000 - \$170,000 + .34B)$$
$$B = \$40,000 - \$13,600 + .0272B$$
$$.9728B = \$26,400$$
$$B = \$27,138.16$$

(4)
$$B = .08(\$500,000 - B - T)$$
$$T = .34(\$500,000 - B)$$
$$B = .08[\$500,000 - B - .34(\$500,000 - B)]$$
$$B = .08(\$500,000 - B - \$170,000 - .34B)$$
$$B = \$40,000 - .08B - \$13,600 + .0272B$$
$$1.0528B = \$26,400$$
$$B = \$25,075.99$$

9-10

PART 7

Employee	Annual Earnings	Employer's FICA Tax	FICA	Employer's Taxes State Unemployment	Employer's Taxes Federal Unemployment	Total
Johnson	$ 55,000	$ 3,750	$ 3,750	$ 210	$ 56	$ 4,016
Jones	12,000	900	900	210	56	1,166
Smith	5,000	375	375	150	40	565
Wilson	52,000	3,750	3,750	210	56	4,016
Total	$124,000	$ 8,775	$ 8,775	$ 780	$ 208	$ 9,763

PART 8

			Debit	Credit
(1) Dec.	31	Vacation Pay Expense	2,950	
		Vacation Pay Payable		2,950
(2) Dec.	31	Product Warranty Expense	3,750	
		Product Warranty Payable		3,750
(3) Dec.	31	Pension Expense	36,000	
		Cash		28,000
		Unfunded Accrued Pension Cost		8,000

PART 9

(1)	Cash	6,000	
	Notes Payable		6,000
(2)	Notes Payable	6,000	
	Interest Expense	165	
	Cash		6,165
(3)	Cash	7,880	
	Interest Expense	120	
	Notes Payable		8,000
(4)	Notes Payable	8,000	
	Cash		8,000

CHAPTER 10

PART 1

1. F	2. I	3. J	4. O
5. B	6. E	7. M	8. D
9. P	10. N	11. Q	12. C

PART 2

1. F	2. T	3. F	4. F
5. T	6. F	7. T	8. F
9. F	10. F	11. T	12. F

PART 3

1. c	2. c	3. c	4. b
5. d			

PART 4

(1)	Cash	300,000	
	Common Stock		300,000
(2)	Equipment	135,000	
	Common Stock		100,000
	Paid-In Capital in Excess of Par—Common Stock		35,000
(3)	Cash	48,000	
	Preferred Stock		40,000
	Paid-In Capital in Excess of Par—Preferred Stock		8,000
(4)	Cash	15,000	
	Common Stock		15,000

PART 5

1.

Year	Total Dividends	Preferred Dividends		Common Dividends	
		Total	Per Share	Total	Per Share
1	$ 4,000	$ 4,000	$ 20	-0-	-0-
2	6,000	6,000	30	-0-	-0-
3	17,000	5,000	25	$ 12,000	$ 6
4	27,000	5,000	25	22,000	11

2.

Year	Total Dividends	Preferred Dividends		Common Dividends	
		Total	Per Share	Total	Per Share
1	$ 4,000	$ 4,000	$ 20	-0-	-0-
2	6,000	6,000	30	-0-	-0-
3	17,000	5,000	25	$ 12,000	$ 6
4	27,000	7,000	35	20,000	10

3.

Year	Total Dividends	Preferred Dividends		Common Dividends	
		Total	Per Share	Total	Per Share
1	$ 4,000	$ 4,000	$ 20	-0-	-0-
2	6,000	5,000	25	$ 1,000	$ 0.50
3	17,000	5,000	25	12,000	6.00
4	27,000	6,000	30	21,000	10.50

PART 6

	Applicable Retained Earnings	Equity per Class	Shares Outstanding	Equity per Share
(1) Preferred	-0-	$ 100,000	2,500	$ 40.00
Common	$ 500,000	900,000	8,000	112.50
(2) Preferred	$ 32,000	$ 132,000	2,500	$ 52.80
Common	468,000	868,000	8,000	108.50
(3) Preferred	-0-	$ 100,000	2,500	$ 40.00
Common	$ 500,000	900,000	8,000	112.50
(4) Preferred	$ 40,000	$ 160,000	2,500	$ 64.00
Common	440,000	840,000	8,000	105.00

PART 7

(1) Oct.	1	Treasury Stock	70,000	
		Cash		70,000
(2) Oct.	31	Cash	37,500	
		Treasury Stock		35,000
		Paid-In Capital from Sale of Treasury Stock		2,500
(3) Nov.	20	Cash	20,100	
		Paid-In Capital from Sale of Treasury Stock	900	
		Treasury Stock		21,000

CHAPTER 11

PART 1

1. D	**2.** C	**3.** Q	**4.** M					
5. H	**6.** B	**7.** I	**8.** N					
9. F	**10.** L							

PART 3

1. B	**2.** B	**3.** B	**4.** D
5. C			

PART 2

1. T	**2.** F	**3.** F	**4.** T
5. T	**6.** T	**7.** F	**8.** F
9. F	**10.** T		

PART 4

(1) Income Tax	180,000	
Income Tax Payable		128,000
Deferred Income Tax Payable		52,000

(2)	Income Tax	. . . .	200,000	
	Deferred Income Tax Payable	. . . .	20,000	
	Income Tax Payable	. . . .		220,000

PART 5

(1)	Income Tax	. . . .	60,000	
	Cash	. . . .		60,000
(2)	Income Tax	. . . .	20,000	
	Income Tax Payable	. . . .		20,000

PART 6

(1)	Retained Earnings	. . . .	500,000	
	Appropriation for Bonded Indebtedness	. . . .		500,000
(2)	Appropriation for Bonded Indebtedness	. . . .	15,000,000	
	Retained Earnings	. . . .		15,000,000

PART 7

(1) Feb. 20	Cash Dividends	. . . .	80,000	
	Cash Dividends Payable	. . . .		80,000
(2) Mar. 22	Cash Dividends Payable	. . . .	80,000	
	Cash	. . . .		80,000
(3) Dec. 15	Stock Dividends	. . . .	201,600	
	Stock Dividends Distributable	. . . .		144,000
	Paid-In Capital in Excess of Par — Common Stock	. . . .		57,600
(4) Jan. 14	Stock Dividends Distributable	. . . .	144,000	
	Common Stock	. . . .		144,000

PART 8

	Column A Before Any Dividend	Column B After Cash Dividend	Column C After Stock Dividend
a. Total number of shares outstanding	200,000	200,000	210,000
b. Total par value of shares outstanding	$ 5,000,000	$ 5,000,000	$ 5,250,000
c. Total paid-in capital	$ 2,000,000	$ 2,000,000	$ 2,050,000
d. Total retained earnings	$ 6,440,000	$ 6,080,000	$ 6,140,000
e. Total stockholders' equity	$ 13,440,000	$ 13,080,000	$ 13,440,000
f. Equity per share	$ 67.20	$ 65.40	$ 64.00
g. Amount required to pay a $1.80 per share cash dividend next year.	$ 360,000	$ 360,000	$ 378,000
h. Percentage of total stock owned by Rafael	.5 %	.5 %	.5 %
i. Total number of shares owned by Rafael	1,000	1,000	1,050
j. Total par value of Rafael's shares	$ 25,000	$ 25,000	$ 26,250
k. Total equity of Rafael's shares	$ 67,200	$ 65,400	$67,200

PART 9

Watley Inc.
Income Statement
For Year Ended March 31, 19—

Sales	$2,000,000
Cost of merchandise sold	1,400,000
Gross profit	$ 600,000
Operating expenses	96,000
Income from continuing operations before income tax	$ 504,000
Income tax	176,000
Income from continuing operations	$ 328,000
Loss on discontinued operations, net of applicable income tax of $14,000	(50,000)
Income before extraordinary item and cumulative effect of a change in accounting principle	$ 278,000
Extraordinary item:	
Loss from earthquake, net of applicable income tax of $48,000	(192,000)
Cumulative effect on prior years of changing to a different depreciation method, net of applicable income tax of $18,000	62,000
Net income	$ 148,000
Earnings per common share:	
Income from continuing operations	$6.56
Loss on discontinued operations	(1.00)
Income before extraordinary item and cumulative effect of a change in accounting principle	5.56
Extraordinary item	(3.84)
Cumulative effect on prior years of changing to a different depreciation method	1.24
Net income	$2.96

CHAPTER 12

PART 1

1.	A	2.	O	3.	D	4.	H
5.	C	6.	E	7.	B	8.	J
9.	F	10.	G				

PART 3

1.	A	2.	B	3.	B	4.	A
5.	C						

PART 2

1.	F	2.	F	3.	F	4.	T
5.	F	6.	T	7.	F	8.	T
9.	T	10.	T				

PART 4

1. (a) Present value of $1 for 20 semiannual

periods at 6% (semiannual rate)	.3118	
Face amount of bonds	x $8,000,000	$2,494,400
Present value of annuity of $1 for 20 periods at 6%	11.4699	
Semiannual interest payments	x $ 480,00	5,505,552
Proceeds of bond (present value)		$7,999,952

Note: The difference of $48 between the face value of the bonds
and the present value is due to rounding.

(b) There is no premium or discount on the bond issue.

2. (a) Present value of $1 for 20 semiannual periods

at 6 1/2% (semiannual rate)	.2838	
Face amount of bonds	x $8,000,000	$2,270,400
Present value of annuity of $1 for 20 periods at 6 1/2%	11.0185	
Semiannual interest payments	x $ 480,000	5,288,880
Proceeds of bond (present value)		$7,559,280

(b) The discount is $440,720 on the bond issuance.

3. (a) Present value of $1 for 20 semiannual periods

at 5 1/2% (semiannual rate)	.3427	
Face amount of bonds	x $8,000,000	$2,741,600
Present value of annuity of $1 for 20 periods at 5 1/2%	11.9504	
Semiannual interest payments	x $ 480,000	5,736,192
Proceeds of bond (present value)		$8,477,792

(b The premium is $477,792 on the bond issuance.

PART 5

(a) Dec. 31	Cash	1,059,724	
	Bonds Payable		1,000,000
	Premium on Bonds Payable		59,724
(b) June 30	Interest Expense ($1,059,724 x 5 1/2%)	58,285	
	Premium on Bonds Payable [($1,059,724 x 5 1/2%)-$60,000]	1,715	
	Cash		60,000
(c) Dec. 31	Interest Expense ($1,058,009 x 5 1/2%)	58,191	
	Premium on Bonds Payable [($1,058,009 x 5 1/2%)-$60,000)]	1,809	
	Cash		60,000
(d) Dec. 31	Bonds Payable	500,000	
	Premium on Bonds Payable [($59,724-$1,715-$1,809)/2] ..	28,100	
	Gain on Redemption of Bonds		13,100
	Cash		515,000

PART 6

(b) June 30	Interest Expense ($60,000-$2,986)	57,014	
	Premium on Bonds Payable ($59,724/20)	2,986	
	Cash		60,000
(c) Dec. 31	Interest Expense ($60,000-$2,986)	57,014	
	Premium on Bonds Payable ($59,724/20)	2,986	
	Cash		60,000
(d) Dec. 31	Bonds Payable	500,000	
	Premium on Bonds Payable [($59,724 - $2,986-$2,986)/2] . .	26,876	
	Gain on Redemption of Bonds		11,876
	Cash		515,000

PART 7

(1) $135,923 ($5,000,000 + 36.7856)

(2)	Sinking Fund Cash	135,923	
	Cash		135,923

PART 8

(a) Jan. 1	Cash	17,507,760	
	Discount on Bonds Payable	2,492,240	
	Bonds Payable		20,000,000
(b) June 30	Interest Expense ($17,507,760 x 5%)	875,388	
	Discount on Bonds Payable [($17,507,760 x 5%)-$800,000]		75,388
	Cash		800,000
(c) Dec. 31	Sinking Fund Cash	275,000	
	Cash		275,000
(d) Dec. 31	Retained Earnings	2,000,000	
	Appropriation for Bonded Indebtedness		2,000,000
(e) Dec. 31	Bonds Payable	20,000,000	
	Cash	18,200	
	Sinking Fund Cash		20,018,200
(f) Dec. 31	Appropriation for Bonded Indebtedness	20,000,000	
	Retained Earnings		20,000,000

PART 9

(a) Oct. 1	Investment in Edy Inc. Bonds ($100,000 x 99)	99,000	
	Interest Income	3,750	
	Cash		102,750
(b) Dec. 31	Cash	7,500	
	Interest Income		7,500
(c) Dec. 31	Investment in Edy Inc. Bonds	30	
	Interest Income		30
(d) Dec. 1	Cash	108,250	
	Investment in Edy Inc. Bonds		99,260
	Interest Income		6,250
	Gain on Sale of Edy Inc. Bonds		2,740

239

PART 10

(a) Jan.	3	Sinking Fund Cash	75,000	
		Cash		75,000
(b) Jan.	6	Sinking Fund Investments	60,000	
		Sinking Fund Cash		60,000
(c) Dec.	31	Sinking Fund Cash	6,150	
		Sinking Fund Income		6,150
(d) Dec.	31	Sinking Fund Cash	69,300	
		Sinking Fund Investments		60,000
		Gain on Sale of Investments		9,300
(e) Dec.	31	Cash	450	
		Bonds Payable	90,000	
		Sinking Fund Cash		90,450

CHAPTER 13

PART 1

1.	F	2.	F	3.	C	4.	L
5.	G	6.	H	7.	N	8.	J
9.	K	10.	I	11.	O	12.	M

PART 3

1.	A	2.	C	3.	D	4.	B
5.	A						

PART 2

1.	T	2.	T	3.	F	4.	F
5.	F	6.	F	7.	T	8.	T
9.	F	10.	T				

PART 4

(a) Investment in Norris Inc. Stock	600,000	
Cash		600,000
(b) Cash (40,000 x $.75)	30,000	
Investment in Norris Inc. Stock		30,000
(c) Investment in Norris Inc. Stock ($900,000 x 25%)	225,000	
Income of Norris Inc.		225,000

(a) Parent:

Investment in subsidiary, 150,000 shares	$600,000	
Subsidiary:		
Net assets	$600,000	
Common stock, 150,000 shares, $4 par		$600,000

(b) Parent:

Investment in subsidiary, 30,000 shares	$800,000	
Eliminate 100% of Subsidiary stock	(540,000)	
Eliminate 100% of Subsidiary retained earnings	(120,000)	
Excess of cost over book equity of Subsidiary interest		$140,000
Subsidiary:		
Net assets	$660,000	
Common stock, 30,000 shares, $18 par		$540,000
Retained earnings		120,000

(c) Parent:

Investment in subsidiary, 20,000 shares	$350,000	
Eliminate 100% of Subsidiary stock	(240,000)	
Eliminate 100% of Subsidiary retained earnings	(200,000)	
Excess of book equity over cost of Subsidiary interest		(90,000)
Subsidiary:		
Net assets	$440,000	
Common stock, 20,000 shares, $12 par		$240,000
Retained earnings		200,000

(d) Parent:

Investment in subsidiary	$1,350,000	
Eliminate 90% of Subsidiary stock	(720,000)	
Eliminate 90% of Subsidiary retained earnings	(360,000)	
Excess of cost over book equity of Subsidiary interest		$270,000
Subsidiary:		
Common stock	$800,000	
Eliminate 90% of Subsidiary stock	(720,000)	
Remainder		$80,000
Retained earnings	$400,000	
Eliminate 90% of Subsidiary earnings	360,000	
Remainder		40,000
Minority interest		$120,000

(e) Investment in Subsidiary	135,000	
Income of Subsidiary		135,000
Cash	45,000	
Investment in Subsidiary		45,000

Parent:

Investment in subsidiary	$1,440,000	
Eliminate 90% of Subsidiary stock	(720,000)	
Eliminate 90% of Subsidiary retained earnings	(450,000)	
Excess of cost over book equity of Subsidiary interest		$270,000

Subsidiary:

Common stock	$800,000	
Eliminate 90% of Subsidiary stock	(720,000)	
Remainder		$80,000
Retained earnings	$500,000	
Eliminate 90% of Subsidiary retained earnings	450,000	
Remainder		50,000
Minority interest		$130,000

(f) Parent:

Investment in subsidiary, 50,000 shares	$1,200,000	
Other net assets	12,780,000	
Common stock, 107,500 shares, $100 par		$10,750,000
Retained earnings		3,230,000

Subsidiary:

Net assets	$1,200,000	
Common stock, 50,000 shares, $15 par		$750,000
Retained earnings		450,000

PART 6

(1)

	Pasteur Inc.	Stertz Inc.	Eliminations Debit	Eliminations Credit	Consolidated Balance Sheet
Investment in Subsidiary ..	350,000			(a)314,500	
				(b) 35,500	
Land	100,000	50,000	(b)35,500		185,500
Other asstes	450,000	350,000			800,000
	900,000	400,000			985,500
Liabilities	200,000	30,000			230,000
Common stock:					
Pasteur Inc.	400,000				400,000
Stertz Inc.		250,000	(a)212,500		37,500 MI
Retained earnings:					
Pasteur Inc	300,000				300,000
Stertz Inc.		120,000	(a)102,000		18,000 MI
	900,000	400,000	350,000	350,000	985,500

(2)   (a) Excess of cost over book equity, $35,500

       (b) Minority interest, $55,500

Pasteur Inc. and Stertz Inc.
Consolidated Balance Sheet
December 31, 19—

<u>Assets</u>

Land	$185,500
Other assets	800,000
Total assets	$985,500

<u>Liabilities and Stockholders' Equity</u>

Liabilities	$230,000
Minority interest in subsidiary	55,500
Common stock	400,000
Retained earnings	300,000
Total liabilities and stockholders' equity	$985,500

PART 7

Mar. 12	Accounts Receivable	. . . .	36,000	
	Sales	. . . .		36,000
Apr. 19	Cash	. . . .	35,000	
	Exchange Loss	. . . .	1,000	
	Accounts Receivable	. . . .		36,000

PART 8

Nov. 8	Purchases	. . . .	800	
	Accounts Payable	. . . .		800
Nov. 20	Purchases	. . . .	1,500	
	Accounts Payable	. . . .		1,500
Dec. 7	Accounts Payable	. . . .	800	
	Exchange Loss	. . . .	200	
	Cash	. . . .		1,000
Dec. 31	Exchange Loss	. . . .	300	
	Accounts Payable	. . . .		300

CHAPTER 14

PART 1

1. R	2. K	3. F	4. L
5. H	6. N	7. E	8. Q
9. C	10. G		

PART 3

1. B	2. C	3. B	4. C
5. D	6. D	7. C	

PART 2

1. T	2. T	3. T	4. T
5. T	6. F	7. F	8. T
9. F	10. T	11. F	12. T
13. F	14. T		

Item	Cash Flows From			Schedule of Noncash Investing and Financing Activities
	Operating Activities	Investing Activities	Financing Activities	
1. Decrease in prepaid expenses	✓			
2. Retirement of bonds			✓	
3. Proceeds from sale of investments		✓		
4. Increase in inventories	✓			
5. Issuance of preferred stock			✓	
6. Purchase of equipment		✓		
7. Cash dividends paid			✓	
8. Acquisition of land in exchange for common stock				✓
9. Amortization of patents	✓			
10. Amortization of discount on bonds payable	✓			

PART 5

Cash flows from operating activities:

Net income, per income statement		$120,000
Add: Depreciation	$36,000	
Decrease in prepaid expenses	2,100	
Increase in accounts payable	13,600	51,700
		$171,700
Deduct: Increase in trade receivables	$ 8,000	
Increase in inventories	12,500	
Decrease in salaries payable	2,400	22,900
Net cash flow from operating activities		$148,800

PART 6

Strauss Inc.
Statement of Cash Flows
For Year Ended December 31, 1991

Cash flows from operating activities:			
Net income, per income statement			$ 95,000
Add: Depreciation	$40,000		
Decrease in inventories	5,000		
Decrease in prepaid expenses	2,000		
Increase in accounts payable	6,000	53,000	
		$148,000	
Deduct: Increase in trade receivables	$10,000		
Gain on sale of land	15,000	25,000	
Net cash flow provided by operating activities			$123,000
Cash flows from investing activities			
Cash received from land sold	$ 45,000		
Less cash paid for purchase of equipment	80,000		
Net cash flow used by investing activities			(35,000)
Cash flows from financing activities:			
Cash used to retire bonds payable	$ 50,000		
Cash paid for dividends	23,000*		
Net cash flow used by financing activities			(73,000)
Increase in cash			$ 15,000
Cash, January 1, 1991			55,000
Cash, December 31, 1991			$ 70,000

*$25,000 + $18,000 - $20,000

CHAPTER 15

PART 1

1.	P	2.	I	3.	l	4.	D
5.	O	6.	B	7.	E	8.	F
9.	M	10.	J	11.	C	12.	H

PART 3

1.	D	2.	C	3.	B	4.	C
5.	D	6.	B				

PART 2

1.	T	2.	F	3.	T	4.	F
5.	T	6.	T	7.	T	8.	F
9.	T	10.	T	11.	T	12.	T
13.	F						

PART 4

Bellamy Inc.
Comparative Income Sheet
For Years Ended December 31, 1991 and 1990

	1991	1990	Increase (Decrease*) Amount	Percent
Sales	$954,500	$830,000	$124,500	15.0%
Sales returns and allowances . .	33,000	30,000	3,000	10.0%
Net sales	$921,500	$800,000	$121,500	15.2%
Cost of goods sold	585,600	480,000	105,600	22.0%
Gross profit	$335,900	$320,000	$15,900	5.0%
Selling expenses	$78,400	$80,000	$1,600*	2.0%*
Administrative expenses	60,000	60,000	—	—
Total operating expenses	$138,400	$140,000	$1,600*	1.1%*
Operating income	$197,500	$180,000	$17,500	9.7%
Other income	17,000	20,000	3,000*	15.0%*
	$214,500	$200,000	$14,500	7.3%
Other expense	75,600	70,000	5,600	8.0%
Income before income tax . . .	$138,900	$130,000	$8,900	6.8%
Income tax	54,600	52,000	2,600	5.0%
Net income	$84,300	$78,000	$6,300	8.1%

Bellamy Inc.
Comparative Balance Sheet
December 31, 1991 and 1990

	1991	1990	Increase (Decrease*) Amount	Percent
Assets				
Cash	$ 88,000	$ 80,000	$8,000	10.0%
Marketable securities	120,000	150,000	30,000*	20.0%*
Accounts receivable (net)	219,300	215,000	4,300	2.0%
Inventory	480,000	400,000	80,000	20.0%
Prepaid expenses	31,800	30,000	1,800	6.0%
Long-term investments	50,000	50,000	—	—
Plant assets (net)	910,000	875,000	35,000	4.0%
Intangible assets	20,000	25,000	5,000*	20.0%*
Total assets	$1,919,100	$1,825,000	$94,100	5.2%
Liabilities				
Current liabilities	$ 143,600	$ 120,000	$23,600	19.7%
Long-term liabilities	480,000	500,000	20,000*	4.0%
Total liabilities	623,600	620,000	$3,600	.6%
Stockholders' Equity				
Preferred 3% stock, $100 par	$ 110,000	$ 100,000	$10,000	10.0%
Common stock, $10 par	520,000	500,000	20,000	4.0%
Retained earnings	665,500	605,000	60,500	10.0%
Total stockholders' equity	$1,295,500	$1,205,000	$90,500	7.5%
Total liabilities and stockholders' equity .	$1,919,100	$1,825,000	$94,100	5.2%

PART 5

Pinnella Inc.
Comparative Balance Sheet
December 31, 1991 and 1990

	1991 Amount	1991 Percent	1990 Amount	1990 Percent
Assets				
Cash	$ 450,000	5.0%	$ 375,000	5.0%
Marketable securities	150,000	1.7	135,000	1.8
Accounts receivable (net)	630,000	7.0	525,000	7.0
Inventory	810,000	9.0	690,000	9.2
Prepaid expenses	54,000	.6	45,000	.6
Long-term investments	400,000	4.4	360,000	4.8
Plant assets (net)	6,506,000	72.3	5,370,000	71.6
Total assets	$ 9,000,000	100.0%	$ 7,500,000	100.0%
Liabilities				
Current liabilities	$ 1,040,000	11.6%	$ 1,000,000	13.3%
Long-term liabilities	2,100,000	23.3	2,000,000	26.7
Total liabilities	$ 3,140,000	34.9%	3,000,000	40.0%
Stockholders' Equity				
Preferred 5% stock, $200 par	$ 300,000	3.3%	$ 300,000	4.0%
Common stock, $10 par	2,500,000	27.8	2,500,000	33.3
Retained earnings	3,060,000	34.0	1,700,000	22.7
Total stockholders' equity	$ 5,860,000	65.1%	$ 4,500,000	60.0%
Total liabilities and stockholders' equity	$ 9,000,000	100.0%	$ 7,500,000	100.0%

Pinnella Inc.
Income Statement
For Year Ended December 31, 1991

	Amount	Percent
Sales	$ 12,750,000	102.0%
Sales returns and allowances	250,000	2.0
Net sales	$ 12,500,000	100.0%
Cost of goods sold	7,500,000	60.0
Gross profit	$ 5,000,000	40.0%
Selling expenses	$ 1,500,000	12.0%
Administrative expenses	750,000	6.0
Total operating expenses	$ 2,250,000	18.0%
Operating income	$ 2,750,000	22.0%
Other income	75,000	.6
	$ 2,825,000	22.6%
Other expense (Interest)	100,000	.8
Income before income tax	$ 2,725,000	21.8%
Income tax	1,100,000	8.8
Net income	$ 1,625,000	13.0%

PART 6

(a) Working capital: $1,054,000

$2,094,000− $1,040,000

(b) Current ratio: 2.0

$$\frac{\$2,094,000}{\$1,040,000}$$

(c) Acid-test ratio: 1.2

$$\frac{\$1,230,000}{\$1,040,000}$$

(d) Accounts receivable turnover: 21.6

$$\frac{\$12,500,000}{\frac{\$630,000+ \$525,000}{2}}$$

(e) Number of days' sales in receivables: 18.4 days

$$\frac{\$12,500,000}{365}= \$34,247$$

$$\frac{\$630,000}{\$34,247}= 18.4$$

(f) Inventory turnover: 10

$$\frac{\$7,500,000}{\frac{\$810,000+ \$690,000}{2}}$$

(g) Number of days' sales in inventory: 39.4 days

$$\frac{\$7,500,000}{365} = \$20,548$$

$$\frac{\$810,000}{\$20,548} = 39.4$$

(h) Ratio of plant assets to long-term liabilities: 3.1

$$\frac{\$6,506,000}{\$2,100,000}$$

(i) Ratio of stockholders' equity to liabilities: 1.9

$$\frac{\$5,860,000}{\$3,140,000}$$

(j) Number of times interest charges earned: 28.3

$$\frac{(\$2,725,000 + \$100,000)}{\$100,000}$$

(k) Number of times preferred dividends earned: 108.3

$$\frac{\$1,625,000}{\$15,000}$$

(l) Ratio of net sales to assets: 1.6

$$\frac{\$12,500,000}{\dfrac{\$8,600,000 + \$7,140,000}{2}}$$

(m) Rate earned on total assets: 20.9%

$$\frac{(\$1,625,000 + \$100,000)}{\dfrac{\$9,000,000 + \$7,500,000}{2}}$$

(n) Rate earned on stockholders' equity: 31.4%

$$\frac{\$1,625,000}{\dfrac{\$5,860,000 + \$4,500,000}{2}}$$

(o) Rate earned on common stockholders' equity: 33.0%

$$\frac{(\$1,625,000 - \$15,000)}{\dfrac{250,000\,shares}{2}}$$

(p) Earnings per share on common stock: $6.44

$$\frac{(\$1,625,000 - \$15,000)}{\dfrac{\$5,560,000 + \$4,200,000}{2}}$$

(q) Price-earnings ratio: 5

$$\frac{\$32.20}{\$6.44}$$

(r) Dividend yield: 3.1%

$$\$250,000 \Big/ \frac{250,000\,shares}{\$32.20}$$

CHAPTER 16

PART 1

1.	F	2.	B	3.	K	4.	I
5.	E	6.	O	7.	J.	8.	M
9.	A	10.	D	11.	G	12.	N

PART 3

1.	d	2.	c	3.	b	4.	c
5.	a	6.	d				

PART 2

1.	F	2.	T	3.	T.	4.	F
5.	F	6.	T	7.	F	8.	T
9.	T	10.	T	11.	F	12.	F

PART 4

(a) Estimated Revenues	5,700,000	
Appropriations		5,450,000
Fund Balance		250,000
(b) Cash	970,000	
Revenues		970,000
(c) Encumbrances	700,000	
Fund Balance Reserved for Encumbrances		700,000
(d) Fund Balance Reserved for Encumbrances	50,000	
Encumbrances		50,000
Expenditures	50,000	
Accounts Payable		50,000
(e) Accounts Payable	50,000	
Cash		50,000

PART 5

Revenues	553,000	
Estimated Revenues		548,000
Fund Balance		5,000
Appropriations	545,000	
Expenditures		530,000
Fund Balance		15,000
Fund Balance	14,000	
Encumbrances		14,000

PART 6

1.

City of Bolton - General Fund
Statement of Revenues, Expenditures, and Changes in Fund Balance
For Year Ended June 30, 1991

	Budget	Actual	Over	Under
Revenues:				
General property taxes	$ 3,135,000	$ 3,125,000		$ 10,000
Sales taxes	1,017,000	1,059,000	$ 42,000	
Motor vehicle licenses	184,000	190,000	6,000	
Interest on savings accounts	30,000	26,000		4,000
Miscellaneous	20,000	18,000		2,000
Total revenues	$ 4,386,000	$ 4,418,000	$ 48,000	$ 16,000
Expenditures:				
General government	$ 1,772,000	$ 1,783,000	$ 11,000	
Police department	897,000	880,000		$ 17,000
Fire department	500,000	495,000		5,000
Streets and roads	450,000	485,000	35,000	
Sanitation	400,000	415,000	15,000	
Public welfare	350,000	340,000		10,000
Total expenditures	$ 4,369,000	$ 4,398,000	$ 61,000	$ 32,000
Excess of revenues over expenditures ...	$ 17,000	$ 20,000		
Fund balance, July 1, 1990		645,700		
		$ 665,700		
Less encumbrances		17,400		
Fund balance, June 30, 1991		$ 648,300		

2.

City of Bolton - General Fund
Balance Sheet
June 30, 1991

Assets

Cash		$ 290,000
Savings accounts		397,600
Property taxes receivable		79,300
Total assets		$ 766,900

Liabilities

Accounts payable	$ 73,700	
Wages payable	27,500	
Total liabilities		$ 101,200

Fund Equity

Fund balance reserved for encumbrances	$ 17,400	
Unreserved fund balance	648,300	
Total fund equity		665,700
Total liabilities and fund equity		$766,900